SYDNEY SMITH

A BIOGRAPHY
& A SELECTION

OTHER BOOKS BY GERALD BULLETT

THE ENGLISH MYSTICS
GEORGE ELIOT: HER LIFE AND BOOKS

☆

POEMS
THE GOLDEN YEAR OF FAN CHENG-TA
WINTER SOLSTICE

☆

THE TESTAMENT OF LIGHT
THE ENGLISH GALAXY OF SHORTER POEMS

and many novels

SYDNEY SMITH

*A biography &
a selection*

—— *by* ——

GERALD BULLETT

London

MICHAEL JOSEPH

First published by
MICHAEL JOSEPH LTD
*26 Bloomsbury Street
London, W.C.1*
1951

*Set and printed in Great Britain by Unwin Brothers Ltd, at the
Gresham Press, Woking, in Baskerville type, ten point, leaded,
on paper made by John Dickinson and bound by James Burn*

PREFACE

BY far the most full account of Sydney Smith is contained in the *Memoir* written in 1855 by his daughter Saba, second wife of Sir Henry Holland, M.D. The present narrative, as will be seen, is heavily indebted to that delightful mass of reminiscence. I have also made use of such memoirs and diaries as those of Brougham, Cockburn, Greville, Tom Moore, and Harriet Martineau, and of S. J. Reid's *Life and Times of Sydney Smith*, 1884. The tale of my indebtedness does not end there: I am very specially grateful to Lady Malise Graham and to Mr Michael Holland, who by generously putting unpublished manuscripts and other family papers at my disposal have enabled me to bring some new facts to light and to present some old facts from a fresh angle. For a wealth of material concerning Smith's relationship with the Hicks Beaches I thank Mrs Hicks Beach, author of *A Cotswold Family* (Heinemann, 1909); and, for a sight of some Hicks Beach letters in her possession, Mrs M. Dudman.

The selection which follows the biography is divided into four parts, each with a brief explanatory introduction. All editorial matter is placed between square brackets. The text used is that of the third (1845) edition of the three volumes prepared by the author in 1839, a supplementary volume of *Sermons* (1846), and the collection of *Letters* edited by Sarah Austin in 1855. A scrutiny of Sydney Smith's holograph manuscript inclines me to believe that the excessively heavy punctuation of the published text was largely the work of his printers; and I have therefore allowed myself, here and there, to lighten it a little, in order to give freer play to that quick flow of energy which is of the essence of his style. In his periodical writing, done in hot haste, there are necessarily passages that can be omitted without loss, to make room for a larger selection of more permanently valuable matter: any such omissions are clearly indicated. *The Letters of Peter Plymley* are given entire.

G. B.

When wit is combined with sense and information, when it is softened by benevolence and restrained by principle, when it is in the hands of a man who loves humour, justice, decency, good nature, morality, and religion, ten thousand times better than wit, wit is then a beautiful and delightful part of our nature. . . . Man could direct his ways by plain reason and support his life by tasteless food; but God has given us wit, and flavour, and brightness, and laughter, and perfumes, to enliven the days of man's pilgrimage and to charm his pained steps over the burning marle.

SYDNEY SMITH

CONTENTS

LIFE OF SYDNEY SMITH

A SELECTION FROM THE WRITINGS OF SYDNEY SMITH

FROM THE EDINBURGH REVIEW

LETTERS OF PETER PLYMLEY

MISCELLANEOUS EXTRACTS

SERMONS AND OTHER OCCASIONS

THE LIFE OF
SYDNEY
SMITH

I

PRELIMINARY PORTRAIT

A GREAT wit, a diner-out, a popular preacher, a zealous champion of reform in a dark age: Sydney Smith was all these. But he was more than these. The public reputation of any man who cuts a conspicuous figure in the world is all too apt to obscure the simple fact that he is also, like everybody else, a private person. The most interesting because the most searching question that can be asked of such a man is what is he like in his solitude, when nobody is looking at him; or among his intimates, unselfconscious and at ease; or in casual encounters with strangers who know nothing about him. The answer, too often, can be supplied only by conjecture, but with Sydney Smith it is otherwise. One dark evening he was on his way to visit the great Henry Brougham, his colleague on the EDINBURGH REVIEW, when two raw Scottish girls got into the coach. 'It's very disagreeable,' said one, 'travelling in the dark. One can't see one's company.' 'Very true, ma'am,' said Smith, 'and you suffer a great loss in not seeing me, for I am a remarkably handsome man.' 'Are you really, sir?' they said. 'Yes,' he assured them, 'and in the flower of my youth, what's more.' They agreed it was a pity they could not see him, and presently, the coach passing near a street lamp, they both darted forward to get a look at him. 'La, sir, you seem very stout!' cried the girls. 'Not at all, ma'am. It's only my great-coat.' They asked where he was going and were told Brougham Hall. 'Why, you must be a very remarkable man', they said, 'to be going to Brougham Hall!' 'I *am* a very remarkable man, ma'am.' At Penrith the girls got out, having talked incessantly and tried in vain, with much laughter, to discover who he was. It was a joyous journey for all three and provides a fair sample of Smith's gay good nature.

Great wit he certainly was; but we do him less than justice

if we emphasize his wit at the expense of his other fine qualities. Wit, in isolation, is apt to shine with a cold inhuman brilliance. It dazzles but does not warm us. Its enchantment is purely intellectual. Sydney Smith's wit was not, or was seldom, of this kind. It was both warmer and merrier: in short, it was fun. When his medical man advised him to take a walk on an empty stomach it was inevitable that he should ask 'Whose?' When he came upon a child who was stroking a tortoise 'to please it' he told him one might as well stroke the dome of St Paul's in the hope of pleasing the Dean and Chapter. And when, as a Canon of that cathedral, he was present at a meeting to discuss a project for laying down a wood pavement, he remarked blandly: 'If my reverend brethren will but lay their heads together, the thing will be done in a trice.' Wit is entrancing; but humour, which springs from the heart, is endearing. Sydney Smith had both in abundance. They flashed like summer lightning in his everyday talk. He was perpetually amusing because perpetually amused, amused by the diverting spectacle of human life and (as his daughter Saba has left on record) by 'the multitude of unexpected images which sprang up in his mind and succeeded each other with a rapidity that hardly allowed his hearers to follow him, but left them panting and exhausted with laughter, to cry out for mercy'. He was no mere professional jester, saving up his good things for display on public occasions. Drollery flowed out of him. In the happiest periods of his life, whether at Doughty Street, at Foston, or afterwards at Combe Florey, his buoyancy of spirit and inexhaustible appetite for fun made him a source of delight and refreshment to all who came near him. He was for many years a poor man, and being in disfavour with the authorities on account of his uncompromising liberalism had no visible prospect of promotion; but his energy of mind was such that neither poverty nor neglect could subdue or finally dishearten him. In the bosom of his family he would let himself go, unbutton his exuberance, and pile absurdity on absurdity in a glittering pyramid of pure nonsense.

He was capable, too, of glorious ingenuous follies. One day he arrived home with two hackney-coach-loads of pictures which he had bought at an auction for no other reason than that they were going 'for absolutely nothing'. His wife, says their daughter,

hardly knew whether to laugh or cry when she saw these horribly
dingy objects in her pretty little drawing-room. She looked at
him as if she thought him half-mad. 'And half-mad he was, but
with delight in his purchase. He kept walking up and down the
room, waving his arms, putting the pictures in fresh lights, and
declaring that they were exquisite specimens of art and, if not
by the very best masters, deserved to be so. He invited all his
friends, displayed the pictures at his suppers, insisted on their
being looked at and admired in every point of view, discovered
fresh beauties for each newcomer; and for three or four days,
under the magic influence of his wit and imagination, these
gloomy old paintings were a perpetual source of amusement and
fun.' At last, however, 'finding he was considered no authority
in the fine arts, and that his pictures made no progress in public
opinion', he got rid of them, to his wife's great relief: but not until he had given them new names, invented on the spur of the
moment, such as 'a beautiful landscape by Nicholas de Falda,
a pupil of Valdeggio, the only painting by that eminent artist'.
It is easy to see how irresistible he must have been in such moods,
and that Mrs Smith found it no hardship to share poverty with
him. In the beginning of their marriage he had nothing to con-
tribute towards the domestic assets but six small silver teaspoons,
much worn by long use. Running joyously into the room he
flung them into his wife's lap, saying: 'There, Kate, you lucky
girl! I give you all my fortune!'

And, with all this, he was a man of very solid and serious
character, animated by 'a passionate love for common justice
and for common sense'. The words are Peter Plymley's and they
accurately sum him up. Common sense implies toleration, and
tolerant he was, of everything except cruelty and humbug and
cant. Humour was his natural mode of expression, ridicule his
chosen weapon. For the unfashionable causes he made his own
he fought unremittingly, against his worldly interests, with gay
ferocity but never with malice. Though he did not spare his
enemies he was at heart the most friendly and least vindictive
of men, with not a particle of hatred or sour envy in his make-up.
Like all very positive and downright people he had prejudices
as well as opinions, and there were things, things of value, which
he did not understand; but he was always a magnanimous
fighter, and his zeal for propagating his own views never took

the form of wishing to persecute or proscribe those of others; indeed much of his superabundant energy was spent in championing the rights of Roman Catholics and Nonconformists, sharply as he disagreed with them both. Living surrounded by landed gentry he was openly and actively the friend of their natural enemies (or victims) the poor, making perpetual war on the vicious Game Laws of his time. As a satirist he has been held to be second only to Swift; but though the tribute is just the comparison is misleading, for combined with his power of devastating mockery he had what Swift conspicuously lacked, a genial gusto. Even in his most severe pages there is no trace of self-enjoying cruelty or 'morose delectation'—the besetting sin of your satirist. In short he was, as Stevenson's Alan Breck said of himself, 'a bonny fighter', never a sour or mean one. He castigated human folly and injustice for love of mankind, not from spleen, not from hatred, above all not (as too many satirists do) from *self*-hatred. All the best of his writings are alive with what his friend Francis Jeffery called his 'brilliancy, benevolence, and flashing decision'.

And when he was alone with himself, what then? High spirits have commonly to be paid for by bouts of depression. With Smith there is no record of black melancholy or ill-temper, but his serenity was not absolute, and not entirely the product of unaided nature. Nature had given him a good start, by endowing him with a quick intelligence and a sanguine humour, but it was his own energy of mind and moral resolution that made of these things a stronghold against despair. He was a man not only of powerful, but of carefully cultivated, common sense. A stoic and a realist, by unflinching recognition of the plain facts of life and death he made the best of a difficult business and helped others to do so. By not pitching his expectations too high he fortified himself against undue disappointment. Illusions no doubt he had, but they were mercifully few. He insisted, to himself and to others, on the wisdom of taking short views of life; for to look too far ahead, into an unknown future, was to make oneself a prey to misery and apprehension. This is a recurring theme with him, both in letters to friends and in notes written for his own private admonition. His 'remedies against nervousness' prescribed for a friend are 'Resolution, Camphor, Cold Bathing, Exercise in the Open Air, Abstinence from Tea and Coffee, and from all distant views of human life except when religious duties call on you to take them'. A large man, inclined to portliness, he lays great stress on the dangers of indolence, whether physical or mental. He evidently found it difficult to get up in the morning: 'Nov. 3rd. Lost a day by indolence. The only method is to spring up at once.' Again: 'A good stout bodily machine being provided, we must be actively occupied, or there can be little happiness.' In a letter to Francis Jeffrey we find this: 'Living a great deal alone (as I now do) will, I believe, correct me of my faults; for a man can do without his own approbation in much society, but he must make great exertions to gain it when he is alone; without it, I am convinced, solitude is not to be endured.' To that end he wrote, in a small (unpublished) note-book, for his own eye alone: 'Remember that every person, however low, has rights and feelings. In all contentions let peace be rather your object than triumph: value triumph only as the means of peace. Remember that your children, your wife, and your servants, have rights and feelings: treat them as you would treat persons who could turn again. Apply these doctrines to the administration of justice as a magistrate. . . . Do not attempt to frighten children and inferiors by putting yourself into a passion. It does more harm to your own character than it does good to theirs. The same thing is better done by firmness and persuasion. . . . Against general fears, remember how very precarious life is, take what care you may; how short it is, last as long as ever it does. Rise early in the morning to avoid self-reproach, to make the most of the little life that remains—not only to save the hours lost in sleep but to avoid that languor which is spread over mind and body for the sake of that day in which you have laid late a bed.' The notebook from which I transcribe these entries is one of two. Though necessarily full of unexplained allusions they go far towards revealing the private self of this very public man, and we shall return to them in a later chapter. But we need look no further than his letters for evidence of his graver moods: not of black melancholy, for that he strenuously resisted, but of the more noble, chastened melancholy, which is inseparable from thoughtfulness. Answering a message of condolence on the death of his mother, he writes, when still a young man: 'Everyone must go to his grave with his heart scarred like a soldier's body— sometimes a parent, sometimes a child, a friend, a husband, or a wife. Thus the bands of this life are gradually loosened, and death at last is more welcome than the comfortless solitude of the world.'

Such things are worth recalling because they show that the gaiety of mind and heart by which he is for ever delighting us is founded on courage and kindness and common sense. Sydney Smith was a living refutation of the popular fallacy that to be 'brilliant' is to be superficial. Nevertheless, and naturally, it is as a never-failing fountain of wit and humour that he is best remembered. Never was there a man of whom so many entertaining stories are told. He took a mischievous pleasure in teasing the literal-minded, to whom all jokes were incomprehensible. A Mrs Jackson remarked how oppressively hot it had been last week. 'Hot, ma'am!' he said. 'It was so dreadful here that I found there was nothing for it but to take off my flesh and sit in my bones.' 'Take off your flesh and sit in your bones, sir? Oh, Mr Smith, how could you do that?' 'Nothing easier, ma'am. Come and see next time.' Another lady, who asked why he chained up his fine Newfoundland dog, was told: 'Because he has a passion for breakfasting on parish boys.' 'Parish boys!' she exclaimed. 'Does he really eat boys, Mr Smith?' 'Yes, ma'am, he devours them, buttons and all.' Her face of horror, said Smith, in telling his family the story, 'made me die of laughing'.

This kind of nonsense was the purest exuberance: his witticisms in general have more body and more point. In what he wrote for publication the point, as we shall see, is sharp, the satire grimly purposeful. But a few examples of the lighter mood, from personal letters, will help to complete this preliminary sketch. 'How very odd, dear Lady Holland, to ask me to dine with you on Sunday the 9th, when I am coming to stay with you from the 5th to the 12th! It is like giving a gentleman an assignation for Wednesday, when you are going to marry him on the preceding Sunday—an attempt to combine the stimulus of gallantry with the security of connubial relations.' Some years earlier he had written to this same Lady Holland, from Howick: 'I take the liberty to send you two brace of grouse—curious, because killed by a Scotch metaphysician; in other and better language, they are mere ideas, shot by other ideas, out of a pure intellectual notion called a gun.' To another lady, writing from Foston, he says: 'I am glad you liked what I said of Mrs Fry [Elizabeth Fry,

Quakeress and prison reformer]. She is very unpopular with the clergy: examples of living active virtue disturb our repose and give birth to distressing comparisons: we long to burn her alive.' To one who had sent him a gift of strawberries: 'What is real piety? What is true attachment to the Church? How are these fine feelings best evinced? The answer is plain: by sending strawberries to a clergyman. Many thanks.' And, for a last example, this, to a child: 'Many thanks for your kind and affectionate letter. I cannot recollect what you mean by our kindness; all that I remember is, that you came to see us, and we all thought you very pleasant, good-hearted, and strongly infected with Lancastrian tones and pronunciations. God bless you, dear child. I shall always be very fond of you till you grow tall, and speak without an accent, and marry some extremely disagreeable person.'

II

HOLY ORDERS

HE was not, however, an embodiment of all the talents and a paragon of all the virtues. His early biographers, in their understandable anxiety to present in the best possible light a man whose nearest relatives were still living, were (as always happens) somewhat partial in their selection from the available facts. Admirable in sum, a man eminently lovable, he had nevertheless certain insensibilities and certain faults of temper. How could it be otherwise? No one as high-spirited, as energetic, as brimful of life as he, could be expected to sustain the monotonous perfection of character sometimes implicitly ascribed to him. He endured his early poverty in 'manly' fashion (to use a favourite word of the period), but did not entirely escape that condition's malign effect on the temper: the less money, the more pride. As a young man he could be touchy, and hasty in his judgments. He could see a slight where none was intended, and become loquacious, even a little pompous, in defence of his dignity. This is certainly more true of the young Sydney Smith than of the man he became, yet even in his benign old age we may find an occasional echo of that youthful stridency, a surviving vestige of that prickly pride. In 1837, his sixty-seventh year, in the course of a correspondence with the Bishop of London, whom he had attacked in his first *Letter to Archdeacon Singleton*, he writes: 'My dear Lord: I hope there was no incivility in my last letter. I certainly did not mean there should be any. Your situation in life perhaps accustoms you to a tone of submission and inferiority from your correspondents which neither you nor any man living shall ever experience from me.' Much as one enjoys this outburst—and on this occasion Sydney had just cause for anger—one cannot help reflecting that the independence it asserts would have been even more impressive if left undeclared, or at any rate declared less aggressively. Yet it does not in the least diminish one's affection for this great-hearted pugnacious man. For with all his quick temper he was always, in the end, magnanimous. A word, provided it were the right word, could disarm him. Generous in victory, he was also generously ready, if fairly defeated, to confess himself to have been in the wrong.

He was born at Woodford, in Essex, in the summer of 1771, the second son of Robert Smith, whose father, originally a man of Devon, had done well in trade and left behind him a thriving business in Eastcheap. Robert was an eccentric, vigorous, self-willed person, an outsize in individualists. On the death of his father he handed over the Eastcheap business to a brother and set off to see the world. He went to America for three or four years and then wandered all over Europe. He was restless, active, unstable, a law unto himself. He had great natural gifts, of humour and eloquence. Catharine Smith, Sydney's wife, in an unpublished memoir of her husband written for her grand-children after his death, gives a lively account of this improbable character. 'An extraordinarily retentive memory, a great gossip; knew who everyone had married, whose lands had been sold or exchanged and from what cause; in short the operations of the whole social world seem'd known to him.' Wherever he went he was so full of anecdote 'that he became everywhere an astonishment and an admiration'. His mode of dressing was 'coxcombically homely, as if purposely to contrast the external appearance with the cultivated and eloquent mind that shone out whenever he spoke'. In old age he was still a very handsome and picturesque figure, white-haired, slight, rather bent, and dressed in the drab-coloured garb of a Quaker, though very far from being one. He 'delighted in making conquests: no woman was ever more vain of them'. While still very young he fell in love with Maria Olier, daughter of a French émigré. She was a very beautiful young woman, with a strong resemblance to Mrs Siddons in feature, 'but join'd to that majestic dignity of Mrs Siddons's face there was an enchanting expression of benevolence that made you feel confident she possessed every moral virtue'. With Robert Smith for a husband the poor girl was to have ample occasion for the exercise of her virtues, especially that of patient forbearance. That masterful young man, having still some business to settle in America, asked for a 'solemn

assurance' from Mrs Olier that on his return after two years
Maria Olier should become his wife. This she refused him, arguing
very sensibly that during so long a separation one or another of
the parties might suffer a change of heart and that then a formal
engagement would prove painful. Finding her as resolute in
decision as himself, he resorted to subterfuge: married the girl,
left her at the church door the moment the ceremony was over,
and went off to America. On his return to England and his wife
some years later, he proceeded further to diminish his considerable
fortune by 'buying, altering, spoiling, and then selling, about
nineteen different places' (Saba Holland), and at last, in old
age, settled at Bishop's Lydiard in Somersetshire, where he died
at the age of eighty-eight. He was excellent company, despite
his egoism. He delighted in laughter and seems to have captivated
all who came near him by the liveliness of his talk. We shall
hear more of him hereafter.

Sydney was luckier in his mother. His gentler qualities can be
traced to her example and influence. He had three brothers:
Robert Percy (nicknamed 'Bobus') his elder by one year, Cecil
a year younger, and Courtenay two years younger. Maria, born
in 1774, completed the family. Five children in five years: it is
possible that Mrs Smith did not always regret her husband's
frequent long absences from home. The boys, who cared little
for games, were omnivorous readers and were for ever arguing
with each other, loudly, vehemently, excitedly, on all manner of
subjects. The result, said Sydney, 'was to make us the most intolerable and overbearing set of boys that can well be imagined, till later
in life we found our level in the world'. With great sagacity, which
the sequel fully justified, their father decided not to send them all
to the same school: accordingly, Robert the eldest and Cecil the
third son went to Eton, Sydney and Courtenay to Winchester.

Public schools in the eighteenth century were run on the
principle of the survival of the toughest. For timid, weakly, or
imaginative boys, they were hell. Sydney Smith was neither timid
nor weakly, and to balance his sensitive imagination he had a
robust self-confidence; yet even in old age he would speak with
horror of the wretchedness he endured at Winchester. Saba
Holland quotes him as saying that 'the whole system was one
of abuse, neglect, and vice'. Near-starvation being the rule, the
predatory habits of the jungle were at a premium. 'There was

never enough provided, even of the coarsest food, for the whole school, and the little boys were of course left to fare as they could.' His brother Courtenay twice ran away, only to be haled back. Both of them survived the grim ordeal; Courtenay, having won the Gold Medal for Latin verse in four successive years, was precluded by Dr Warton from competing again, in response to a petition from the other boys; and Sydney became captain of the school. But these family triumphs did not reconcile him to the viciousness of the system, and to the end of his life he regarded his school career as largely time wasted. At school, he said, he 'made above ten thousand Latin verses, and no man in his senses would dream in after-life of making another'. One day an eminent visitor to the school, chancing to find him reading Virgil when the other boys were at play, patted his head, gave him a shilling, and said: 'Clever boy! That's the way to conquer the world.' It gives the measure of young Sydney's general misery, during at any rate the earlier part of his school career, that he always remembered this trifling incident with warm gratitude and dated his progress from it; for up till then the only incentive to learning, in his experience, had been fear of the cane. On leaving Winchester he was sent to Normandy to perfect his knowledge of French. The Revolution being then in full spate, he thought it prudent to join a local Jacobin Club, where he was duly enrolled as 'Le Citoyen Smit, Membre Affilié au Club des Jacobins de Mont Villiers': a precaution that stood him in good stead when two English friends of his insisted on sketching the fortifications at Cherbourg and were caught in the act by a gendarme. After six months in France he went to Oxford, as a Scholar of New College, and was in due time elected to a Fellowship. From that moment he received no further financial help from his father. One is sometimes tempted to suppose that Robert Smith harboured an obscure resentment against his second son; but it may be merely that his lavish expenditure on the eldest, Bobus, had frightened him into caution. Bobus, distinguished for his classical scholarship and especially for his facility in Latin verse, went from Eton to King's College, Cambridge, where his father gave him an allowance of £250 a year. He studied law and in due time was called to the Bar, where, however, he made little headway, being 'too full of delicate scruples to push his fortunes as an advocate', as his sister-in-law Catharine puts it. But influential friends got him the appointment of Advocate General at Calcutta, and there, during eight years, he amassed a handsome fortune. An eminent contemporary said of him: 'I never knew a mind with so gigantic a grasp.' For Cecil and Courtenay their father secured lucrative positions in the East India Company, the one at Madras, the other at Calcutta. Cecil was an amiable person: everybody liked him. But he was wildly extravagant; his large income as Accountant General at Madras never sufficed for his wants; and he was forced by debts and ill-health to return to England. He died in 1814, his forty-second year. Courtenay, at Catcutta, rose to great eminence. He became a considerable Orientalist and as Supreme Judge of the Adawlut Court wielded large powers. He spent not a tenth part of his noble income and so died a wealthy man. Returning to England with a fortune of a hundred and fifty thousand pounds, he lived during his remaining years the life of a recluse, rarely consenting even to dine with his two remaining brothers, Bobus and Sydney, though he had had no shadow of a difference with either.

All this, however, belongs to the future: we are at present with Sydney, newly elected to a Fellowship of his College at Oxford. His father's help peremptorily withdrawn, he managed, on an income of about £100 a year, not only to support himself but to pay off a debt incurred at Winchester by Courtenay, who flinched from disclosing it to their father. According to Catharine Smith, this loan was never repaid. The question of Sydney's profession came up for discussion. His father's project of sending him as a supercargo to Maccao (Robert Smith was a great hand at expatriating his sons) miscarried, so—'You may be either a College Tutor or a Parson,' said Mr Smith. As a parson, he added, Sydney might get a living from his college. Sydney's own strong inclination was for the law, a profession for which nature had brilliantly endowed him. But Smith senior, who either could not or would not afford to indulge that preference, pointed out to him that if he chose to be a lawyer he could expect nothing at his father's death, for he would have eaten up his patrimony in advance. Reluctantly, therefore, but with a characteristic resolve to make the best of a bad job, he took holy orders, and in 1794, at the age of twenty-three, accepted a curacy at Netheravon, a village on Salisbury Plain.

For a spirited young man, with an immense appetite and talent
for good talk, it was an unenviable situation. He was cut off
from every external thing that could help to make life enjoyable.
His solitude, at first, was unalleviated. The village consisted
only of a few scattered cottages; the house was in bad repair;
he was forced to live meanly, on a diet largely of potatoes
sprinkled with mushroom ketchup; he could not afford to buy
books; and for the bleak grandeur of the Plain he had no taste.
But, so far from sinking into despondency, he at once set about
doing what he could to help his parishioners. He petitioned his
father for a horse. 'A horse! Are you mad? Ask Beach—he'll
jump to give you a horse.' Michael Hicks Beach, the local squire,
did no such thing, but he did prove himself a very good friend
and benefactor. These Michael Hicks Beaches were much absent
from Netheravon, either in London, where they had a house in
Harley Street, or at their home in Gloucestershire. Very conscious
of the moral obligations which the possession of great wealth
must entail, with the old social order in decay and a new one
not yet struggling to be born, they were no doubt glad to have
someone on the spot who could be relied on to carry out their
plans for helping the villagers. In a letter to Mrs Hicks Beach
the young curate refers to a conversation he had had with her
about the poor of Netheravon in which she had agreed with him
that some of the boys and girls might possibly be prevented from
attending church by lack of proper clothing. He is now in a
position to confirm that conjecture. 'On Sunday last there were
three or four children with their feet on the cold stones, without
any shoes; and one came, a perfect *sans-culotte*, or at least with
only such grinning remnants of that useful garment as were just
sufficient to show that he was so clad from necessity and not
from any ingenious theory he had taken up against a useful
invention. If the Sunday school had begun, I should have
imagined that the poor boy thought it his duty to come ready for
whipping, as a fowl is sent from the poulterer's trussed and ready
for roasting. In whatsoever manner, to whatsoever extent, you may
choose to alleviate this species of misery, be so good as to remember
that I am on the spot, and shall be happy to carry your benevolent
intentions into execution in the best manner I am able.'

The Sunday school, which was to teach the art of reading
as well as piety and good behaviour, had not yet been brought

into being; but in April 1795 the project is taking shape. Who
is to be the schoolmaster? 'Andrew Goulter, whom you mentioned as a man likely to undertake it, is going to quit the place,'
writes Smith to Hicks Beach. 'Bendall the blacksmith, Harry
Cozens (a tailor and cousin to the clerk), and Giles Harding,
have all applied for the appointment. The last I consider quite
out of the question; his wife cannot read, and he has no room
fit to receive the children. Henry Cozens, in my opinion, is the
most eligible. His wife reads, his brother reads, and his appren-
tice reads; he has a good kitchen, which may be filled with
overflowings of the school, if it ever should overflow.' Next comes
the question of salary. 'I have mentioned the salary you arranged
with me to the applicants, namely 2s per Sunday, and two score
of faggots. The children will attend on Christmas Day and Good
Friday. Is the master to be paid for those days? It is impossible
to find two rooms in the same house for boys and girls; if they
are put to different houses the divided salary will be too small
to induce any reputable man to accept it.' Then, what of the
curriculum? He has not the smallest doubts on that point. 'The
books that are wanted will be about sixty spelling-books (with
easy lessons in reading at the end), beginning from the letters
and going on progressively in syllables; twenty New Testaments;
and twenty Prayer-books.' He adds a warm recommendation
of Hannah More's books, which can be obtained at five shillings
a hundred. It is clear from what follows in this letter that Smith
had succeeded in infecting others with his enthusiasm for this
highly novel scheme, which must have effected a species of
revolution in the village of Netheravon, that 'pretty feature in
a plain face', as he called it. The people who had sittings in
the great pew, he reports, have given it up; and Farmer Munday
is going to fit it up for the children's use. Moreover, 'the people
all express a great desire of sending their children to the school'.
He will talk to the farmers collectively at the vestry, and individually out of it. A few benches will be wanted for the Sunday-
school: will Mr Hicks Beach empower him to order them? Then
another practical point occurs to him. 'In the very hot weather,
why might not the children be instructed in the church before
and after service, instead of the little hot room in which they
would otherwise be stuffed? I shall mention it to the church-
wardens, with your approbation.'

So much for the Sunday school. Later we find him busy on another scheme, a 'school of industry' for the village girls, suggested by Mrs Hicks Beach. He sets about it with the same singleminded resolution and the same engaging attention to practical details. 'I have selected one girl from every family in the parish whose poverty entitled them to such relief. They amount to twenty. I have set them, first of all, upon making a coarse canvas-bag each, to hold their work in; which bags will be numbered, and hung up round the room when they leave school. We have divided the week between darning, sewing, and knitting; spinning is postponed for the present. I have weighed out materials to Mr Bendam; his salary is fixed at four shillings per week, and firing.' With his abundant good nature, fortified by a powerful sense of duty, this brilliant young man of four or five and twenty gave himself without stint to these homely sensible activities, and still found time, it is said, for 'theological studies'. He had not wanted to be a parson, but since destiny had cast him for that part he was resolved to be a good one. By now, however, a brighter personal prospect was unfolding before him. 'Nothing,' he had told Hicks Beach, 'can equal the profound, the immeasurable, the awful dullness of this place, in which I lie, dead and buried, in hopes of a joyful resurrection in the year 1796.' He did not know then that the Squire would propose to him that he should resign the curacy of Netheravon at the end of two years and become personal tutor to young Michael, his eldest son. It was arranged that he and Michael should go to the University of Weimar, in Saxony. 'We set out; but before reaching our destination, Germany was disturbed by war, and, in stress of politics, we put into Edinburgh, where I remained five years.'

III

MIGRATION TO EDINBURGH

A GERMAN courier engaged for the Weimar expedition, by name Mithoffer, accompanied Smith and his pupil to Edinburgh and lodged with them in Hanover Street, whence they commanded 'a view of the Firth shipping and opposite shore' and had a whole furnished floor to themselves, with a kitchen and a servant, for about forty-one shillings a week, or nine guineas a calendar month. The woman of the house, Smith tells Mrs Hicks Beach, was extremely civil all the summer, when lodgings were of no value; but at the approach of winter, when the town was filling up, 'because I would not give her twelve guineas instead of nine, she called me a Levite, a scourge of human nature, and an extortioner, and gave me notice to go out instantly, bag and baggage, without beat of drum or colours flying. I refused to stir; and after a severe battle, in which I threatened to carry it through all the courts of law in England, and from thence to Russia, she began to make the amiable, and to confess that she was apt to be a little warm, that she had the most perfect confidence in my generosity, and the old story. I made her sign an agreement, with subscription of two witnesses; and I am now lord of the castle for the time I tell you'. Not long afterwards, however, they moved round the corner into Queen Street.

Sydney's time was spent not only in directing the studies of Michael, his eighteen-year-old pupil, but in housekeeping, with Mithoffer's help. Mithoffer was at first a very poor judge of meat, but he improved under instruction from Sydney Smith, who several times went to the market with him. One day they tried to make a pie—the cook, Mithoffer, and Sydney himself; but the crust turned out to be as hard as biscuit and uneatable. 'There is always some beef in the salting tub; and I look into the family affairs like a fat old lady of forty'—he himself being a plump young man of twenty-six. To Michael he stood *in loco parentis*. He reports on progress from time to time, and it is evident that in spite of his predilection for laughter he took his job very seriously and did it very thoroughly. Perhaps too seriously, too thoroughly. He seems to have managed Michael, on the whole, with a nice blend of authority and friendliness; but it is possible that the boy was at first somewhat overwhelmed by his tutor's all-too-ready wit and crushing common sense. Was he sometimes made to feel a fool? The author of *A Cotswold Family: Hicks and Hicks Beach* thinks he was, and as evidence that Sydney Smith was not the ideal tutor for this particular pupil adduces the fact that Michael's letters to his parents from Edinburgh, in marked contrast to those he had written from Eton, are affected in calligraphy and stilted in manner. But though this may have been partly, and indirectly, Smith's fault, it may equally well have been a mere symptom of adolescent selfconsciousness. Nevertheless it does seem likely that his parents' too anxious desire to improve him, coupled with Smith's conscientious efforts in the same direction, tended for a while to defeat itself.

Two occasions of conflict between pupil and tutor are recorded in the above family history, the first a breeze, the second a storm, and both concerned with Michael's predilection for self-adornment. 'Our beginning has been very auspicious,' writes Sydney to Mrs Hicks Beach. 'I am extremely pleased and satisfied with Michael. My first serious conversation with him was upon the subject of his toilette, and the very great portion of time he daily consumed in adorning himself. This Michael took in high anger, and was extremely sulky. And upon my renewing the conversation some time after, he was still more so. Without the smallest appearance of anger or vexation on my part, I turned his sulkiness into ridicule, and completely laughed him into good humour. He acknowledged it was very foolish and unmanly to be sulky about anything, promised that he would hear any future remarks of mine about his conduct with cheerfulness and that he would endeavour to dress himself as quickly as he could.' A year later, however, something occurred which provoked Smith into writing to Michael's father, with sledgehammer solemnity, as follows: 'I am sure that you will do me the justice to say that it has not been my habit to harass you with trivial complaints of your son's conduct, and indeed as I never troubled you before upon the subject you may believe I should not *now* do it, unless the occasion appear'd to me to be such, as fully called for your interference. . . . You have no conception of his frivolous minuteness and particularity in everything which concerns his dress and person—it is more than feminine. And upon venturing the other morning to make some observation about the inutility of his troubles with his own boot-jack, his behaviour was so extremely improper and disrespectful, that I *did not open my lips to him for two days*—in all this time no sort of apology.' The italics (mine) reflect one's astonishment that so sensible a man as Sydney Smith should have thought offended silence a likely way of effecting his purpose. 'This morning,' he continues, 'I had a very long and serious conversation with him on the subject, and though he knew I intended to write to you, not a syllable of apology. Perhaps my dear Sir a few observations from you on that politeness and respect which he owes to those to whom you delegate your authority would do him more good than I am sorry to say any advice of mine can do. You expect, and have an undoubted right to expect, from me, the strictest attention to everything which goes to make up the character of your son as a man and a gentleman, and I am sure you will use your influence and authority to protect me from insult and injury. One single word of apology on the part of your son would have prevented you from ever hearing what passed between us. I was the more hurt on this occasion as Mithoffer was present during the whole of his improper behaviour. I have read over this letter to your son, but he heard without the least notice and without a single word.'

Michael had behaved badly, and a rebuke was inevitable. But one can hardly resist the impression that Sydney made unnecessarily heavy weather of the affair. In the sequel, however, they both emerge with credit. Michael's answer to his father's letter is full of genuine contrition. It also, incidentally, and I think accidentally, throws light on 'the cause of my misbehaviour'. It surely argues a failure of imagination on Sydney's part that he did not divine that cause—the presence of Mithoffer. 'I lost all command over myself when questioned and reprimanded before him,' says Michael. But if Michael made ample amends, so did Sydney, by the characteristic generosity with which he cut short the eventual apology. 'I have at last attempted to make a proper apology, but Mr Smith was so good he would not suffer me. He said, "My dear friend, one word by way of apology is enough". I shall never forget those words, and only hope that I may prove what he then called me.' The hope was fulfilled. Having taken each other's measure, and learnt give-and-take, the two became better friends than they had ever been. Michael had no taste for books, and his tutor no taste for the more frivolous social amusements that Michael enjoyed; but henceforward by mutual tolerance they seem to have got along together very well, and frequent reports went to Mrs Hicks Beach in Gloucestershire saying that Michael was 'in the essential points of character an extremely good young man, honest, honourable, and friendly, without the smallest tendency to any one vice whatsoever'. Sydney wisely abandoned the hope of making him a scholar or of forcing literature upon him. That 'useful and ornamental' addition to gentility was something he was too evidently resolved to do without.

Sydney Smith had arrived in Edinburgh at a most propitious time. That queen of cities was rich in eager, friendly, talented young men, many of them destined to win distinction as lawyers, statesmen, doctors, men of affairs, and men of letters. Erskine, like Brougham a future Lord Chancellor, was already eminent. Light and learning radiated from Dugald Stewart, Professor of Moral Philosophy—'one of the greatest of didactic orators . . . to me his lectures were like the opening of the heavens', says Henry Cockburn in his memoirs. The choicest spirits in Edinburgh were, in Saba Holland's words, 'neither rich, nor ashamed of being poor'. Jeffrey, Horner, Brougham, Murray (afterwards Lord Advocate), Walter Scott, Thomas Campbell: these and others received the newcomer with great kindness and soon recognized in him an acquisition to a society in which plain living and high thinking was the rule. Nothing could have been more exactly suited to Sydney's tastes or in more congenial contrast to the intellectual starvation he had endured at Netheravon. The friends met two or three times a week, either in each other's houses or in oyster-cellars, and talked to their hearts' content about every subject under the sun. 'When shall I see Scotland again?' wrote Sydney in after life. 'Never shall I forget the happy days passed there, amidst odious smells, barbarous sounds, bad suppers, excellent hearts, and most enlightened and cultivated understandings.' He attended Dugald Stewart's lectures with delight and much profit; continued medical studies begun at Oxford, thus acquiring a knowledge and skill that came in very handy later on; and did duty as an occasional preacher. All this in addition to his tutoring, which was never neglected. Anglo-Scottish friendship has always thrived on banter, a commodity in which Sydney Smith, wherever he might be, dealt lavishly; but his pleasantries, unlike Dr Johnson's, are always mixed with warm appreciation. Their temper stands everything, he says of the Scots, except an attack on their climate. 'They would have you believe they can ripen fruit; and, to be candid, I must own that in remarkably warm summers I have tasted peaches that made most excellent pickles; and it is upon record that at the siege of Perth on one occasion, the ammunition failing, their nectarines made admirable cannon-balls.' Though he calls Scotland 'that garret of the earth, that knuckle-end of England, that land of Calvin, oat-cakes, and sulphur', and gives countenance to the traditional half-truth that it requires a surgical operation to get a joke well into a Scottish understanding, he warmly declares that 'no nation has so large a stock of benevolence of heart: if you meet with an accident, half Edinburgh immediately flocks to your door', and offers an illuminating comparison between Scotland and England. 'The clergy of England have no more influence over the people at large than the cheesemongers of England. In Scotland the clergy are extremely active in the discharge of their functions, and are, from the hold they have on the minds of the people, a very important body of men. The common people are extremely conversant with the Scriptures; are really not so much pupils as formidable critics to their preachers; many of them are well read in controversial divinity.' No one who has read the novels of Walter Scott can question the justice of that pronouncement, or of the sentences that follow it: 'They are perhaps in some points of view the most remarkable nation in the world; and no country can afford an example of so much order, morality, economy, and knowledge, amongst the lower classes of society.'

His sojourn in Edinburgh was interrupted in his thirtieth year by a visit to England for the purpose of getting married. His bride was Catharine Amelia Pybus, a girlhood friend of his sister Maria's, and the betrothal was of long standing. Catharine, in the account she wrote for her grandchildren, does not even mention the courtship. 'The intimacy between our families continued, dear Maria and myself remaining strongly attached to each other. At last, when Mr Hicks Beach was desirous that his eldest son should go abroad in 1798 under Sydney's charge, it was agreed that on his return Sydney and I should marry.' That is all she has to say on this crucial matter. Of Sydney's 'love story', therefore, nothing is known, nor of his marriage either except that it brought happiness to everyone concerned, with the exception of his preposterous father, Robert Smith senior, and Charles Pybus, the bride's brother. Sydney, putting it to his father that he would forfeit his New College Fellowship by marrying, petitioned for a small allowance from him. 'Not one penny!' said the old man, implying that if he was fool enough to throw away his Fellowship he must take the consequences. It was not that he disliked Catharine Pybus. 'I believe he liked me as much as his selfish nature was capable of loving anyone who did not minister to his own comforts.' Despite this set-back, Sydney insisted that all her fortune at that time, and more that was ultimately to come to her, should be placed in trust for her sole use, and that she should have the entire disposal of it at her death and the interest arising from it during her life. Both she and her mother opposed him on this point, saying that it was impossible to know what contingencies might arise that would make it desirable for the young couple to have access to some of the money. 'With the greatest difficulty she [Mrs Pybus] at last prevailed; and £1,000, at our jointly expressed wish, my trustees were empowered to make over to us.' Sydney's earnest request that his wife's money should be placed beyond his reach was not actuated solely by a wish to demonstrate his own disinterestedness: he knew, and declared, that if he were known to have the smallest control over it the old man, with his mania for acquiring property, would demand loans from him for the financing of yet another crazy enterprise. 'This notion,' says Catharine, 'we ridiculed as quite an overdrawn picture.' But they soon had reason to think otherwise. After the honeymoon she and Smith paid a visit to Beauchamp, 'where Mr Smith, his dear wife, and Maria, then lived. We really had not been a week there, when the most furious outburst took place. His father abused Sydney violently for having so tied up my money as that he could not lend it to him to purchase an estate. "You know I

C

wished to purchase a farm. Your father should have been first thought of. What right had *you*, where you had it in your power to benefit *me*, to indulge in such silly romantic notions of securing to her her property? Could it be anywhere safer than in the hands of your *father*?" ' And so on. Poor Mrs Smith, when told of this, could only say pathetically: 'Oh my dear, Sydney has mistaken him! It cannot be!'

The visit continued without further explosions, and at the end of a fortnight the two families parted, apparently good friends. But in the sequel Robert Smith seems to have behaved like one of the more improbable characters in Dickens. For two years later, in 1802, Sydney's mother died. Sydney, deeply grieved, wrote to his father 'in the most affectionate manner, begging him and dear Maria would come to him in Edinburgh, that change of scene would relieve the heavy sorrow he well knew she would suffer from her mother's death, and that it should be the study of his life to make him happy and comfortable'. It was, in short, 'such a letter as [only] a heart full of the tenderest affection for the dead, and soften'd too by grief for her loss, could suggest'. The answer, 'though I cannot repeat the excess of its abuse', was to this effect, says Catharine: 'So long as poor Jona lived (the name he always gave Mrs Smith) I have borne patiently with you because I knew that if I had quarrel'd with you it would have broken her heart; but now that she is gone I never will see you more; for I never will forgive and never shall forget your d——d selfishness in so tying up your wife's fortune as to put it out of your power to assist your father.' Owing to the gentle influence of Maria, father and son did meet after some years; but until then almost every week had brought an abusive letter. Moreover, this eminently comic character not only abused his son but—in the same letters—made use of him, 'sending Sydney to the furthest parts of the City [of London, where by this time they were living] about some trifling article that he thought might be purchased there better than elsewhere'. The most charitable construction one can put upon all this is that Robert Smith, at any rate in his later years, was more than a little mad. It suggests, too, the conjecture that Sydney's character and behaviour must have been much influenced, in a negative sense, by the example of his father, and in particular by the spectacle of that father's married life. Even had he not inherited something of his mother's gentleness, patience, and sympathetic imagination, by asking himself 'What would my father do?' and then doing the exact opposite he could have made himself the considerate husband and understanding father which in fact he was.

But to return to 1800. The only undisguised opponent of Sydney's marriage was Charles Pybus, who was indignant that the sister of so important a personage as himself—he became a Lord of the Admiralty in the Pitt administration—should throw herself away on a penniless nobody. His attitude led to a complete and final breach between them: they never saw each other again. For the girl herself had courage and sense. She was twenty-two, and presumably in love. With her mother's encouragement she faced undismayed the prospect of forgoing the comforts and luxuries to which she had been accustomed all her life. Mrs Pybus declared that she wished for nothing but her daughter's happiness. She 'had long known and loved Sydney', and if to marry him was Catharine's resolve she would not oppose it. 'Now, dear children,' remarks Catharine in old age, with endearing complacency, 'this is not a decision for you and others to follow. There never before *was*, and never again *will be*, another Sydney!!' She adds that her resolution to marry him was not so rash as at first sight it appeared to be; for to her, in her youthful assurance, 'it was *impossible* but that his success should in the end be perfect'. Such a mind, such versatility of talents, 'such a bold and fearless love of truth, such an ardent love of human happiness that no feelings of selfish prudence could ever controul, *must* eventually break through all obstacles and gain for itself honour and distinction.—*And so it did*!' she writes exultantly, in double-sized characters, underscored, and followed by two exclamation marks. The triumphant words leap up from her page of beautiful, slanting calligraphy.

The marriage took place in July. The situation of the young couple was tolerably comfortable even in a mercenary sense. Mr Hicks Beach made them a handsome gift of government stock. The early biographers insist much on Smith's poverty in early life, and there is no gainsaying that he had some very difficult and anxious times; but when actual figures are quoted they provoke the reflection that poverty is after all a comparative term, and that as the son of an affluent country gentleman he had perhaps inherited larger ideas of what was due to him than he would have today. Within a few years he was to have two pupils: Michael's young brother William, and Alexander Gordon, son of the Earl of Edinburgh. For each of these he was paid £400 a year, 'which made us for a time very rich', says his wife; and in view of the high value of the pound in those days, compared with our own, we may believe her. Sydney, it is evident, was a great stickler for his rights. His often-declared gratitude to the Hicks Beaches did not deter him from speaking his mind, at prodigious length, when he fancied, on what looks like very slender foundation, that a slight had been put upon his wife. In the late summer of the marriage-year, 1800, before they finally settled down together in George Street, Edinburgh, Sydney and Catharine accompanied the Hicks Beaches on a holiday tour in England. There followed a painful correspondence between Sydney and Mrs. Hicks Beach on the subject of bedrooms. In one letter, evidently not the first of the series, after pompously remarking that 'when people of good breeding and education travel together they share equally the pleasures and inconveniences of the journey', Sydney writes: 'You uniformly through the whole of our tour put Mrs Smith in the worst room and took the best for yourself—without the smallest apology, or any one softening expression whatever. Is this not to say in language *too plain to be mistaken*—I do not think this woman worthy of being treated with the common forms of politeness?— If there *is* any other interpretation to be put upon this, it has escaped my attentive consideration. My wife is of a disposition that she would not complain if she were to be placed in a dungeon —but am I to feel for her less because her disposition is amiable? I should be unworthy your notice if I thought for a moment whether my bed were good or bad, of if the bad accommodation to which every person is exposed in travelling could for a moment ruffle my temper; but I want the consideration, and the politeness, not the accommodation. I want not the thing itself but the offer, and I want these much more for my wife than myself.' This, from guest to hostess, from a young man to a woman considerably his senior and with whom he had enjoyed a pleasant epistolary friendship for some six or seven years, might by anyone less hotheaded than Sydney Smith have been thought almost enough. But not by him: he goes on and on, rebuking, moralizing, laying down the law. Unfortunately the whole correspondence is not available, but from Smith's next letter it may be inferred that Mrs Hicks Beach, being of a milder and more forbearing disposition than he, contented herself with denying his accusation and (perhaps) expressing astonishment that it had been brought against her. 'My dear Madam,' he says, 'I lay down this simple principle that under all the circumstances of our journey, and from every principle of good breeding with which I am acquainted, a fair share of the accommodation experienced on the road ought to have been *offered* to Mrs Smith. If such, as you say, was the fact—or *nearly* the fact—my conduct has been quite unpardonable, by myself and by you.'

In the course of her reply to this further letter the defendant writes: 'Your letter has not offended me, on the contrary I think you have done well in accounting for your very extraordinary behaviour at Bank House. But . . . you are much mistaken in supposing that Mrs Smith had always the worst bedroom during our journey, I do assure you her room was sometimes equal to mine and sometimes better. . . . I must do myself the justice to say good Sir, that after a strict review of my late behaviour from the commencement of our acquaintance, I can fairly acquit myself of having at any time treated you or Mrs Smith with negligence or disrespect, I have uniformly endeavour'd to pay you both every proper attention and can only add, I am sorry to find I have not succeeded better in her opinion and in yours. . . . Mr Hicks Beach unites with me in compliments to Mrs Smith and love to William. I am, dear Sir, Your obedient Servant, H. M. Hicks Beach.' No man could fail to be mollified by that. Smith's reply, though still somewhat wordy, is temperate and somewhat chastened in tone. He is bound, he says, in view of what she has said, to believe her *intention* to have been irreproachable. But even now he will not quite give up his point. Even if Mrs Smith *was* (his argument runs) given as good a bedroom as her hostess, it remained true that she was never offered a choice of accommodations, as 'in conformity to established usages' she should have been. Had that been done it would have 'settled and sweetened everything in a moment, would have convinced *you* of the disposition of the woman you had to deal with and would have prevented me from misconceiving the conduct of my old and respected friends and benefactors'.

A further strain was put upon the friendship, which however survived it, when a few months later the question of Smith's remuneration for tutoring William was raised, Michael having by now gone on to a university. The tutor was invited to assess the value of his time, and did so in some detail, though he said he found the task an embarrassment. Delighted with his new pupil, he ends by saying: 'If Mr Beach shall differ in opinion with me on this offer, and should rather prefer placing William with Mr [Dugald] Stewart, my reluctance in parting with so truly amiable a young man will be in some degree mitigated by the pleasure I shall have in forwarding by my mediation any wish Mr Beach and you may entertain for the welfare of your son.' If this was an ultimatum, it was answered with a counter-ultimatum. An extra £200 a year is offered, instead of the extra £300 demanded. Evidently a little hurt by Sydney's saying that five of the best years of his life will have been given up to the education of their children, the Hicks Beaches point out that he has been an entirely free agent in the matter. The letter is courteous, but the offer has an air of finality. 'My dear Madam,' answers Sydney, with a civility that thinly disguises hot haste: 'The contents of your letter did not require that deliberation which you were so kind as to allow me to give them. I confess I had great objections to propose terms myself because I thought it unprecedented and incorrect, but having so done in compliance with your desire I cannot allow myself even to think of accepting any others, or to consider the question of interest when the question of decency and propriety (which should always be prior in the order of reflections) is so very plain and obvious. I shall therefore in the spring resign my charge into your hands, with that reluctance for his loss which his charming understanding and admirable disposition will most unfeignedly inspire.' He goes on to regret that Dugald Stewart, whose address he sends, is unfortunately unable to undertake the charge of William, being 'completely full', and adds that he will do everything in his power to find some other suitable person. Finally: 'You shall hear from me in a day or two. . . . If contrary to all probability you should not meet with an eligible situation for William by the time I am settled in London, my services to superintend his education till you can succeed in placing him elsewhere are most entirely at your disposal and I shall conceive myself

amply rewarded by the pleasure of improving so good a
young man.'

There seemed nothing more to be said. But at this point,
certainly without Sydney's knowledge, his father intervened,
writing to Mrs Hicks Beach, from Bath, a letter which exhibits
him at his paternal best. He has written to her husband and
now begs her to intercede with him, 'offended as he has the
justest reason to be with Sydney's conduct. . . . I had not the
most distant information of the business from Sydney till last
week; he too well knew my sentiments of your past goodness
and the eternal gratitude it so truly merited; and it is with
grief I confess I feel myself very much hurt from this pointed
neglect so recent after his marriage, to which and all its arrangements I was equally an utter stranger. Yet I am convinced he is
a good Man holding you and Mr Beach in the highest esteem
and attached to your son William warmly. Nor do I believe
there exists another who would more honourably devote his time
and faculties and the trust you have repos'd in him. He has
mistaken the point of honor, of which he thinks improperly,
and, fearful of sinking in your opinion, had not courage to recede
from a point to which he should never have committed himself.
Mr Beach's offer was of a piece with his former friendship and
ought not to be increas'd, but Madam it will be shewing such
superiority over this false parade of Sydney's to indulge me in
the proposal I have taken the liberty of making to him [Mr Beach]
as must have most beneficial effect in future. Added to which'—
the addition will suggest to a suspicious mind that Robert Smith
preferred to have his son at a distance—'I am convinc'd his
coming either to London or Bath will be followed with the
consequences I dread of all others.' What those consequences
were one can only conjecture. Mr Smith ends by confessing to
'a weight of shame' and saying: 'I will yet hope for a favorable
turn at the earnest intercession of, Dear Madam, Your ever
Faithful and obliged humble Servant, Robert Smith.' The
upshot of it all was that Sydney was empowered by Mr Hicks
Beach to draw on him for whatever he thought fair, over and
above his expenses—'and thus everyone's dignity was saved',
remarks the author of *A Cotswold Family*.

Whatever view one may take of this episode, it was certainly
wise and courageous of Sydney to decline, in 1803, the suggestion

that he should stay in Edinburgh, tutoring William, for yet another year. 'It is a matter of real regret to me,' he writes to Mrs Hicks Beach, 'that I should be compelled to decline any proposal which it would give you pleasure that I should accept. I have one child, and I expect another : it is absolutely my duty that I should make some exertion for their future support. The salary you give is liberal; I live here in ease and abundance; but a situation in this country leads to nothing. I have to begin the world, at the end of three years, at the very same point where I set out from; it would be the same at the end of ten. I should return to London, my friends and connexions mouldered away, my relations gone and dispersed, and myself about to do at the age of forty what I ought to have begun to do at the age of twenty-five.' He goes on to speak of the kindness with which he has been treated by the Hicks Beaches. 'That kindness I shall never forget; and I shall quit this country with a very large balance of obligation on my side, which I shall always be proud to acknowledge. But I could not hold myself justified to my wife and family if I were to sacrifice, any longer, to the love of present ease, those exertions which every man is bound to make for the improvement of his situation.'

IV

THE EDINBURGH REVIEW

D URING the latter part of his time in Edinburgh he had initiated an enterprise which was to play an important part not only in his own life but in the intellectual and political life of Britain for many years to come. For Sydney Smith was the chief progenitor of the EDINBURGH REVIEW, the second of that name. It was on a stormy night in March 1802 that he first announced his idea, in Buccleuch Place, to his two friends Francis Jeffrey and Henry Brougham, lawyers both. The proposal, he says, was agreed to with acclamation. The motto he suggested—*Tenui musam meditamur avena:* 'We cultivate literature on a little oatmeal'—was however turned down in favour of a grave quotation from Publius Syrus, 'of whom none of us had, I am sure, read a single line'. According to Brougham's account of the matter the expression 'with acclamation' is an overstatement; for, while Brougham entered warmly into the scheme, Jeffrey was full of doubts and fears. 'It required all Smith's overpowering vivacity to argue and laugh Jeffrey out of his difficulties. There would, he said, be no lack of contributors. There was himself, ready to write any number of articles, and to edit the whole; there was Jeffrey, *facile princeps* in all kinds of literature; there was myself, full of mathematics, and everything relating to colonies; there was Horner for political economy, Murray for general subjects.' Despite all this, and more to a similar effect, Jeffrey was with difficulty persuaded, and in the weeks and months that followed he continued to prophesy failure and 'seemed only anxious to be freed from the engagement he and the rest of us had entered into with Constable to guarantee him four numbers as an experiment'—which throws an interesting sidelight on that forthright and sometimes wrongheaded literary critic. After many delays the first number appeared, in October. Smith's wildest hopes were exceeded, and Jeffrey's fears utterly confounded, by its instant success. So far the editorial work had fallen to Smith, but now, on the point of leaving Edinburgh, he urged upon Constable that a permanent editor at a liberal salary should be appointed, and that every contributor, whether he would or no, should be paid, at not less than a standard rate. The rule against gratuitous contributions, which today would need no enforcement, at any rate upon writers, was both wise and necessary in an age when professional journalism was regarded, especially it seems in legal circles, as an occupation unfit for a gentleman, notwithstanding that some distinguished men were already engaging in it. Jeffrey himself, when offered the editorship, was beset by fears of 'vexation and trouble, interference with professional employment and character, and risk of general degradation'. Nor were such fears groundless, for the historian Walpole tells us, in a passage quoted by Smith's early biographer Reid, that as late as 1808 the Benchers of Lincoln's Inn made a by-law excluding all persons who had written for the daily press from being called to the Bar, and that more than twenty years later a Lord Chancellor gave great offence to his supporters by asking the editor of THE TIMES to dinner. An incidental effect of Jeffrey's brilliant management of the EDINBURGH REVIEW was to raise the social status of periodical journalism. All articles being anonymous, many able men who would have shrunk from confessing to the indiscretion were persuaded to write for print, and encouraged moreover to write in a style that could catch the attention of the general public; and by allowing no one to refuse payment the proprietors were able to ensure that no private axes should be ground in their pages. 'The severity of the criticism on books and their authors,' says Brougham, 'was much, and often justly, complained of;* but no one could accuse it of personal malice, or any sinister motives. The rule was inflexibly maintained, never to suffer the insertion of any attack by a writer who was known, or even justly suspected

---

* This should not be forgotten, and Sydney Smith must have some share of the blame. Harriet Martineau in her autobiography tells how, many years later, she taxed him with the fact, saying: 'It is all very well to talk sensibly now of the actual importance of reviews and the real value of reviewers' judgments: but the fact remains that spirits were broken, hearts were sickened, and authorship was cruelly discouraged, by the savage and reckless condemnations passed by the EDINBURGH REVIEW in its early days.' Quoted by Dr J. A. Greig in his *Francis Jeffrey of the Edinburgh Review* (Edinburgh, 1948).

to have a personal difference with the author, or other sinister motive.' He also asserts, with justice, that the REVIEW not only raised the character and increased the influence of periodical criticism, but in the long run effected 'vast reforms and improvements in all our institutions, social as well as political'. It contributed, incalculably but decisively, to such reforms as the establishment of parliamentary representation in Scotland, the emancipation of the Catholics, the repeal of the Test Acts, the abolition of the death penalty for stealing, the allowing a prisoner accused of a capital crime to be represented by counsel, and the abolition of the slave trade. Smith's share in this work seemed to Brougham never to have been sufficiently recognized. And that verdict stands. Smith, with his emphasis on reason and good sense, his warm humanity, his passion for justice, his distrust of anything that smacked of fanaticism, embodied many of the characteristic virtues of the two centuries in which he lived. He was a great fighter in good causes, and he never lost his head.

That truth is better than lying and freedom better than slavery have for long been accepted as self-evident propositions by all men of good will; but we today have witnessed, are witnessing, a resolute and powerful attempt to disestablish them; the simple truths we took for granted, and perhaps despised as mere truisms, have now to be defended with a zeal generally reserved for more novel and exciting opinions. Smith's example, therefore, should have more than an historical interest for us: it has a special pertinence in an age like ours, when the pure lust for power, aided by modern techniques, threatens the destruction of all human values. A great lover of freedom, says Brougham of Smith, and a still more fervent lover of truth, he 'was not led away by the false appearance of liberty which the dangerous and mischievous doctrines of the French Revolution too widely spread. He looked upon all that had been going on in France with calm good sense; and in all his writings, while he was the unflinching advocate of every sound principle, he earnestly protested against the dangers to which true liberty was exposed by the mistaken zeal of its first worshippers'. Acton's famous dictum that all power corrupts had not yet been uttered, but Smith, we may be sure, was very much alive to its truth. He knew that individual liberty can only be preserved by a distribution of power and is inevitably destroyed when too much power becomes concentrated in a clique or a class, so that to dethrone one set of men in favour of another, though it may be a necessary temporary expedient, can of itself effect nothing, in the long run, but a change of tyrannies. Only angels can be trusted with unrestricted power; and the supply of angels, even among politicians, has always been limited.

To the first four numbers of the REVIEW Smith contributed eighteen long articles. Long they were, nothing scrappy or sketchy about them: book-reviews nominally, they were more like leisurely dissertations on a chosen theme than the kind of reviewing we are accustomed to today. He did not as a rule venture into the realm of pure literary criticism: that was Jeffrey's department. He concerned himself most with moral, social, and political questions. It was not expert or specialist knowledge that was required of him: there were others in the team who could supply that. He was that rare kind of born writer, so highly valued by hardworked editors, one who could be relied on to write sensibly and wittily on any subject that interested him, and at short notice. He continued for some twenty-five years to write for the EDINBURGH REVIEW, and these articles constitute the largest part of his published work. They nearly all have the speed and vigour, the wit and clarity, of first-rate pamphleteering. Like all writers in that kind, he hammers away at his points with what sometimes seems unnecessary iteration; but this repetitiveness, the exuberant overflow of a full mind, is redeemed by his good humour and buoyant self-confidence. He was always a very active man: activity of both body and mind was the regimen he prescribed for himself, to keep his weight down and his spirits up. As his insistence on 'short views' shows, he was keenly alive to the danger of sinking, through worry augmented by indolence, into despondency. In middle life he spent an hour or two every day digging in his Yorkshire garden, 'to avoid sudden death', as he said. His daughter Saba Holland has testified that he was hardly ever unoccupied. He was always reading, or writing, or talking. He read so quickly that his family often laughed at him when he shut up a thick quarto and declared his morning's work done; but when, in response to his challenge, they examined him on the book, they would find that he knew all that was worth knowing about it. As in reading, so in writing. 'When he had any subject in hand he was indefatigable in reading, searching, inquiring, seeking every source of information, and discussing it with any man of sense or cultivation who crossed his path. But, having once mastered it, he would sit down, and he might be seen committing his ideas to paper with the same rapidity that they flowed out in his conversation—no hesitation, no erasures, no stopping to consider and round his periods, no writing for effect, but a pouring out of the fullness of his mind and feelings, for he was heart and soul in whatever he undertook. One could see by his countenance how much he was interested or amused as fresh images came clustering round his pen.' Impatient of revision, when he had finished he would often toss the manuscript to his wife saying: 'There, it's done. Do look it over, Kate, and dot the i's and cross the t's'—and then he would go out for a brisk walk.

V

A FREELANCE IN LONDON

IT was partly Catharine's persuasions that decided him to leave Edinburgh, where he had so many good and influential friends, and try his luck in London. She tells her grandchildren that it is the one occasion of her life of which she is really proud. Not content that he should squander his talents in tutoring and periodical journalism, she was willing to risk having to endure a long period of poverty in the hope of his making ultimate headway in his chosen—though reluctantly chosen—profession, the Church. The family settled down once again in a small house in Doughty Street, Mecklenburgh Square, where in 1804, to add to their joys and anxieties, a son was born. One of Catharine's early measures of economy after settling in London was to sell some pearls which she had recently inherited from her mother. During the negotiations with the jeweller Sydney was in a state of comical anxiety lest mankind should suddenly wake up to the folly of paying large prices for 'such glittering baubles', and when the deal was completed he pretended to suffer some twinges of conscience at having helped to perpetuate the illusion of their high value. The pearls fetched five hundred pounds: some years later Catharine saw them offered for sale at fifteen hundred.

Smith came as a stranger to London, but quickly made friends. Among the first to welcome him was Francis Horner, an EDIN-BURGH REVIEW colleague, who had left Scotland before him to become a member of the English Bar, and who, as an expert economist with the power of making his subject interesting to the uninitiated, was to enjoy a distinguished though brief career (he died young) in the House of Commons. The very thing that blocked Sydney's ecclesiastical advancement would commend him to precisely the kind of men whose society he most enjoyed; but his years in London were years of struggle and anxiety, as well as of tremendous intellectual stimulation; he had difficulty in obtaining employment as a preacher; and it can only be supposed that he supported himself and his family largely on his wife's pearls and what money he had been able to save from the Edinburgh days. He gave joyous if frugal supper parties once a week, but would never subscribe to the vanity of trying to keep up an appearance beyond his means. In a letter to Jeffrey written from Doughty Street in July 1805, he says: 'You ask me about my prospects. I think I shall long remain as I am. I have no powerful friends. I belong to no party. I do not cant. I abuse canting everywhere. I am not conciliating, and I have not talents enough to force my way without these laudable and illaudable auxiliaries. This is as true a picture of my situation as I can give you. In the meantime I lead not an unhappy life, much otherwise, and am thankful for my share of good. My kindest regards to all my old friends. Ever yours, my dear Jeffrey, with the truest affection, Sydney Smith.' He did however acquire at least one powerful friend, of the ruling class though not of the ruling party, in the person of Lord Holland, who had been at school at Eton with his brother Bobus; he began to be more and more widely valued as a preacher; and he achieved a *succès fou* with a series of lectures at the Royal Institution on moral philosophy, a subject in which his competence, he considered, was so slight that he described the episode as 'the most successful swindle of the season'. These were years of public tumult and anxiety. Napoleon was overrunning Europe and threatening this island with invasion. The triumph of Trafalgar was followed, within a matter of weeks, by the disaster at Austerlitz. Pitt died; Grenville formed his famous 'ministry of all the talents'; George the Third, against the national interest as well as in defiance of plain justice, stubbornly vetoed the proposal to let Roman Catholics hold commissions in the army; and Grenville's administration gave place to men of coarse fibre and no principles. These events formed the political background of Sydney Smith's first London period.

His meeting with Lord Holland led to three important results: (i) a warm and permanent friendship with Holland and his formidable but amusing wife, (ii) access, through the gates of Holland House, to the best literary and political society of the day, and (iii) appointment to the living of Foston in Yorkshire, his first real taste of economic security. Henry Richard Fox, third baron Holland and nephew of Charles James Fox, had made scandalous history in his young manhood by running away with the wife of a baronet, Sir Godfrey Webster: their first (illegitimate) son distinguished himself, in his turn, by marrying a daughter of William the Fourth and Mrs Jordan. Young Lord Holland and his lady were enabled by her divorce in 1797, his twenty-fourth year, to regularize their position; and after some four years spent in France, where during the Peace of Amiens they were received by Napoleon, for whom Lady Holland professed a fervid admiration, they became conspicuous members of London society, he as a vigorous Whig politician and patron of literature, she as a hostess of enterprise and genius. Holland House, when Smith first entered it, was already famous for the brilliance of its assemblies. It was a *salon* after the French style, to which scientists, statesmen, philosophers, diplomats, poets, painters, and eminent visitors from Europe, were glad to resort. Such men as Byron, Macaulay, Tom Moore, Samuel Rogers were frequent and favourite guests. Unable to afford a coach, Smith made a practice of going to these gatherings on foot, often with muddy shoes which he changed on arrival, at risk of being despised by the proud liveried flunkeys who guarded the door. It is said that he was shy and embarrassed in manner at his first entry into this brilliant society: which suggests that with all his cleverness he was anything but cocksure and overbearing. But he soon found his feet and became a prime favourite. When Lady Holland, in her brusque peremptory fashion, one day commanded him to ring the bell—'Ring the bell, Sydney!'— he coolly replied: 'Certainly. And shall I sweep the floor as well?'

To possess wealthy friends is not an unmixed blessing to a poor man unless he is also an exceptionally sensible man. By being always himself, and never trying to cut a dash, Sydney continued to get the best out of any situation he found himself in. Years later he once remarked: 'The observances of the Church concerning feasts and fasts are tolerably well kept upon the whole, since the rich keep the feasts and the poor the fasts'. But the period of his fasting was now nearly at an end. Holland was Lord Privy Seal in the short-lived Grenville administration and used his influence with Erskine, the Lord Chancellor, to get Smith appointed to the living of Foston in 1806. Before we follow him there, however, it will perhaps be well to give one concrete example of the obstacles to earning a livelihood that he had encountered in London.

It seems to have been the curious practice, in the preaching trade, for chapels or meeting-houses to be owned by private persons and leased to individual preachers: subject, however, to the rule that no Church of England clergyman could enjoy the use of such a place without the formal permission of the local rector. Smith was offered, by the proprietor, a chapel occupied by an obscure dissenting sect. He therefore addressed himself in persuasive terms to the Reverend Dr Monopoly (the real name is not recorded), asking whether, 'under any restrictions and upon any conditions', he would allow him to preach there. 'I cannot doubt,' he says, 'that where a place of worship is to exist in your parish you would rather that the worship of the Church of England were carried on there, than that it should belong to such sectaries as the Christians of the New Jerusalem (as they entitle themselves). I should have greater reluctance in making this request if the places of worship in your parish were thinly attended, or if they were more than sufficient for the population of the parish; but, on the contrary, numbers are sent away every Sunday from your church, for want of room.' He then mentions the names of some distinguished clerics to whom reference can be made, gives an account of his personal situation, and ends with an earnest appeal. 'A few years ago, my dear Sir, when your situation was what mine is, such considerations would have touched you, and you would have acknowedged their force. You know well the difficulties and the miseries of a curate's life; and I am sure you are the last man in the world to forget them, merely because you have overcome them with so much honour and distinction.' But was he sure? If so it was perhaps hardly necessary to say so. Anyhow, his request was refused, on the specious plea that Dr Monopoly was reluctant to impose an obligation on his successors. To this Smith replied: 'Would you then object to give me leave to preach during your life, leaving it entirely open, by such limited concession, to those who succeed you, to continue or suspend the permission? . . . I appeal to you again, whether anything can be so enormous and unjust, as that that privilege should be denied to the ministers of the Church of England which every man who has folly and presumption enough to differ from it can immediately enjoy?' But the rector was deaf

D

to argument, and all Smith got for his pains was a pompous snub. Though for a time he preached a weekly evening sermon at the Foundling Hospital (at £50 a year), and on Sunday mornings in one of two other places, where he drew large congregations, he evidently had difficulty in making ends meet. Happily, brother Robert came to his help by giving him a hundred a year for a few years.

As a preacher he was lively and eloquent, and, as always, eminently practical. He took theology for granted and was content that his sermons should be vivid, homely, and humane. The preaching of applied Christianity, the insistence that religion is a dead letter unless it promotes charity, toleration, and active benevolence, was a decided novelty in Smith's day. In the preface to a selection of his sermons published as early as 1801 he sets forth his considered opinion on the subject. 'Preaching has become a byword for long and dull conversation of any kind, and whoever wishes to imply, in any piece of writing, the absence of anything agreeable and inviting, calls it a sermon. One reason for this is the bad choice of subjects for the pulpit. The clergy are allowed about twenty-six hours every year for the instruction of their fellow-creatures; and I cannot help thinking this short time had better be employed on practical subjects, in explaining and enforcing that conduct which the spirit of Christianity requires, and which mere worldly happiness commonly coincides to recommend.' Scriptural exegesis and learned dissertation on points of doctrine 'do well for publication but are ungenial to the habits and tastes of a general audience'. They are of high importance, he concedes, in their own place, but—'God forbid it should be necessary to be a scholar, or a critic, in order to be a Christian!' To the multitude, 'whether elegant or vulgar', only the results of erudition can be of any consequence: 'with the erudition itself they cannot meddle, and must be fatigued if they are doomed to hear it'. He is impatient of the distinction set up between moral and religious subjects of discourse. 'If Christianity concern itself with our present as well as our future happiness, how can any virtue, or the doctrine which inculcates it, be considered as foreign to our sacred religion? Has our Saviour forbidden justice, proscribed mercy, benevolence, and good faith? Or, when we state the more sublime motives for their cultivation, which we derive from revelation, why are we not to display the temporal motives also, and give solidity to elevation by fixing piety upon interest?'

His personal creed was almost comically simple and straightforward. He accepted the cardinal doctrines of Christianity as unquestioningly as he accepted the multiplication table, and in much the same spirit. A scheme of present happiness and future salvation had been provided, and it was only common sense to take advantage of it. He had a great dislike of militant atheism or 'infidelity', and never for a moment doubed that tthe cosmic arrangements were based on his own guiding principles of benevolence and good sense. He distrusted anything that savoured of mysticism or 'enthusiasm' (in the eighteenth-century sense of that term), discouraged speculation about the ultimate mysteries both in himself and others, and in short, while firmly persuaded that a well-appointed paradise existed for the reception of all reasonably good people, irrespective of creed, kept his feet firmly planted on the earth. Above all—and this is the secret of his appeal as a preacher—he was himself a good and lovable person: large-minded, warm-hearted, high-spirited, quick of understanding, and generous in sympathy. He had a keen eye for folly and a delight in exposing it, but was ready to be any man's friend. Envy and hatred, his daughter tells us, were so foreign to his nature that he hardly discerned them when they existed in others. The tribute he paid to his friend Henry Grattan, the Irish statesman, might with equal truth have been written of himself: 'He thought the noblest occupation of a man was to make other men happy and free; and in that straight line he kept for fifty years.' Indeed, among his formal writings, never intended for publication, there are many touches of unconscious self-portraiture. The slighting reference to dissenters, in the letter to Dr Monopoly which I have quoted, is not truly characteristic of him; for though he had a hearty dislike both of Dissent and of Roman Catholicism, and wrote scathingly of fervid extravagant follies which he lumped together under the misleading title of Methodism, he was implacably opposed to anything in the shape of persecution. Tolerance of opinion and courtesy to individuals was his fixed rule; and these virtues shine the more brightly in him because they did not proceed from indifference, absence of principle, or lack of decided opinions. A notebook entry declares: 'The religious mistakes of mankind have been: that there are spirits mingling with mankind, hence demons, witchcraft; that God governs the world by present judgments, hence ordeals; that there is a connexion between the fate of particular men and the heavenly bodies at the time of their birth, hence astrology; that God is to be worshipped by the miseries and privations of the worshippers, hence monasteries, stylites, flagellants.' But, however much he despised these errors, for the people who embraced them he demanded full toleration.

At the request of a young woman, daughter of the Archbishop of York, he wrote some sentences defining hardness of character. 'Hardness is a want of minute attention to the feelings of others. It does not proceed from malignity or a carelessness of inflicting pain, but from a want of delicate perception of those little things by which pleasure is conferred or pain excited. A hard person thinks he has done enough if he does not speak ill of your relations, your children, or your country; and then, with the greatest good humour and volubility, and with a total inattention to your individual state and position, gallops over a thousand fine feelings, and leaves in every step the mark of his hoofs upon your heart.' A similar character is sketched in one of the note-books: 'He is always treading on your gouty foot, or talking in your deaf ear, or asking you to give him something with your lame hand.' A man's character is revealed equally by his likes and dislikes, his hopes and his fears. Sydney Smith hated discourtesy, whether casual or deliberate. He enjoyed honest fighting. He had a dread of physical indolence. He was a great believer in work. 'You may do anything with industry. A friend of mine has mastered Greek, Latin, mathematics, and music, in an extraordinary degree, together with all the *ologies;* and yet without any remarkable abilities, by industry alone.' And his own 'plans of study', which we shall glance at later, show that he practised what he preached. Like all men who combine imagination with high animal spirits, he was no stranger to depression and was keenly alive to its perils. Again and again he insists on the importance of taking short views of life and avoiding melancholy thoughts. 'Never give way to melancholy. Resist it steadily, for the habit will encroach. I once gave a lady two-and-twenty recipes against melancholy. One was a bright fire; another, to remember all the pleasant things said to and of her; another, to keep a box of sugar-plums on the chimney-piece and

a kettle simmering on the hob.' Profound melancholy can be
induced by such trifles as injudicious feeding. 'My friend sups
late; he eats some strong soup, then a lobster, then some tart,
and he dilutes these esculent varities with wine. The next day
I call on him. He is going to sell his house in London and retire
into the country. He is alarmed for his eldest daughter's health.
His expenses are hourly increasing, and nothing but a timely
retreat can save him from ruin. All this is the lobster; and when
over-excited nature has had time to manage this testaceous
encumbrance, the daughter recovers, the finances are in good
order, and every rural idea effectually excluded. In the same
manner old friendships are destroyed by toasted cheese, and
hard salted meat has led to suicide.'

To his wit, his gift of phrase, it is fitting that we should constantly recur. 'When so showy a woman as Mrs So and So appears
at a place,' he remarked in casual conversation, 'even though
there is no garrison within twelve miles the horizon is immediately clouded with majors.' A good example of his talent for
cumulative nonsense is his comment on the report that a young
gentleman was about to marry a widow who was twice his age
and of very ample person. 'Marry her? Impossible!' said Smith.
'A part of her perhaps—he couldn't marry all of her by himself.
There's enough of her to furnish wives for a whole parish. You
might people a colony with her, or give an assembly with her,
or take your morning's walk round her provided there were
frequent resting-places and you were in rude health. Or you
might read the Riot Act and disperse her. In short you might do
anything with her but marry her.'

VI

YORKSHIRE PARSON

THE appointment to Foston-le-Clay was a matter for much rejoicing and some misgiving. For his children's sake he was glad to move to the country, though reluctant to go so far. He had many good friends in London, and many others in Edinburgh: now he was to be fixed at a point impossibly distant from both. Visiting Foston to see what was in store for him he found that the parsonage-house was an uninhabitable hovel: mean, dingy, in sad disrepair. There had been no resident clergyman there for generations: Smith was to have the arduous privilege of putting an end to that scandal. The ancient parish clerk who met him and showed him round saw at once that he was no fool and bluntly said so, much to his amusement. The Clergy Residence Bill of 1808 promoted by Spencer Perceval was in principle a piece of delayed justice which no fairminded person could quarrel with, in that it required clergymen to live and preach in their own parishes instead of farming the work out to underpaid curates; but like so many well-intentioned Acts of Parliament it imposed great hardships on individuals. Roughly one-third of the parsonages in England had fallen into decay, and a single generation of clergymen were now compelled to build new ones out of their own private means, helped only by a loan from Queen Anne's Bounty repayable with interest year by year. The house at Foston consisted of one brick-floored kitchen, with a room above it that was in imminent danger of falling down. It was flanked by a foal-yard on one side and the churchyard on the other. The village carpenter valued it at fifty pounds, the stonemason at forty-eight. For the first year of Smith's tenure of the living he was allowed to stay in London to continue his preaching at the Foundling Hospital, a curate from York acting as his deputy at Foston; but with the passing of the Residence Bill into law that arrangement must come to an end.

He did however obtain permission from Dr Markham, Archbishop of York, to live at Heslington, about thirteen miles from his church. A notebook entry written at this time incidentally reinforces our suspicion that Sydney Smith's 'poverty', of which we hear so much, was not quite what we understand by poverty today. 'As I have resolved to quit London,' the entry begins, 'I think it right to put down those motives which have influenced me in this decision, that when I am shut up in the country I may appeal to it for my comfort and convince myself that I have done for the best.' The gist of the ensuing argument is that he cannot afford *not* to leave London. 'Without the New River company, which it is disgraceful to retain, and without borrowing every year an hundred pounds from Bobus, which I have no sort of right to do, my income would be little more than a thousand pounds per annum, upon which I am quite sure I could not subsist in the way I should like without running into debt, as I have spent for the last 2 years £1400 per annum.' Remembering that a thousand pounds in 1807 would be equal to three or four thousand today, and that income tax had not been invented, we may infer that Sydney was not unduly modest in his requirements.

The removal into Yorkshire took place in 1809. In the summer of an earlier year, 1807, Smith had given his young family their first taste of rural pleasures by taking a house at Sonning in Berkshire: and it was probably there that he wrote the first few of the immortal Peter Plymley letters, addressed 'to my brother Abraham who lives in the country'. The first letter, or pamphlet, appeared in the autumn of 1807 and at once became the talk of the town. The friends of Catholic Emancipation were enchanted; the Tories, now back in power with the Duke of Portland and Spencer Perceval at their head, found themselves pelted with ridicule and were greatly incensed, but their efforts to discover who was the author met with no success. Smith wisely refrained from confiding the secret even to his friends. Nine more letters followed in rapid succession, to be hungrily snapped up by a delighted public; and very soon a small volume containing all ten appeared on the market and sold like hot cakes. It was certainly one of the most successful pieces of pamphleteering in our political history. The cause for which Smith fought is now won, but the spirit he fought *against* we have always with us, and the quality of his mind—the wit, the irony, the scathing satire, the humour, drollery, the unfailing literary skill—preserves these letters from the dull oblivion that commonly (and mercifully) overtakes political controversy. An enemy of Roman Catholicism, seeing its peculiar tenets as a compound of intellectual error and crude superstition, Sydney Smith was yet the the most zealous and persistent champion of the civil rights of Roman Catholics, for no reason but that he had a disinterested passion for freedom and justice. In this he is the embodiment of that liberalism which today, in some influential Catholic circles, is so disdainfully regarded as oldfashioned and ineffectual.

He lived at Heslington for some five years, driving over Sunday by Sunday to conduct the services at Foston. Though almost entirely cut off from his urban pleasures, chief among which was conversation with congenial friends, he maintained an undaunted cheerfulness. The monotony of his new existence was alleviated however by occasional visitors from London, and by some new friendships. The local squire, a staunch Tory, first regarded him with suspicion because of his reputation as a man of subversive opinions, but was soon won over. Saba Holland quotes her father as saying of this worthy: 'He was a perfect specimen of the Trullibers of old. He smoked, hunted, drank beer at his door with his grooms and dogs, and spelt over the county paper on Sunday. At first he heard that I was a Jacobin'—which he never was—'and a dangerous fellow, and turned aside when we met; but at length, when he found the peace of the village undisturbed, harvests much as usual, Juno and Ponto uninjured, he first bowed, then called, and at last reached such a pitch of confidence that he used to bring the papers that I might explain the difficult words to him. He actually discovered that I had made a joke, laughed till I thought he would have died of convulsions, and ended by inviting me to see his dogs.' A visit to Howick led to an intimacy with Charles Grey, second Earl of that name, the Whig statesman who was destined to collaborate with the formidable Brougham in forcing the Reform Bill through the House of Lords. It was Grey who in 1831 appointed Smith a Canon Residentiary of St Paul's. Another friendship made in Yorkshire was with the new Archbishop of York, Dr Vernon Harcourt, to whose daughter, 'my dear Georgiana', some of his liveliest letters are addressed. Though never a monopolist of the conversation, for he had strong views on the folly and incivility of long speeches, Smith was, as he confesses, fond of talking; and at the Archbishop's table he acquired the self-protective habit of holding on to his plate while discoursing, in order to prevent the servants snatching it away, which they had a trick of doing.

With all his gregariousness, and his talent for amusing any company he might find himself in, he was a great enjoyer of simple family life. He had a particular fondness for children, and endless patience with them. One of his own children, at a very early age, used for a time to wake every evening and sob bitterly, haunted by imaginations of death. Unable to bear 'this unnatural union of childhood and sorrow', Sydney made a point of being present at this moment of waking to charm the child back to happiness; and this happened night after night, until at length the evil spell was broken. One of the domestic joys at Heslington was the possession of a young donkey which the family had had from its birth and which under their tuition became a most accomplished animal. 'It would walk upstairs,' says Saba, 'pick pockets, follow us in our walks like a huge Newfoundland dog, and at the most distant sight of us in the field, with ears down and tail erect would set off in full bray to meet us.' She tells a pleasant story of how one day, when she and her eldest brother were playing with this donkey in the garden, Jeffrey unexpectedly arrived, and finding Smith not at home promptly joined in the sport, mounted, careered round the lawn in triumph, and in this posture was presently discovered by Sydney and Catharine returning from their walk. From Catharine's manuscript it would seem that Brougham, Horner, and Murray were also there. The donkey remained with the Smiths for thirteen years, and on their leaving Yorkshire for Combe Florey was given the freedom of a private park, Lord Carlisle's, where to the end of his life he enjoyed complete idleness and 'an unbounded command of thistles'.

During the early years at Heslington Sydney made repeated efforts to exchange the Foston living for something more congenial and nearer London, but without success. He then resolutely addressed himself to the task of building a Foston rectory. A diner-out, a wit, and a popular preacher fresh from London, he was 'compelled to farm three hundred acres and without capital to build a parsonage-house'. His pretence of 'not knowing a turnip from a carrot', however, must be taken with more than the usual grain of salt; for Catharine tells her grand-children that he had acquired some knowledge of farming with the Hicks Beaches and in Scotland. He was a man who did nothing by halves, and since there was no escape he threw himself into the new life with a good heart. 'I lived in the country for twenty years,' he remarks somewhere, 'and was never bored.' Before he had been many months in Yorkshire he was saturated in rural lore and could talk on more or less equal terms with all sorts and conditions of countrymen, from cow-herds to master farmers. He quickly acquired a knowledge of baking, brewing, poultry-keeping, butter-making, and much besides, partly to satisfy his own ever-eager curiosity, and partly because only so could he enter fully into the interests of his parishioners. Even had he not conceived that his position required him to be everybody's friend, his own good sense and good nature would have impelled him to be so. It was a maxim of his that friendships should be formed with persons of all ages and conditions and with both sexes. He speaks of the great happiness to be derived from 'sincere friendship with a woman', adding: 'The austerity of our manners hardly admits such a connexion', though it is 'compatible with the most perfect innocence and a source of the highest possible delight to those who are fortunate enough to form it.' In addition to the new rural accomplish-ments, the medical skill acquired in Edinburgh now came in useful. He was village doctor, as well as village parson, village comforter, village magistrate, and Edinburgh Reviewer: 'so you see I had not much time left on my hands to regret London'. His house at Foston, he says, was considered the ugliest in the country, but all admitted that it was one of the most comfortable. He designed it himself, with Catharine's help, handing back the architect's plans with a consolatium of five-and-twenty pounds and the remark: 'You build for glory, Sir; I for use.'

The story of the building and its sequel is best told in the words ascribed to him by his daughter. On the advice of neigh-bours he bought four oxen to haul bricks and timber for him, but they took to fainting and lying down in the mud. 'So I did as I ought to have done at first: bought a team of horses, and at last, in spite of a frost which delayed me six weeks, in spite of walls running down with wet, in spite of the advice and remon-strance of friends who predicted our death, in spite of an infant

of six months old who had never been out of the house, I landed
my family in my new house nine months after laying the first
stone, on the 20th of March 1814; and performed my promise
to the letter to the Archbishop, by issuing forth at midnight with
a lantern to meet the last cart, with the cook and the cat, which
had stuck in the mud, and fairly established them before twelve
o'clock at night in the new parsonage-house—a feat, taking
ignorance, inexperience and poverty into consideration, re-
quiring, I assure you, no small degree of energy. It made me a
very poor man for many years, but I never repented it. I turned
schoolmaster, to educate my son, as I could not afford to send
him to school. Mrs Sydney turned schoolmistress, to educate my
girls, as I could not afford a governess. I turned farmer, as I
could not let my land. A manservant was too expensive, so I
caught up a little garden-girl made like a milestone, christened
her Bunch, put a napkin in her hand, and made her my butler.
The girls taught her to read, Mrs Sydney taught her to wait, and
I undertook her morals. Bunch became the best butler in the
county.' The problem of furnishing was solved in equally
characteristic fashion. A carpenter named Jack Robinson, with
a face like a full moon, came to Smith for parish relief. Smith
took him into his service, established him in a barn, provided him
with 'a cartload of deals', and said: 'Jack, furnish my house!'—
which he promptly did. Soon they found they needed a carriage.
'After a diligent search I discovered in the back settlements of
a York coachmaker an ancient green chariot, supposed to have
been the earliest invention of the kind. I brought it home in
triumph to my admiring family. The village tailor lined it. The
village blacksmith repaired it. The result was wonderful. Each
year added to its charms; it grew younger and younger—a new
wheel, a new spring; I christened it the *Immortal*. It was known
all over the neighbourhood. The village boys cheered it, and the
village dogs barked at it. But *faber meae fortunae* was my motto,
and we had no false shame.'

Catharine's account of their removal from Heslington to the
half-finished Foston house makes a pleasant supplement to the
story. They had to be out by Lady Day. For eight weeks or more
the country had been in the grip of a hard frost. The last things
left at Heslington were the bedding, two or three chairs, and a
table. On their last night there they all slept on the floor, the

bedsteads having been sent away the previous day. Next day, on a bleak March morning, they were all up at five o'clock in order to release the bedding, which had to be sent ahead of them. A close carriage was hired to convey Catharine, her six-months-old son Wyndham, Annie Kaye the servant girl, and the three other children. Some waggonloads of furniture had set out before them; others followed. All went well for a while, but presently Wyndham began wailing with hunger and was with difficulty pacified. There was no made road to the new parsonage, only a field track; and here the carriage stuck fast. With the baby in her arms Catharine got out, lost a shoe in the stiff clay, and walked on without it to the house. 'There were no doors yet to the drawing-room and dining-room, the plaistering of which latter room was not even begun; but I remember in spite of it all there was a very merry tea-making upon some of the boxes piled up in the drawing-room. Large fires were kept in all the rooms day and night. The house-maid three or four times a day wiped the steam off the windows, which looked like ground glass, and wiped up the streams that came dripping down the walls on to the boards, for *carpets* in this early stage of our Robinson Crusoe establishment we had none. So very fearful was I that the fires should get low during the night that I used like an unquiet Ghost to go from room to room to see that they burnt well, and in every room was a good depot of coals to renew them. The living in this warm vapour was really not as unpleasant as might be imagined. No one suffer'd, not even the Baby or its Mother. Summer was coming on, each day improved our condition, its gradual amendment was an affair of daily interest: and with dear Sydney's incessant activity and contrivance for hastening our comforts we all took a cheerful and earnest interest in these improvements. In time it became as perfect for its size as any reasonable person could desire.'

Though Sydney always did his best to radiate cheerfulness, it was sometimes more than he could manage. Catharine's detailed account of their economic situation would not strike a present-day reader as anything out of the way, for that kind of anxiety most of us, after two world wars, have always with us. They did, for all that, have a hard struggle for some years. Sydney wrote his EDINBURGH REVIEW articles, now more than ever necessary, with wit, wisdom, good sense, and apparent cheer-

fulness (says Catharine), 'though trembling at his heart's core
for the future comfort and stability of myself and of his children'.
No one but herself, she adds, 'who saw, and knew, and listen'd
to his despondence, can have any notion of what his sufferings
and his sorrows were'. All difficulties, however, were vigorously
met and grappled with. Salvation from despondency lay in
ceaseless activity of mind and body. Into farming, as well as
into domestic arrangements, Smith introduced some ingenious
novelties. He would stand at the door of the house, a telescope in
his hand, and shout instructions to the farm-hands through a
large speaking-trumpet; and for the comfort and relief of his
animals, whose habits like everything else he had carefully
studied, he had a number of stout scratching-posts erected. The
extreme poverty of some of his neighbours set him trying to
determine which were the most nourishing of inexpensive foods,
'and many a hungry labourer was brought in and stuffed with
rice, or broth, or porridge, to test the relative effects of these
kinds of food on the appetite'. For a while, until dissuaded by
the protests of his family who found the smell disagreeable, he
indulged a fancy for burning mutton-fat in little tin lamps
instead of using candles; and he invented a successful device for
dealing with smoky chimneys. These are samples of his lighter
pursuits: plenty of more serious problems engaged him. In the
winter of 1816 a poor harvest and the consequent scarcity and
badness of the food led to a local pestilence among the needier
part of the population. Smith went unwearyingly from cottage to
cottage with food and medicine, comfort and counsel. His chief
problem, at first, was how to prevent people from crowding into
the infected houses; but later on, says Saba (she was about
fourteen at the time), the deaths were so frequent that he had
equal difficulty in persuading anyone to go near the sick and the
dying, or to carry the dead to their graves, 'till he shamed them
into it, by threatening to become one of the bearers himself'.
He was deeply impressed by the behaviour of some Quakers in
the village: they, uninfected by the panic, quietly continued their
work among the sick. When he asked them if they didn't realize
the danger, they answered mildly: 'We are in the hands of
God.'

In his writings Sydney never mentions Quakers except with
high respect. He himself, though perhaps a stranger to their

serenity, had no lack of courage. His was the heroic, hard-won courage of a man too imaginative to be unafraid. One wonders whether during this time of pestilence his mind went back to a previous experience of such dangers. Brother Bobus and family, back from India, had paid the Sydney Smiths a visit at Hesling-ton. From there they went to Hinckley to consult a specialist about Bobus's daughter Caroline, who was thought to have a slight curvature of the spine. At Hinckley Caroline was seized with a malignant fever (unspecified) which was 'afterwards communicated to little Henrietta', her sister. Henrietta died of it. So did her two nurses. The distracted parents then left the sick child, Caroline, in the care of two devoted aunts, Mrs Bobus being in a panic lest her husband should contract the fever. They had got no further than Northampton when her fears were realized: he too was struck down. She at once sent to Sydney, begging him to come. It was an appeal to which he felt bound to respond. Catharine had three young children and was soon to be confined again. She thought it madness that he should expose himself to infection, risking his life to no good purpose; but nothing would deflect him from what he conceived to be his duty to a beloved brother. He wrote to Dr Allen, an Edinburgh friend who had since become librarian and physician at Holland House. Allen replied with some simple precautionary rules and added: 'But above all, don't be afraid.' 'Your rules,' answered Sydney, 'I will faithfully observe. But not to be afraid I cannot promise, for I am very much afraid.' He went, nevertheless, 'directed everything, thought of everything, rarely left his brother's room by night or day, anticipated every want and every risk', his sister-in-law being rendered quite incapable of thought or exertion by her distress. Bobus recovered, and Sydney returned home in safety.

From these biographical scraps a clear portrait of the man begins, I hope, to emerge. He was no milk-and-water saint. His benevolence did not preclude either stubbornness or hot impatience. He was capable not only of anger against manifest injustice but of losing his temper on more trivial occasions. When that dilapidated newly-bought carriage was delivered to him after being locally repaired he called on the village tailor and accused him of not carrying out instructions. The tailor indignantly denied the charge, and a quarrel ensued which

culminated in the tailor's hurling a great pair of scissors across
the room at him. But within an hour or so Smith was back, with
a smiling apology, to explain that there had been a misunder-
standing: Mrs Smith, without Sydney's knowledge, had in fact
given the order which the tailor had faithfully performed. On
the bench, though by no means always lenient, he spent much
time pleading 'like a lawyer' with his brother-magistrates for
clemency to poachers: his views on the iniquitous Game Laws
are set forth in more than one EDINBURGH REVIEW article.

Another matter with which he actively concerned himself
was prison reform. On at least one occasion he accompanied
Elizabeth Fry on her rounds and was moved to tears by the sight
of her goodness and its effect on the prisoners. On this subject
too he wrote at some length (see page 169); but the proposals
he submitted to the Marquis of Lansdowne in 1819, when the
question arose in Parliament, are worth noting for the additional
light they shed both on his attitude to it and on the state of affairs
then prevailing. He recommends: (1) that the names of the
visiting magistrates and their places of abode should be printed
and stuck up in all rooms where prisoners are confined, under
penalty to jailors; (2) names of visiting magistrates to be called
over by the clerk of the peace, or clerk of assize, in open court,
on the first day of any assize and quarter sessions, and the judge
or chairman to ask in open court whether they have visited the
prisons, and have any observation to offer upon their condition;
(3) a book to be kept by the jailor, noting down the visits of
magistrates to the prison, to be read in open court in the same
manner; (4) more power to visiting magistrates to make alterations between session and session, subject to the approbation of
magistrates assembled at quarter sessions or assizes; (5) accused
persons not to be confined with persons already committed, nor
young offenders with old; (6) neither beer nor spirits to be allowed
without order of the apothecary or permission of magistrates in
visiting, under heavy penalties; (7) no Roman Catholic or
Dissenter to be compelled to attend the prison worship if he
objects to do so and expresses himself willing to attend a clergyman of his own persuasion; (8) power in two magistrates to
confine for two or three days in solitary confinement any refrac-
tory prisoner; (9) no prisoner to be locked up in sleeping-room
for more than ten hours at night (to which Smith adds a note:

'they are now locked up in small rooms in winter from four in the evening till eight in the morning, without fire or candle, to avoid the trouble and expense of watching, lighting, and warming them'); (10) no male prisoner after conviction to have less than two pounds of bread per diem, women not less than a pound and a half, if the diet is bread alone; and prisoners before conviction to have at least the same allowance, and twice a week one pound of meat each; (11) money allowance to be put on a more rational footing.

As we have seen, he made a great point of never being idle and not harbouring melancholy thoughts. To all outward appearance he always enjoyed good spirits. Yet we find him in 1820 writing to a woman friend who had complained that she was suffering from depression: 'Nobody has suffered more from low spirits than I have done.' He proceeds to prescribe remedies for her: 'ıst Live as well as you dare. 2nd Go into the shower-bath with a small quantity of water at a temperature low enough to give you a slight sensation of cold, 75° or 80°. 3rd Amusing books. 4th Short views of human life—not further than dinner or tea. 5th Be as busy as you can. 6th See as much as you can of those friends who respect and like you. 7th And of those acquaintances who amuse you. 8th Make no secret of low spirits to your friends, but talk to them freely—they are always worse for dignified concealment. 9th Attend to the effects tea and coffee produce upon you. 10th Compare your lot with that of other people. 11th Don't expect too much from human life—a sorry business at the best. 12th Avoid poetry, dramatic representations (except comedy), music, serious novels, melancholy, sentimental people, and everything likely to excite feeling or emotion not ending in active benevolence. 13th *Do good*, and endeavour to please everybody of every degree. 14th Be as much as you can in the open air without fatigue. 15th Make the room where you commonly sit, gay and pleasant. 16th Struggle by little and little against idleness. 17th Don't be too severe upon yourself, or underrate yourself, but do yourself justice. 18th Keep good blazing fires. 19th Be firm and constant in the exercise of rational religion. 20th Believe me, dear Lady Georgiana, very truly yours, Sydney Smith.'

All these precepts he himself put into practice. The first part of number 12 in the list exposes a limitation and a weakness in him: it suggests that his brisk common sense was in part a mode of what is now called escapism. To resist melancholy and avoid self-indulgent emotionalism is an excellent rule; but to include poetry, tragic drama, music and serious fiction in the same proscription indicates either a morbidly repressed sensibility or some confusion of mind, possibly both; for no mature person, in normal psychological health, is plunged into a state of depression by listening to a Beethoven symphony or by reading *Hamlet*; nor is there any reason why such listening or reading should not lead, indirectly, to 'active benevolence'. Smith's preference for a degree of emotional anaesthesia can only have been a self-protective measure. So also, perhaps, was his somewhat excessive delight in laughter and in exciting laughter in others: on the principle of the famous maxim that life is a tragedy to him who feels and a comedy to him who thinks. He was anything but deficient in feeling, but he was, perhaps, a little afraid of it, and not least in the realm of religion; with the happy result that his compassion, his love of mankind, his very genuine piety, were instantly translated into action and so never degenerated into sickliness and sentimentality. As for his exuberant humour, everyone who came near him was the better for what his friend Samuel Rogers (the banker-poet) calls his 'power of turning everything into sunshine and joy'. Rogers had been ill for some weeks, confined to his bed. 'Sydney heard of it, found me out, sat by my bed, cheered me, talked to me, made me laugh more than I ever thought to have laughed again.' Next day he arrived armed with a medical report on the case, written by himself. The day after he brought a second and worse report, and on the fourth day he declared that there was no hope. 'England would have to mourn the loss of her sweetest poet. Then I died, amidst weeping friends. Then came my funeral. And lastly a sketch of my character. . . . Sydney never forgot his friends.'

Among his friends were his servants, whom, as Jeffrey has recorded, it was his mischievous pleasure to reduce to abject laughter, so that they had to run out of the room. He was capable, too, of schoolboyish tricks. A lady having remarked that the one thing wanting to make Foston perfect was a herd of deer, on her next visit he paraded before her a pair of donkeys with antlers fastened to their heads. 'Excuse their long ears,' he said. 'It's a little peculiarity belonging to parsonical deer.' The little

E

girl called Bunch who waited at table was evidently a prime favourite. 'Come here, Bunch, and recite your crimes to Mrs Marcet.' Gravely, without the least hesitation, the child answered: 'Plate-snatching, gravy-spilling, door-slamming, fly-catching, and curtsey-bobbing.' 'Explain to Mrs Marcet what fly-catching is.' 'Standing with my mouth open and not attending, Sir.' 'And what is curtsey-bobbing?' 'Curtseying to the centre of the earth, please Sir.' 'Good girl! Now you may go.' Family jokes, in general, are best kept for the family. Smith's published wit, in writing and conversation, shines with a brighter lustre; but in an intimate portrait these homelier moments are worth preserving. For, as Macaulay has testified, he was not 'one of those show-talkers who reserve all their good things for special occasions. It seems to be his greatest luxury to keep his wife and daughters laughing for two or three hours every day'. Tom Moore in his diary speaks of his 'natural and overflowing exuberance'. Here are a few quotations from Moore. 'Dined at Rogers's. A distinguished party. Smith particularly amusing. Have rather held out against him hitherto, but this day he conquered me, and I am now his victim, in the laughing way, for life. His imagination of a duel between two doctors, with oil of croton on the tips of their fingers trying to touch each other's lips, highly ludicrous. What Rogers says of Smith very true, that whenever the conversation is getting dull he throws in some touch which makes it rebound and rise again as light as ever. . . . Breakfasted at Rogers's. Smith full of comicality and fancy; kept us all in roars of laughter. In talking of the stories about dram-drinkers catching fire, pursued the idea in every possible shape. Imagined a parson breaking into a blaze in the pulpit; the engines called to put him out; no water to be had, the man at the waterworks being a Unitarian or an Atheist. Left Rogers's with Smith, to go and assist him in choosing a grand pianoforte. Found him (as I have often done before) change at once from the gay, uproarious way, into as solemn, grave, and austere a person as any bench of judges or bishops could supply. This I rather think his natural character. Called with him at Newton's to see my picture. Said, in his gravest manner, to Newton: "Couldn't you contrive to throw into his face somewhat a stronger expression of hostility to the Church establishment?"' (Moore was a Roman Catholic.) 'September 16. Sydney at breakfast made me actually cry with laughing. I was obliged to start up from the table.' 'October 16. Some agreeable conversation after breakfast with Smith and Lord Lansdowne. In talking of O'Connell, of the mixture there is in him of high and low, formidable and contemptible, mighty and mean, Smith summed up all by saying, "The only way to deal with such a man is to hang him up and erect a statue to him under his gallows." This *balancing* of the account is admirable.' Moore gives the text of a letter written by Smith after he had exchanged the Foston living for Combe Florey. 'August 11th, 1831. My dear Moore, From hence till the 1st September (when men of large fortune put men of no fortune in prison on account of partridges), I shall be absent. I shall be at Sidmouth till the 12th, and then a week at Lord Morley's, returning to Sidmouth for the rest of the month. I shall be at home all October. At Sidmouth we are no farther from the sea than the focus of Rogers's voice. Nothing intervenes between us and the coast of France. The noise of persons chattering French on the opposite coast is heard. Flat fish and mackerel have been known to leap into the drawing-room; and in the dreadful storm of 1824 the four Miss Somebodies were taken out in the lifeboat without petticoats by men who, in the hurry of the occasion, were without small clothes. Come to Sidmouth, and make Rogers come, and come to C.-Florey too and make Rogers come. Ever yours, S. Smith.'

It is possible that the riot of fun that Smith carried about with him was sometimes a little overwhelming. Charles Greville hints as much in the note on him written on February 25th, 1845: 'Yesterday we heard of the death of Sydney Smith. It is the extinction of a great luminary, such as we shall hardly see the like of again, and who has reigned without a rival in wit and humour for a great length of time. It is almost impossible to overrate his wit, humour, and drollery, or their effect in society. Innumerable comical sayings and jokes of his are or have been current, but their repetition gives but an imperfect idea of the flavour and zest of the original. His appearance, voice, and manner added immensely to the effect, and the bursting and uproarious merriment with which he poured forth his good things never failed to communicate itself to his audience, who were always in fits of laughter. If there was a fault in it, it was that is was too amusing.' Very possibly. But when Greville goes on to say that people 'so entirely expected to be made to die of laughing, and he was so aware of this, that there never seemed to be any question of conversation when he was of the party, or at least no more than just to afford Sydney pegs to hang his jokes on', one feels, in the light of other testimony, that this statement needs qualification, that it can be true only of the more public occasions when he found himself one of a numerous company. 'I have very little doubt,' adds Greville, 'that Sydney often felt oppressed with the weight of his comical obligations, and came on the stage like a great actor, forced to exert himself but not always in the vein to play his part.' But, though it is true that a reputation for wit can become something of a burden to its possessor, one cannot believe that among a small gathering of intimates Smith would have felt obliged to be for ever exhibiting his talent: he was never the vain, shallow, tedious kind of person that that would imply. Moreover, all the best things attributed to him have a fresh, spontaneous quality. Greville declares it to be well known that he was subject at home to frequent fits of depression (which would account for his so often prescribing remedies against it for himself and his friends); 'but I believe in his own house in the country he could often be a very agreeable companion, on a lower and less ambitious level, for his talk never could be otherwise than seasoned with his rich vein of humour and wit, as the current, though it did not always flow with the same force, was never dry. He was full of varied information, and a liberal, kind-hearted, charitable man. The favourite objects of his jokes were the men of his own cloth, especially the bishops, among whom he once probably aspired to sit. I do not suppose he had any dogmatic and doctrinal opinions in respect to religion, and [I think] that in his heart of hearts he despised and derided all that the world wrangles and squabbles about; but he had the true religion of benevolence and charity, of peace and good-will to mankind, which let us hope (as I firmly believe) to be all-sufficient, be the truth of the great mystery what it may.'

VII

CANON OF ST PAUL'S

———

HE had expected to end his days at Foston, but an exchange
of livings took him to Combe Florey near Taunton in
1829, his fifty-eighth year. During the previous year he
had been appointed a canon of Bristol Cathedral by Lyndhurst,
the new Lord Chancellor, possibly at the instance of Sydney's
friend Lord Lansdowne. Lyndhurst, though opposed to him
in politics, appreciated his fine personal qualities. The new
canon's first sermon before the Mayor and Corporation, on Guy
Fawkes day, 1828, was nicely calculated to give offence in
official quarters, and did so. Instead of launching the usual
attack on Roman Catholicism he chose for his subject religious
toleration, his text being: 'Put on, as the elect of God, kindness,
humbleness of mind, meekness, longsuffering, forbearing one
another, and forgiving one another.' It was a very temperate and
persuasive discourse, quite free of rancour or deliberate provo-
cation. A 'wise and lawful use of this day', he says, 'is an honest
self-congratulation that we have burst through those bands which
the Roman Catholic priesthood would impose upon human
judgment . . . but I should be to the last degree concerned if a
condemnation of theological errors were to be construed into an
approbation of laws which I cannot but consider as deeply
marked by a spirit of intolerance'. He urges his hearers to
'imitate the forbearance and longsuffering of God, who throws
the mantle of his mercy over all, and who will probably save, on
the last day, the piously right and the piously wrong, seeking
Jesus in humbleness of mind'. While he agrees in resisting 'the
errors and follies and superstitions of the Catholic church', he
is most of all concerned with 'the sacred principles of Christian
charity', adding, in a moving passage: 'That charity which I ask
of others, I ask also for myself. I am sure I am preaching before
those who will think (whether they agree with me or not) that

I have spoken conscientiously, and from good motives, and from honest feelings, on a very difficult subject—not sought by me, but devolving on me in the course of duty—in which I should have been heartily ashamed of myself (as you would have been ashamed of me) if I thought only how to flatter and please, or thought of anything but what I hope I always do think of in the pulpit: that I am placed here by God to tell the truth and to do good.' He ends by quoting, from memory, a sublime anecdote from Jeremy Taylor of how Abraham received in his tent a wayfaring old man weary with age and travail, washed his feet, gave him supper, made much of him, and then, finding him to be of a different religion from his own, a fire-worshipper, angrily threw him out and exposed him to all the evils of the night. And the voice of God came to Abraham saying: 'Where is the stranger?' 'I thrust him away,' said Abraham, 'because he did not worship thee.' And the voice of God answered: 'I have suffered him these hundred years, though he dishonoured me; and wouldst thou not endure him one night, when he gave thee no trouble?'

Five months later the civil disabilities imposed on Roman Catholics were removed by the passing into law of an Emancipation Bill; but Smith's rejoicing in this triumph of a cause for which he had so long fought must have been all but obliterated by the death, during that same week, of his eldest son. The story of Douglas Smith, as Catharine tells it, is a harrowing one. By prodigious efforts, in spite of ill-health, the boy won a King's Scholarship to Westminster, much to the joy of his parents. His first year at the school was a nightmare. The junior King's Scholars had to fag for their seniors. Douglas had two fag-masters, one of them 'a very great Brute'. He was forced to spend much of his time 'blacking shoes, brushing coats, washing-up tea-things, dressing beefsteaks', any neglect being visited with disgustingly cruel chastisement. One day he lost the key of his fag-master's desk, for which offence that spirited young gentleman 'compelled him every day for a month to hold out his hand, and with a heavy walking stick he beat him so intolerably that at one time he really thought his thumb was broken and it was days before he could use his hand'. The senior boys had also the engaging habit of taking all the bedclothes from the smaller ones' beds, and of monopolizing the fireplaces, 'the fires of wood kept up of course by the Slaves'. Finally, for some trifling offence,

young Douglas was so brutally beaten about the head, and his
eye so badly injured, that he wrote in confidence to his father
declaring that unless some excuse could be invented for calling
him home he would be obliged to run away. Sydney thereupon
wrote to Dr Goodenough, the headmaster, saying that his
daughter Emily was ill (as she was) and most anxious to see her
brother. Douglas came home and begged to be allowed to stay
until the end of term, when his chief persecutor would be leaving.
He went back next term and in due time rose to be captain
of the school: in which office, like the true son of his father, he
made it his business to remove the worst of the intolerable wrongs
which the smaller boys had to endure. From Westminster he went
to Christchurch, Oxford, where he took his degree. Like his
uncle Bobus he was to have been a lawyer, but in his twenty-
fourth or twenty-fifth year he died. It was the sharpest personal
grief of Sydney's life. 'The first great misfortune I ever suffered,'
he wrote in his diary, 'and one which I shall never forget.' It
perhaps made him welcome the distraction of having to move
himself and his family to Combe Florey.

'I am extremely pleased with Combe Florey, and pronounce
it to be a very pretty place in a very beautiful country,' he tells
Lady Grey, in July 1829. 'The house I shall make decently
convenient. I have sixty acres of land round it. The habit of the
country is to give dinners and not to sleep out, so this I shall
avoid. . . . My spirits are very much improved, but I have now
and then sharp pangs of grief. I did not know I cared so much for
anybody; but the habit of providing for human beings, and
watching over them for many years, generates a fund of affection,
of the magnitude of which I was not aware.' And to Lord
Lansdowne a month later: 'I have very few years to live, and
therefore I cannot afford to waste time in building. I have ten
carpenters and ten bricklayers at work. Part of my house has
tumbled down, the rest is inclined to follow. We sleep upon
props; an enemy or a dissenter might saw me down in the night.'
Francis Jeffrey was one of the earliest visitors at the Smiths' new
home. Having been appointed Dean of the (Scottish) Faculty of
Advocates ('In England,' said Sydney, 'our Deans have no
faculties'), he had resigned the editorship of the EDINBURGH
REVIEW and was free for a while to enjoy the company of his old
friend. Jeffrey was a very small man, and when in 1834 he was

raised to the Scottish Bench, Smith remarked: 'His robes will cost him little. One buck-rabbit will clothe him to the heels.'

Smith held the living of Combe Florey for the rest of his life. During his latter years, after his appointment as Canon of St Paul's, he had also a town house, in Green Street. His 'very few years to live' amounted in fact to sixteen, and from 1839 onwards, owing to his having inherited fifty thousand pounds from his brother Courtenay, they were years of such affluence as he had never expected to enjoy, and of growing fame. As a high dignitary of the Church which had for forty years looked askance at him he was not only, as he had always been, an influential person, but a figure who commanded automatic respect from the conventionally-minded. The possession of wealth gave him unaffected satisfaction. 'Moralists tell you of the evils of wealth and station, and the happiness of poverty. I have been very poor the greatest part of my life, and have borne it as well, I believe, as most people; but I can safely say that I have been happier with every guinea I have gained. I well remember, when Mrs Sydney and I were young, in London, with no other equipage than my umbrella, when we went out to dinner in a hackney-coach, and the rattling step was let down, and the proud powdered red-plushes grinned, and her gown was fringed with straw, how the iron entered into my soul.' His St Paul's appointment was an incidental result of Grey's accession to power. He had been promised a vacancy at Westminster Abbey likely to be created by the death of Dr Andrew Bell. But Dr Bell had refrained from dying, and in September 1831 Smith received a letter dated from Downing Street. 'My dear Sydney: You are much obliged to Dr Bell for not dying, as he had promised. By the promotion of the Bishop of Chichester to the see of Worcester, a Canon Residentiary of St Paul's becomes vacant. A snug thing, let me tell you, being worth full £2000 a year. To this the King, upon my recommendation, has signified his pleasure that you should be appointed, and I do not think it likely that you can be *dis*-appointed a second time by the old bishop coming to life again, like Dr Bell. Mr Harvey, tutor to Prince George of Cambridge, will have your stall at Bristol. I am, my dear Sydney, Yours very sincerely, Grey. P.S. I must take care that your appointment is placed out of possibility of being recalled—before we are turned out!'

When this letter was written, Grey had been for ten months
at the head of a coalition ministry in which Whigs and Canning-
ites were united against the ultra-Toryism of the Duke of
Wellington, the great question at issue being parliamentary
reform. Wellington had committed political suicide by declaring,
in face of the growing and no longer resistible popular demand
for reform, that the system of representation possessed the full
and entire confidence of the country and that to improve upon it
was beyond the power of human wisdom. This preposterous
statement alienated some of his most influential supporters. He
fell in November 1830, and Grey was called upon to form a
ministry. The 'system of representation' belauded by Wellington
was in fact largely a system of non-representation. Only a small
fraction of the population (something under 3 per cent) had
votes; parliamentary seats could be bought and sold; bribery was
rampant; and many large populous towns were not represented
at all. The grossest scandal of all was the existence of the 'rotten
boroughs', in respect of which men were nominated to seats in
parliament without any pretence of popular election. The
reforms proposed (and eventually carried through) by Grey and
Brougham were to abolish fifty-six nomination boroughs with a
total complement of a hundred and eleven members, dock some
thirty other boroughs of one member each, and redistribute the
seats thus gained on a more equitable, proportional basis. It was
a plan that only privilege and corruption could quarrel with.
Both Grey and Lord Chancellor Brougham enjoyed the confidence of the King, William the Fourth, who, unlike his pre-
decessor, seems to have been an honest and eminently approach-
able person, keenly alive to the dangers of the situation and much
concerned that a violent collision between the two extremes of
opinion should be avoided. But though personally amiable he was
weak and vacillating: he had the indiscreet habit of talking too
freely with the opposition leaders; and strong pressure had to be
applied before he would consent to take the steps which his
advisers considered necessary. It was Brougham who applied the
pressure, with Grey as his instrument. The second reading of the
first Reform Bill was carried in the Commons by a majority of
one. In view of the known hostility of the Lords this was rightly
regarded as tantamount to defeat, and the King was persuaded
to dissolve parliament. These were bold tactics. The state of the

country was such that even the opposition dreaded the resignation of Grey's ministry. In the new Parliament the Bill passed its second reading by a majority of 136. The Lords promptly rejected it. A third Reform Bill, in the following session, was carried in the Commons by an even larger majority; but the Lords had still to be dealt with. It was a desperate situation calling for desperate remedies. The issue was no longer between Reform and No-Reform but between Reform and Revolution. The temper of the nation was roused; riots had already occurred and worse was threatened; there were fanatics on both sides who, if constitutional methods failed, would not have shrunk from civil war. Brougham proposed the creation of a sufficient number of new peers to swamp the Lords' opposition, his hopes being that the mere threat to do so would prove effective. The Lords met this new situation by giving the Bill a narrow majority with the intention of mutilating it in committee. But the demand of people and Commons was for the whole Bill: nothing short of that would be acceptable. The King, foolishly hoping for compromise, allowed himself to be persuaded by the enemies of Reform that if the Commons should reject the Lords' mutilations, and Grey's ministry resign, the emasculated Bill, a mere sham, would be brought in and passed by a Tory government. Confronted by the demand that he should either create new peers to carry the Bill through or accept the resignation of Grey's ministry, he chose the latter course. Wellington was ready to undertake the task of forming an administration which in view of the state of public feeling could only have been an imposture; but Robert Peel, the only man who could have tackled the odious job with even a frail chance of success, refused to have anything to do with it; and after a week of intense excitement and indignation throughout the country the King was forced to recall Grey and Brougham. They told him at once that they could not undertake the responsibilities of government unless he consented in advance to the creation of peers. He was forced to give way. Moreover, Brougham insisted on having the royal consent in writing, thereby scandalizing the less resolute or more reverent Grey. 'The King grants permission to Earl Grey, and to his chancellor Lord Brougham, to create such a number of peers as will be sufficient to ensure the passing of the Reform Bill, first calling up peers' eldest sons. William, R., Windsor, May 17, 1832.' When the

substance of this document became known, the anti-Reform
party knew that the game was lost. The actual creation of new
peers proved to be unnecessary: the power to do so was enough
to ensure the Bill's passage through the Lords.

This sequence of events is reflected in Smith's letters to Lady
Grey. 'Once for all,' he writes to her, early in 1831, 'I take it for
granted that neither Lord Grey nor you think me such an absurd
coxcomb as to imagine that, with inferior information, experience,
and talents, I can offer any advice to Lord Grey: the truth is,
that I attach such very little importance to my own opinions, that I
have never the slightest objection to give them. And so, without
any more preamble, or any repetition of preamble, I will tell
you from time to time what occurs to me.' What first occurs to
him is the expedient which, in fact, Brougham finally persuaded
the Cabinet to adopt. 'I take it for granted,' Smith continues,
'you are prepared to make peers, to force the measure if it fail
again, and I would have this intention half-officially communicated in all the great towns before the Bill was brought in. If
this is not done—I mean, if peers are not made—there will be a
general convulsion, ending in a complete revolution. Do not
be too dignified, but yield to the necessity of demi-official
communications. If the Huskisson party in the Cabinet are refrac-
tory about making peers (should such a creation be necessary),
turn out the Huskisson party. Their power is gone; they are
entirely at your mercy.' Again, on March 5th: 'I am now quite
at my ease about Lord Grey and yourself. Whether Lord Grey
will go out or not I cannot conjecture, as I know so little of the
way Parliament is leaning; but if he is driven out it will be with
an immense increase of reputation, with the gratitude and best
wishes of the country, and with the sincere joy of his friends that
he has ventured upon office, because they must know that he will
be a happier man for all that has taken place. The plan is as
wise as it is bold. I call it a magnificent measure, and am heartily
glad it is understood to be his individually. God bless you, dear
Lady Grey.' On October 6th he sends her a copy of a speech
he had recently made on the subject at Taunton. 'I send my
speech, which missed you the last time I sent it. It is of little
value, but honest. I found public meetings everywhere, and the
utmost alarm at the idea of the Bill being thrown out; coachmen,
ostlers, inside and outside passengers, barmaids, and waiters, all

eager for news.' And in an undated letter, perhaps a month or two later, he returns to the attack. 'Is there a strong probability, amounting almost to a certainty, that the Bill will be carried *without* a creation of peers? No.—Then make them. But the King will not?—Then resign. But if the King *will* create, we shall lose more than we gain?—I doubt it. Many threaten, who will not vote against the Bill. At all events you will have done all you can to carry it. If you *do* create, and it fail, you are beaten with honour; and the country will distinguish between its enemies and its friends. . . . If you wish to be happy three months hence, create peers. If you wish to avoid an old age of sorrow and reproach, create peers. If you wish to retain my friendship, it is of no sort of consequence whether you create peers or not; I shall always retain for you the most sincere gratitude and affection, without the slightest reference to your political wisdom or your political errors; and may God bless and support you and Lord Grey in one of the most difficult moments that ever occurred to any public man.'

The Taunton speech he refers to above was far from being 'of little value', though soon to be eclipsed in popularity by the famous Dame Partington speech. 'They tell you, gentlemen, that you have grown rich and powerful with these rotten boroughs, and that it would be madness to part with them, or to alter a constitution which had produced such happy effects. There happens, gentlemen, to live near my parsonage a labouring man, of very superior character and understanding to his fellow-labourers, and who has made such good use of that superiority that he has saved what is (for his station in life) a very considerable sum of money, and if his existence is extended to the common period he will die rich. It happens, however, that he is (and long has been) troubled with violent stomachic pains, for which he has hitherto obtained no relief, and which really are the bane and torment of his life. Now if my excellent labourer were to send for a physician, and to consult him respecting this malady, would it not be very singular language if our doctor were to say to him, "My good friend, you surely will not be so rash as to attempt to get rid of these pains in your stomach? Have you not risen under them from poverty to prosperity? Has not your situation, since you were first attacked, been improving every year? You surely will not be so foolish and so indiscreet as to part with the pains in your stomach?"—Why, what would be the answer of the rustic to this nonsensical monition? "Monster of Rhubarb!" he would say, "I am not rich in consequence of the pains in my stomach, but in spite of the pains in my stomach; and I should have been ten times richer, and fifty times happier, if I had never had any pains in my stomach at all." Gentlemen, these rotten boroughs are your pains in the stomach; and you would have been a much richer and greater people if you had never had them at all. Your wealth and your power have been owing, not to the debased and corrupted parts of the House of Commons, but to the many independent and honourable members whom it has always contained within its walls.'

Once again he found himself fighting for a cause that was hateful to his brethren of the cloth. As the great mass of the clergy had stubbornly and bitterly opposed Catholic Emancipation, so now with equal stubbornnesss, with equal bitterness, they resisted parliamentary reform. In the briefest and best of his Taunton speeches Smith referred to this fact. 'I feel most deeply the event which has taken place, because, by putting the two Houses of Parliament in collision with each other, it will impede the public business and diminish the public prosperity. I feel it as a churchman, because I cannot but blush to see so many dignitaries of the Church arrayed against the wishes and happiness of the people. I feel it more than all because I believe it will sow the seeds of deadly hatred between the aristocracy and the great mass of the people. The loss of the Bill I do not feel, and for the best of all possible reasons—because I have not the slightest idea that it *is* lost. I have no more doubt that before the expiration of the winter this Bill will pass, than I have that the annual tax bills will pass; and greater certainty than this no man can have, for, as Franklin tells us, there are but two things certain in this world—death and taxes.' There follows the celebrated jest which, eagerly seized on by the newspapers and repeated with joy all over the country, injected a much-needed element of gaiety into the prevailing anger against the Lords and has since attained proverbial status. 'As for the possibility of the House of Lords preventing ere long a reform of Parliament, I hold it to be the most absurd notion that ever entered into human imagination. I do not mean to be disrespectful, but the attempt of the Lords to stop the progress of Reform reminds me very forcibly of the great storm of Sidmouth and of the conduct of the excellent Mrs Partington on that occasion. In the winter of 1824 there set in a great flood upon that town; the tide rose to an incredible height; the waves rushed in upon the houses; and everything was threatened with destruction. In the midst of this sublime and terrible storm Dame Partington, who lived upon the beach, was seen at the door of her house with mop and pattens, trundling her mop, squeezing out the sea-water, and vigorously pushing away the Atlantic Ocean. The Atlantic was roused. Mrs Partington's spirit was up. But I need not tell you that the contest was unequal. The Atlantic Ocean beat Mrs Partington. She was excellent at a slop or a puddle, but she should not have meddled with a tempest. Gentlemen, be at your ease—be quiet and steady. You will beat Mrs Partington.'

VIII

THE LAST CONTROVERSY

T HE last public controversy in which he engaged is of far less interest today. In 1836 the Ecclesiastical Commission, business department of the Church of England, was set up by Act of Parliament. Sydney Smith both resented its constitution and sharply criticized its powers and recommendations. The gravamen of his attack, made in a series of *Letters to Archdeacon Singleton* (1837–1839), was that the Commission was packed with bishops, who were busy appropriating power to themselves and robbing the inferior clergy of their few traditional privileges. A special grievance, which was incidentally a personal one, was that patronage, the gift of offices and livings, was to be taken out of the hands of Deans and Chapters.

We do not need to fight our way through the thicket of this somewhat tediously technical dispute, still less to take sides in it. Smith's writing is as spirited and in general as amusing as ever, and his main point, the danger of an excessive centralization of power, is pertinent enough to our own times. But though in principle he was right, his arguments sometimes strike one as reckless. The Commission proposed to confiscate a number of Prebends and apply the proceeds to a central fund from which the value of the poorer livings could be increased. Smith's contemptuous retort that if the whole income of the Church were equally distributed among all the clergy each man would get no more than the wages of a nobleman's 'upper domestic' seems wilfully to miss the point; for that is not what was proposed. Simple arithmetic might have convinced him that to take, say, a hundred thousand pounds and divide it among two or three hundred meagre livings would in fact have precisely the effect aimed at, of rescuing a number of struggling incumbents from near-starvation. But he will have none of this. No Welfare State for him! Though presumably he would not have denied, under

challenge, that priesthood should imply a special vocation,
Sydney with his uncompromising realism treats it throughout
these letters as a career like any other, and surprisingly seems
more concerned that ambitious men should be lured into the
Church by the prospect of worldly advancement than that the
condition of the lowest-paid clergy should be bettered. He
declares roundly that 'it is impossible to make a fund which will
raise the smaller livings into anything like a decent support for
those who possess them', and, further, 'that the respectability
of the Church, as well as of the Bar, is almost entirely preserved
by the unequal division of their revenues'. The whole income
of the Church, if equally divided, would give each minister about
£250, he says. And why not, one may ask: in those days £250
was a substantial sum. But in fact no one had suggested an equal
division of the income. What was proposed was a slightly more
equitable distribution of it, in the interests of the all-but-destitute
poorer clergy. The only true method in any profession, Smith
contends, is the method of Blanks and Prizes. 'At present men
are tempted into the Church by the prizes of the Church, and
bring into that Church a great deal of capital, which enables
them to live in decency, supporting themselves not with the
money of the public but with their own money, which but for
this temptation would have been carried into some retail trade.
The offices of the Church would then fall down to men little
less coarse and ignorant than agricultural labourers—the clergyman of the parish would be seen in the squire's kitchen; and all
this would take place in a country where poverty is infamous.'
To those who may tell him that this is a Mammonish view of
the subject he retorts: 'Shall the Gospel be preached by men
paid by the State? shall these men be taken from the lower
orders, and be meanly paid? shall they be men of learning and
education? and shall there be some magnificent endowments to
allure such men into the Church? Which of these methods is
the best for diffusing the rational doctrines of Christianity? Not
in the age of the apostles, not in the abstract, timeless, nameless,
placeless land of the philosophers, but in the year 1837, in the
porter-brewing, cotton-spinning, tallow-making kingdom of Great
Britain, bursting with opulence, and flying from poverty as the
greatest of human evils.' To attract into the Church a 'lower
and worse educated set of men' would be disastrous. 'You will

have a set of ranting, raving Pastors, who will wage war against all the innocent pleasures of life, vie with each other in extravagance of zeal, and plague your heart out with their nonsense and absurdity: cribbage must be played in caverns, and sixpenny whist take refuge in the howling wilderness. In this way low men, doomed to hopeless poverty and galled by contempt, will endeavour to force themselves into station and significance.'

There was some excuse for these fears: the squalid pietism of some dissenting sects may have seemed to justify them. But the evils he predicted did not come to pass; the Ecclesiastical Commission went its own way in spite of him; and he took his defeat goodhumouredly, even going so far as to offer an olive branch to the Bishop of London, by writing to a friend: 'I like the Bishop and like his conversation. The battle is ended, and I have no other quarrel with him and the Archbishop but that they neither of them ever ask me to dinner. You see a good deal of the Bishop, and as you have always exhorted me to be a good boy, take an opportunity to set him right as to my real dispositions towards him, and exhort him, as he has gained the victory, to forgive a few hard knocks.'

This was certainly magnanimous. He had attacked the Bishop in the Singleton pamphlets, and there had ensued an exchange of private letters between them in which a good deal of heat was generated. Not content with trying to defend himself, the Bishop had rashly said: 'At a meeting of the ecclesiastical commissioners, one of their number made known to them your willingness to abstain from all further opposition to their measures, *provided that your own individual rights were not interfered with.*' The person referred to was Lord John Russell. 'You cannot really mean,' replies Smith, 'that Ld J. Russell told you that I wanted for myself what was not given to my Brother Prebendaries of St Paul's, or for St Paul's what was not given to other Cathedrals. . . . What he *did* say, I presume, was that I should not interfere about Church arrangements if the vested interests and patronage of Cathedrals were not meddled with, and this perhaps is true enough; if the Commission had not been *unjust*, I should not, I am afraid, have attacked them for being *unwise*!' The Bishop's answer is equivocal. In two subsequent letters he fails to withdraw the implied accusation that Sydney Smith's concern was for himself and his cathedral alone, and not 'for

F

every cathedral in England'. He insists that he had given the precise terms of Lord John Russell's statement, and did not 'feel obliged to declare the sense in which I understood it'. At this point Sydney begins to lose patience. And who can blame him? 'You know perfectly well,' he says bluntly, 'what Lord J. R. meant by attention to my own interests. You ought not in your letter to me to have used any ambiguous terms which might convey another meaning, or having done so and being called upon for an explanation, it should have been given frankly and immediately. When I ask you about facts, you deviate into intentions; I have never said a syllable to you about my concern for the vested rights and patronage of Chapters in general, but whether I had asked anything from Lord John for myself and my own Cathedral which was not [to be] extended to all other Prebendaries and Cathedrals. You *know* very well I *did not*, and *so* you ought immediately to have said.' The letter is signed, as usual, 'I remain, my dear Lord, respectfully your obedient Servant, Sydney Smith'. Even at his most heated, the conventional forms of courtesy are scrupulously adhered to.

The Singleton pamphlets reinforce one's general impression: that zealous though he was for social justice and individual freedom, his zeal was tempered by more respect for traditional institutions than is popular today. The reverence with which he speaks of 'property', a word now commonly regarded as a synonym for sin, has an oldfashioned ring. An embarrassing example occurs in his EDINBURGH REVIEW essay on Chimney Sweepers, where, after giving a harrowing account of the terrors and dangers to which climbing boys were subjected, he concludes (and, alas, without irony): 'We should have been very glad to have seconded the views of the Climbing Society, and to have pleaded for the complete abolition of climbing boys, if we could conscientiously have done so. But such a measure, we are convinced from the evidence, could not be carried into execution *without great injury to property* and great increased risk of fire' (my italics). Ergo, little boys must continue to die of terror or suffocation until property-owners can be persuaded to adopt the (already available) mechanical method of sweeping chimneys. The plea that 'there are many chimneys in old houses which cannot possibly be swept in any other manner' (than by boys) seems surely frivolous, or at any rate strangely complacent,

in view of the fact that ancient houses still exist and climbing
boys do not. It was obviously not beyond human wit to contrive
other means of sweeping oldfashioned chimneys: what was
lacking was the will to do so.

Sydney Smith, in short, was conservative in his outlook as
well as liberal. He had the vice, as well as the virtue, of 'moderation'. The Reform Acts of 1832 have long been recognized by
all parties as a welcome but inadequate first instalment of remedies
long overdue. It makes one rub one's eyes, therefore, to read,
in a long footnote appended to one of the Taunton speeches in
his first collected writings (1839), that 'it was a great deal too
violent'. He says: 'I was a sincere friend to Reform; I am so
still. It was a great deal too violent—but the only justification
is, that you cannot reform as you wish, by degrees; you must
avail yourself of the few opportunities that present themselves.
The Reform carried, it became the business of every honest man
to turn it to good, and to see that the people (drunk with their
new power) did not ruin our ancient institutions. We have been
in considerable danger, and that danger is not yet over.' This
makes us smile, but the sentence that follows has some pertinence
even for us today: 'What alarms me most is the large price paid
by both parties for popular favour.' He cites the spending of
a million pounds of revenue on 'the nonsensical penny-post
scheme' as one of the concessions which are 'sad and unworthy
marks of weakness, and fill reasonable men with just alarm'.
In this same year, 1839, he wrote a pamphlet ridiculing the
proposal of a secret ballot. 'Lady Grey,' he says in a letter,
'writes me word that my pamphlet on the ballot made Lord
Grey laugh heartily, which is to me the pleasantest thing I have
heard about it. When I come out with my universal suffrage
I hope to put him in convulsions.' But whatever one may think
of his minor opinions, there can be no quarrel with the guiding
principle of statesmanship which he laid down. 'There is only
one principle of public conduct—*do what you think right, and take
place and power as an accident.* Upon any other plan, office is
shabbiness, labour, and sorrow.' Here, surely, is a plain message
for our own times.

IX

THE MAN WITHIN

IN spite of gout and other infirmities, which increased with the approach of old age, he kept his courage and humour to the end. In January 1843, his seventy-second year, he writes to Harriet Martineau: 'What an admirable provision of Providence is the gout! What prevents human beings from making the body a larder or a cellar but the gout? When I feel a pang I say, "I know what this is for. I know what you mean. I understand the hint!"—and so I endeavour to extract a little wisdom from pain.' These two had become acquainted, she tells us, after 'a great music-party, where the drawing-room and staircases were one continuous crowd'. She, being deaf, had a seat upstairs, next to the piano. A message was brought to her from Sydney, saying that he understood they desired one another's acquaintance, and that he was awaiting it at the bottom of the stairs. 'He put it to my judgment whether I, being thin, could not more easily get down to him than he, being stout, could get up to me: and he would wait five minutes for my answer. I really could not go, under the circumstances; and it was a serious thing to give up my seat and the music; so Mr Smith sent me a good-night, and promise to call on me, claiming this negotiation as a proper introduction. He came, and sat down, broad and comfortable, in the middle of my sofa, with his hands on his stick as if to support himself in a vast development of voice; and then he began, like the great bell of St Paul's, making me start at the first stroke. He looked with shy dislike at my trumpet, for which there was truly no occasion. I was more likely to fly to the furthest corner of the room. It was always his boast that I did not want my trumpet when he talked with me.' Tom Moore, on a visit to Combe Florey, was met by Sydney in a gig, but taking alarm at the friskiness of the horse got out and walked. He writes on his return: 'I was persuaded to get into a gig with Lady Kerry, and let her drive me some miles. Next day I found out that, but a day or two before, it had run away with her!—no bad taste, certainly, in the horse, but it shows what one gets by consorting with young countesses and frisky ecclesiastics.' With this letter Moore enclosed some verses:

> Rare Sydney! thrice honour'd the stall where he sits,
>   And be his every honour he deigneth to climb at!
> Had England a hierarchy form'd of all wits,
>   Whom but Sydney would England proclaim as its primate?
>
> And long may he flourish, frank, merry, and brave,
>   A Horace to feast with, a Pascal to read!
> While he laughs, all is safe; but, when Sydney grows grave,
>   We shall then think the Church is in danger indeed.

He continued to laugh. He continued to be frank, merry, and brave. Calling on a certain Dr Blake of Taunton, medical man and staunch Unitarian, to ask after his health, he found him complaining of a cold aguish feeling which even a roaring fire could not drive away. 'I can cure you,' said Sydney. 'Cover yourself with the Thirty-nine Articles, and you will soon have a delicious glow all over you.' All witnesses agree that even his most audacious quips seldom gave offence. Samuel Rogers, in his latter years a man of cadaverous appearance, asked him what attitude he had best assume when sitting for his portrait. 'There is a very expressive attitude that we of the clergy adopt on first getting up into the pulpit. I think it might suit you very well. Like this,' said Sydney, and put his hands before his face, as in prayer. There was not one of his friends he did not quiz, says Harriet Martineau, 'but I never heard of any hurt feelings'. She quotes some pleasant examples. His praise of Macaulay: 'Macaulay improves. I have observed in him, of late, flashes of silence.' His characterization of a celebrated scientist: 'Science is his forte, omniscience his foible.' His description of an argumentative friend at a dinner-party: 'There was Hallam, his mouth full of cabbage and contradiction.'

Practical and conscientious as ever, as a canon of St Paul's he gave close attention to every detail, being in all matters of cathedral business, says Catharine, as cautious, prudent, and distrustful, 'as the dullest Clerk in a Merchant's compting house'. Sometimes he was pigheaded, as when he peremptorily dismissed a proposal that the cathedral should be warmed, with the remark that one might as well try to warm the county of Middlesex, and put a veto on having any music in the minor key because he found it dispiriting; but his kindness in personal relationships never failed. He had no patience with 'Newmania' (the Tractarian Movement), which, as a sturdy no-nonsense Protestant, he seems to have disliked mainly because of its emphasis on ritual. Writing news of England to Sir Humphry Davy's wife, who was abroad, he says he has not yet discovered what he is to die of, but rather believes he will be burnt alive by the Puseyites. 'Nothing so remarkable in England as the progress of these foolish people. I have no conception what they mean, if it be not to revive every absurd ceremony, and every antiquated folly, which the common sense of mankind has set to sleep. You will find on your return a fanatical Church of England.' To Miss Martineau, three months later: 'I am just come from London, where I have been doing duty at St Paul's, and preaching against the Puseyites—(1) Because they lessen the aversion to the Catholic faith, and the admiration of Protestantism, which I think one of the greatest improvements the world has ever made. (2) They inculcate the preposterous surrender of the understanding to Bishops. (3) They make religion an affair of trifles, of postures, and of garments.'

He was now, at last, a wealthy man. Fifty thousand pounds from Courtenay, ten thousand from his father (increased from six thousand in a codicil added at Bobus's insistence), together with minor legacies and the emoluments of his office, had made him as rich and powerful as he could wish. Probably he would have liked a bishopric as well, and in any other political climate would have got one; but he had the satisfaction of knowing that throughout a long life he had maintained his integrity and independence, had never tried to curry favour by soft speeches, never trimmed his sails to the prevailing wind, never abstained from speaking his mind. No sooner had his friends the Whigs attained power than he began quarrelling with them, about the Ecclesiastical Commission. Though prominent in the ranks of nineteenth-century reformers, much of the eighteenth-century spirit survived him. He was a liberal but no radical. With the doctrines of egalitarian democracy he had less than no sympathy.

'You may as well attempt to poultice off the humps on a camel's back,' he wrote in a notebook. The sentence is unfinished, but the words that follow, on the next line, give the clue to his meaning: 'Natural inequalities like the humps on a camel's back'. He might or might not have conceded, under pressure, that the existence of natural inequalities affords no excuse for imposing artificial ones; but most likely he regarded the long-established social hierarchy as itself 'natural'.

I have said in an earlier chapter that these unpublished note-books throw a light on his private self, as indeed they do. But it is necessarily a somewhat fitful light, if only because one cannot, short of literary omniscience, be sure of always distin-guishing quotations (never specified) from original remarks. Many quotations there are which show by inference his quick appreciation of great things in literature. He was evidently well read in Shakespeare and Milton, as well as in the Latin texts drilled into him at school; but it is a safe guess that the Romantic movement of his time left him cold; probably he agreed with his friend Jeffrey's despairing verdict on *The Excursion*—'This will never do'. Certainly the mystical element in Wordsworth could not have appealed to him. There are also, however, intimations of a delicacy of perception such as the published works hardly reveal. 'I am glad that I am shielded from your beauty by the insensibility of age. I rejoice that I shall never live to see the decay of your charms but shall die with that unfaded image.' To whom and by whom? If Sydney is himself the author we have here a moving personal avowal. And again: 'His life while there was as dazzling and promising as a rainbow. Love had no wings there, and June no scythe.' Such fragments, however tantalizing, and whatever their source, argue a gentleness of spirit in the man who wrote them down. Another one might have been (but was not) written of himself: 'And when he was crushed with misfortune there came out an aromatic smell of wisdom.'

But as to the main lines of his character as a private person the evidence of the notebooks is conclusive. There is a 'plan of study' noted down for 1820 and another for 1821. They were Foston years. He was about fifty. 'Translate every 10 Lines of the de officiis and retranslate into Latin. 5 Cap of Greek Testament. Theological studies. Plato's apology for Socrates. Horace's Epodes, Epistles, Satires, and Ars Poetica.' The next year's programme is more detailed. It includes reading of 'either Polybius or Diodorus Siculus—or some tracts of Xenophon or Plato—and, for Latin, Tebull, Catull & Propert'. There follows a lay-out for each day of the week. 'Monday write Morning— read Tasso evening. Tuesday Latin or Greek M—Evening Theology.' And so on, with this general postscript: 'Read every day a Chap in Greek Testament and translate 10 Lines of Latin.' In addition to all this he wrote sermons and reviews, supervised the work on his farm, looked after his parishioners like a father, kept up a lively correspondence with absent friends, and did a great deal of talking and laughing. Some of his private 'maxims and rules of life' have been quoted earlier. They are methodically set out, a series of numbered paragraphs, under 'Cap 1' and 'Cap 2'. Here are some of them. '7 If you wish the common people to treat you as a Gentleman you must conduct yourself as a Gentleman should do to them. 8 Rank poisons make good medicines. Error and misfortune may be turned into wisdom and improvement. 9 When you meet with neglect, let it rouse your exertion instead of mortifying your pride. Set about lessening those defects which expose you to neglect, and improve those excellencies which command attention and respect. 10 Where no kindness is due, take any, and do not quarrel with it because it is not more. And where you have not all you think yourself entitled to, consider if it is not better to have a little than none. You cannot extort Love. 12 If you want to improve in the corageous defence of a cause take care to be moderate and just.' Numbers 19 and 20 in this first series concern the dangers of lying late in bed. 'If you don't get up in the Morning you will be overtaken by ignorance and by poverty. Some effort must be made after all. Sloth will take as much as you will give. I once laid a bed till 4 o'clock. I have heard of people who have laid a bed for 6 months. If the effort must be made at some moment, make it at the right moment.'

The unique interest of these admonitions is that they are addressed to himself and are therefore intimately self-revealing. The second series, a few pages on, begins with three related items. '1 Passion gets less and less powerful after every defeat. 2 If you will not terminate gratification where reason points out you will terminate it in death and destruction. Passions always encroach. 3 Husband energy for the real demands which the

dangers of life make upon it.' The next concerns faultfinding.
'Find fault, where you must find fault, in private if possible, and
some time after the offence rather than at the time. The blamed
are less inclined to resist when they are blamed without Witnesses, and both parties are more calm when the matter is
investigated after the delict is burnt out, and the party accused
is struck with the forbearance of the accuser who has seen the
fault and watched for a private and proper time for mentioning
it.' There follow cautions about laughter, religion, and anger.
'5 You must not only not laugh at sacred things, but in this
serious Country you must not laugh at anything even distantly
connected with sacred things. 6 Not only is religion calm and
tranquil, but it has an extensive Atmosphere round it where
calmness and tranquility must be preserved if you wish to avoid
misrepresentation.' He bids himself keep up the 'habit of being
respected', not attempt to be more amusing and agreeable than
is consistent with the preservation of respect, subdue anger on
account of the misery and self-reproach which it entails to him,
and cultivate calmness for the sake of the satisfaction which the
successful struggle with anger produces. He is not to be uneasy,
however, at quarrelling with individuals, provided he has done
his best to avoid it, because to avoid it always is impossible
'unless you are utterly insignificant'. And finally, a recurring
theme: 'Take short views—hope for the best—trust in God.'

The numbered maxims end there, but there are others scattered
about in these miscellaneous pages. They are all to much the
same purpose, and all reflect a sensitive conscience and a lively
common sense. The means of happiness are: humility, philanthropy, temper, occupation. 'Keep doing. Expect little from
others, and be thankful for any thing. Fight against the devils
of temper. Cherish a frank confidence in the good will of others.'
He warns himself against the vice of worrying. 'Wyndham writes
word he is unhappy at School. But 1st There is much unhappi-
ness in human life, how can School be exempt—2, Boys are
apt to take a particular moment of depression for a general
feeling, but they are in fact rarely unhappy—at the moment I
write perhaps he is playing about in the highest Spirits. 3rdly,
When he comes to state his grievance it will probably have
vanished or be so trifling that it will yield to argument or
expostulation. 4thly, At all events, if it is a real Evil that makes

him unhappy I must find out what it is and proceed to act upon it, but I must wait till I can either in person or by Letter find out what it is.' Other items from the notebooks are to be found under *Miscellaneous Extracts*, in the selection which follows this biography. Incidentally the letter to Lady Dacre, given in the same section, suggests that he had experienced the miseries, as well as the happiness, of romantic love.

Among his chief pleasures as a canon of St Paul's was the bestowal of livings on needy or deserving men. He had a frank delight in 'doing good'. One of these acts of patronage was the occasion of a scene truly Dickensian in its arch irony and unrestrained sentiment. The death of a brother clergyman at St Paul's, Canon Tate, left the living of Edmonton vacant; and by the rules of the Chapter it rested with Sydney Smith either to take it himself or present it to some person of his choice. For him the first alternative can hardly have existed, since he happened to know that the bereaved family were reduced to poverty by their loss, and that Tate's eldest son had been acting as his father's curate at Edmonton. Having by inquiry satisfied himself that young Tate was a fit person for the job, he took the obvious course, and then wrote from Green Street to his wife to tell her about it. 'Dearest Kate: I meant to have gone to Munden today, but am not quite stout, so have postponed my journey there till next Saturday, the 28th. I went over yesterday to the Tates, at Edmonton. The family consists of three delicate daughters, an aunt, the old lady, and her son, the curate of Edmonton. The old lady was in bed. I found there a physician, an old friend of Tate's, attending them from friendship, who had come from London for that purpose. They were in daily expectation of being turned out from house and curacy. . . . I began by inquiring the character of their servants; then turned the conversation on their affairs, and expressed a hope that the Chapter might ultimately do something for them. I then said: "It is my duty to state to you" (they were all assembled) "that I have given away the living of Edmonton, and have written to our Chapter clerk this morning to mention the person to whom I have given it; and I must also tell you that I am sure he will appoint his curate." (A general silence and dejection.) "It is a very odd coincidence," I added, "that the gentleman I have selected is a namesake of this family; his name is Tate. Have you any relations of that name?" "No, we have not." "And, by a more singular coincidence, his name is Thomas Tate. In short," I added, "there is no use in mincing the matter. You are vicar of Edmonton." They all burst into tears. It flung me also into a great agitation of tears, and I wept and groaned for a long time. Then I rose and said I thought it was very likely to end in their keeping a buggy, at which we all laughed as violently. The poor old lady, who was sleeping in a garret because she could not bear to enter the room lately inhabited by her husband, sent for me and kissed me, sobbing with a thousand emotions. The charitable physician wept also. . . . I never passed so remarkable a morning, nor was more deeply impressed with the sufferings of human life, and never felt more thoroughly the happiness of doing good.'

X

A LIGHT EXTINGUISHED

'I AM come to the age of seventy, and have attained enough reputation to make me somebody. I should not like a vast reputation: it would plague me to death. I hope to care less for outward things.'

Death came a few years later. It was preceded by months of sickness and pain, patiently borne. Some of his thoughts about the ultimate mystery he had noted down some eight years before. '1 It must come some time or another. 2 It has come to all, greater better and wiser than me. 3 Who shall say that I may not avoid more evil by dying than I lose of good. 4 I have lived 66 years. 5 I have done very little harm in the world. 6 I have brought up my family and I leave every body well off. 7 I have seen all that is worth seeing. 8 It would only be the same thing over again.' Other entries touch on the same theme. 'Great care must be taken that life does not become wearisome before it is time to depart.' And: 'Time which changes all has altered me in soul and aspect. It has taken the fire from my mind and the vigor from my limbs.'

But this last was perhaps only half true, for within a few months of the end he was writing with grim humour about his condition in letters to friends. 'October 11, 1844. My dear Lady Grey: I rather think that last week they wanted to kill me, but I was too sharp for them. I am now tolerably well, but I am weak, and taking all proper care of myself: which care consists in eating nothing that I like and doing nothing that I wish.' 'October 21, 1844. My dear Lady Carlisle: From your ancient goodness to me, I am sure you will be glad to receive a bulletin from myself, informing you that I am making a good progress; in fact I am in a regular train of promotion. From gruel, vermicelli, and sago, I was promoted to panada, from thence to minced meat, and thence (such is the effect of good conduct)

I was elevated to a mutton-chop. My breathlessness and giddiness are gone—chased away by the gout. If you hear of sixteen or eighteen pounds of human flesh, they belong to me. I look as if a curate had been taken out of me.' 'Dear Holland [his son-in-law] : I am only at broth at present, but Lyddon thinks I shall get to pudding tomorrow, and mutton-chops the next day. I long for promotion.' To one of these letters is appended a series of news-items under the title *Combe Florey Gazette* : 'Mr Smith's large red cow is expected to calve this week. Mr Gibbs has bought Mr Smith's lame mare. It rained yesterday, and, a correspondent observes, is not likely to rain today. Mr Smith is better. Mrs Smith is indisposed. A nest of black magpies was found near the village yesterday.' In November he was taken to his London house, to be under the care of Dr Holland, for whom he had a great regard. 'I should like to get well,' he told Saba, 'were it only to please Dr Holland.'

He died on the 22nd of February 1845, 'at peace with himself and with all the world'. The last person to see him alive was Bobus, who himself died within a fortnight. 'And now dear Children I have done,' writes Catharine Smith at the end of her narrative. 'After passing nearly half a century with *such* a Man I am alone . . . the Light of my Life is extinguished.' Yet for her as she writes of him, as for us who may still enjoy his ghostly company, his courage and gaiety and goodness, something of that light lives on; and from the shattered lamp there rises, subtle and pervasive, 'the aromatic smell of wisdom'.

A SELECTION
FROM THE WRITINGS
OF
SYDNEY SMITH

FROM THE EDINBURGH REVIEW

[Many of the articles contributed by Sydney Smith to the EDINBURGH REVIEW are reviews only in name, the book in question—mere pretext for a discourse on a chosen theme—being generally disposed of in a brief first paragraph. In the present selection therefore, except in the case of 'The Suppression of Vice' which is given entire, we begin at the second paragraph, or later. Other minor cuts are indicated by a triple or quadruple point, more substantial ones by the § sign. Any footnotes that appear between square brackets are by the present editor: the other footnotes are the author's, inserted by him in the collected edition of his writings. In reading the EDINBURGH REVIEW articles, allowance must be made not only for the more formal prose manners of the period but for the pompousness inherent in any anonymous writing that involves the use of the editorial 'we'. It should be remembered too that they had all been sub-edited by Jeffrey, whom Smith goodhumouredly accused of spoiling some of his best jokes. In another letter to Jeffrey he enumerates his motives for writing reviews. 'First, the love of you. Second, the habit of reviewing. Third, the love of money. To which I may add a fourth, the love of punishing fraud and folly.']

TOLERATION

IF a prudent man sees a child playing with a porcelain cup of great value, he takes the vessel out of his hand, pats him on the head, tells him his mamma will be sorry if it is broken, and gently cheats him into the use of some less precious substitute. Why will Lord Sidmouth meddle with the Toleration Act, when there are so many other subjects in which his abilities might be so eminently useful—when enclosure bills are drawn up with such scandalous negligence, turnpike roads so shamefully neglected, and public conveyances illegitimately loaded in the face of day and in defiance of the wisest legislative provisions? We confess our trepidation at seeing the Toleration Act in the hands of Lord Sidmouth; and should be very glad if it were fairly back in the statute-book, and the sedulity of this well-meaning nobleman diverted into another channel.

The alarm and suspicion of the Dissenters upon these measures is wise and rational. They are right to consider the Toleration Act as their palladium; and they may be certain that in this country there is always a strong party ready, not only to prevent the further extension of tolerant principles, but to abridge (if they dared) their present operation within the narrowest limits. Whoever makes this attempt will be sure to make it under professions of the most earnest regard for mildness and toleration, and with the strongest declarations of respect for King William, the Revolution, and the principles which seated the House of Brunswick on the throne of these realms—and then will follow the clauses for whipping Dissenters, imprisoning preachers, and subjecting them to rigid qualifications, etc. The infringement on the militia acts is a mere pretence. The real object is, to diminish the number of Dissenters from the Church of England, by abridging the liberties and privileges they now possess. This is the project which we shall examine; for we sincerely believe it to be the project in agitation. The mode in which it is proposed to attack the Dissenters is, first, by exacting greater qualifications in their teachers; next, by preventing the interchange or itinerancy of preachers and fixing them to one spot.

It can never, we assume, be intended to subject dissenting ministers to any kind of *theological* examination. A teacher examined in doctrinal opinions, by another teacher who differs from him, is so very absurd a project, that we entirely acquit Lord Sidmouth of any intention of this sort. We rather presume his Lordship to mean, that a man who professes to teach his fellow-creatures should at least have made some progress in human learning, that he should not be wholly without education, that he should be able at least to read and write. If the test is of this very ordinary nature it can scarcely exclude many teachers of religion; and it was hardly worth while, for the very insignificant diminution of numbers which this must occasion to the dissenting clergy, to have raised all the alarm which this attack upon the Toleration Act has occasioned.

But, without any reference to the magnitude of the effects, is the principle right? or, What is the meaning of religious toleration? That a man should hold, without pain or penalty, any religious opinions, and choose, for his instruction in the business of salvation, any guide whom he pleases—care being taken that the teacher and the doctrine injure neither the policy nor the morals of the country. We maintain that perfect religious toleration applies as much to the teacher as [to] the thing taught; and that it is quite as intolerant to make a man hear Thomas, who wants to hear John, as it would be to make a man profess Arminian, who wished to profess Calvinistical principles. What right has any government to dictate to a man who shall guide him to heaven, any more than it has to persecute the religious tenets by which he hopes to arrive there? You believe that the heretic professes doctrines utterly incompatible with the true spirit of the Gospel. First you burnt him for this; then you whipt him; then you fined him; then you put him in prison. All this did no good; and for these hundred years last past you have let him alone. The heresy is now firmly protected by law; and you know it must be preached. What matters it, then, who preaches it? If the evil must be communicated, the organ and instrument through which it is communicated cannot be of much consequence. It is true, this kind of persecution, against persons, has not been quite so much tried as the other against doctrines; but the folly and inexpediency of it rest precisely upon the same grounds.

Would it not be a singular thing, if the friends of the Church of England were to make the most strenuous efforts to render their enemies eloquent and learned?—and to found places of education for Dissenters? But, if their learning would not be a good, why is their ignorance an evil?—unless it be necessarily supposed, that all increase of learning must bring men over to the Church of England; in which supposition, the Scottish and Catholic Universities, and the [nonconformist] College at Hackney, would hardly acquiesce. Ignorance surely matures and quickens the progress, by insuring the dissolution, of absurdity. Rational and learned Dissenters remain: religious mobs, under some ignorant fanatic of the day, become foolish overmuch, dissolve, and return to the Church. The Unitarian who reads and writes gets some sort of discipline, and returns no more.

What connection is there (as Lord Sidmouth's plan assumes) between the zeal and piety required for religious instruction and the common attainments of literature? But, if knowledge and education are required for religious instruction, why be content with the common elements of learning? why not require higher attainments in dissenting candidates for orders, and examine them in the languages in which the books of their religion are conveyed?

A dissenting minister, of vulgar aspect and homely appearance, declares that he entered into that holy office because he felt a call; and a clergyman of the Establishment smiles at him for the declaration. But it should be remembered that no minister of the Establishment is admitted into orders before he has been expressly interrogated by the bishop whether he feels himself called to that sacred office. The doctrine of calling, or inward feeling, is quite orthodox in the English church; and in arguing this subject in Parliament it will hardly be contended that the Episcopalian only is the judge when that call is genuine and when it is only imaginary.

The attempt at making the dissenting clergy stationary, and persecuting their circulation, appears to us quite as unjust and inexpedient as the other measure of qualifications. It appears a gross inconsistency to say: 'I admit that what you are doing is legal, but you must not do it thoroughly and effectually. I allow you to propagate your heresy, but I object to all means of propagating it which appear to be useful and effective.' If there are any other grounds upon which the circulation of the dissenting clergy is objected to, let these grounds be stated and examined; but to object to their circulation merely because it is the best method of effecting the object which you allow them to effect, does appear to be rather unnatural and inconsistent.

It is presumed, in this argument, that the only reason urged for the prevention of itinerant preachers is the increase of heresy; for, if heresy is not increased by it, it must be immaterial to the feelings of Lord Sidmouth, and of the Imperial Parliament, whether Mr Shufflebottom preaches at Bungay, and Mr Ringletub at Ipswich; or whether an artful vicissitude is adopted, and the order of insane predication reversed.

But, supposing all this new interference to be just, what good will it do? You find a dissenting preacher, whom you have prohibited, still continuing to preach,—or preaching at Ealing when he ought to preach at Acton. His number is taken, and the next morning he is summoned. Is it believed that this description of persons can be put down by fine and imprisonment? His fine is paid for him; and he returns from imprisonment ten times as much sought after and as popular as he was before. This is a receipt for making a stupid preacher popular, and a popular preacher more popular, but can have no possible tendency to prevent the mischief against which it is levelled. It is precisely the old history of persecution against opinions turned into a persecution against persons. The prisons will be filled, the enemies of the Church made enemies of the State also, and the Methodists rendered ten times more actively mad than they are at present. This is the direct and obvious tendency of Lord Sidmouth's plan.

Nothing dies so hard and rallies so often as intolerance. The fires are put out, and no living nostril has scented the nidor of a human creature roasted for faith; then, after this, the prison-doors were got open, and the chains knocked off; and now Lord Sidmouth only begs that men who disagree with him in religious opinions may be deprived of all civil offices and not be allowed to hear the preachers they like best. Chains and whips he would not hear of; but these mild gratifications of his bill every orthodox mind is surely entitled to. The hardship would indeed be great if a churchman were deprived of the amusement of putting a dissenting parson in prison. We are convinced Lord Sidmouth is a very amiable and well-intentioned man: his error is not the error of his heart, but of his time, above which few men ever rise. It is the error of some four or five hundred thousand English gentlemen, of decent education and worthy characters, who conscientiously believe that they are punishing, and continuing incapacities, for the good of the State; while they are, in fact (though without knowing it), only gratifying that insolence, hatred, and revenge, which all human beings are unfortunately so ready to feel against those who will not conform to their own sentiments. . . .

[1811]

GAME LAWS

[Sydney Smith wrote two articles under this title. The first, in 1819, contends that game should be the property of the landowner, irrespective of the value of his holding, and that he should be allowed to sell the game, or to grant shooting rights, to whomsoever he please. The second article, in 1823, begins by citing evidence, from a Report on the Game Laws issued by a committee of the House of Commons, that the law against the buying and selling of game was being treated with the contempt it deserved. All classes, from lords of the manor and their gamekeepers at one end of the scale down to country higglers and poachers at the other, were engaged in the illegal traffic. Even 'the most respectable' poulterers had declared that in the then state of the Game Laws it was absolutely necessary for them to take part in it, because their regular customers for poultry would leave them if they refused to supply game as well; and Bow Street officers had given evidence that in some villages all the inhabitants, including the constable, were united against the gamekeepers, and that the people of all kinds and classes who were setting these particular laws at defiance had no sense of wrongdoing in the matter.]

THE inferences from these facts are exactly as we predicted, and as every man of common sense must have predicted—that to prevent the sale of game is absolutely impossible. If game is plentiful, and cannot be obtained at any lawful market, an illicit trade will be established which it is utterly impossible to prevent by any increased severity of the laws. There never was a more striking illustration of the necessity of attending to public opinion in all penal enactments. Mr Bankes (a perfect representative of all the ordinary notions about forcing mankind by pains and penalties) took the floor. To buy a partridge (though still considered as inferior to murder) was visited with the very heaviest infliction of the law; and yet, though game is sold as openly in London as apples and oranges, though three years have elapsed since this legislative mistake, the officers of the police can hardly recollect a single instance where the information has been laid or the penalty levied: and why? because every man's feelings and every man's understanding tell him that it is a most absurd and ridiculous tyranny to prevent one man, who has more game than he wants, from exchanging it with another man, who has more money than he wants; because magistrates will not (if they can avoid it) inflict such absurd penalties; because even common informers know enough of the honest indignation of mankind, and are too well aware of the coldness of pump and pond to act under the bill of the Lycurgus of Corfe Castle.

The plan now proposed is, to undersell the poacher, which may be successful or unsuccessful; but the threat is, if you attempt this plan there will be no game, and if there is no game there will be no country gentlemen. We deny every part of this enthymeme, the last proposition as well as the first. We really cannot believe that all our rural mansions would be deserted although no game was to be found in their neighbourhood. Some come into the country for health, some for quiet, for agriculture, for economy, from attachment to family estates, from love of retirement, from the necessity of keeping up provincial interests, and from a vast variety of causes. Partridges and pheasants, though they form nine-tenths of human motives, still leave a small residue which may be classed under some other head. Neither are a great proportion of those whom the love of shooting brings into the country of the smallest value or importance to the country. A Colonel of the Guards, the second son just entered at Oxford, three diners-out from Piccadilly; Major Rock, Lord John, Lord Charles, the Colonel of the regiment quartered at the neighbouring town, two Irish Peers, and a German Baron;— if all this honourable company proceed with fustian jackets, dog-whistles, and chemical inventions, to a solemn destruction of pheasants, how is the country benefited by their presence? or how would earth, air, or sea, be injured by their annihilation? There are certainly many valuable men brought into the country by a love of shooting, who, coming there for that purpose, are useful for many better purposes; but a vast multitude of shooters are of no more service to the country than the ramrod which condenses the charge or the barrel which contains it. We do not deny that the annihilation of the game laws would thin the aristocratical population of the country; but it would not thin that population so much as is contended; and the loss of many of the persons so banished would be a good, rather than a misfortune. At all events, we cannot at all comprehend the policy of alluring the better classes of society into the country by the temptation of petty tyranny and injustice, or of monopoly in sports. How absurd it would be to offer to the higher orders the exclusive use of peaches, nectarines, and apricots, as the premium of rustication; to put vast quantities of men into prison as apricot eaters, apricot buyers, and apricot sellers; to appoint a regular day for beginning to eat, and another for leaving off; to have a lord of the manor for greengages, and to rage with a penalty of five pounds against the unqualified eater of the gage! And yet the privilege of shooting a set of wild poultry is stated to be the bonus for the residence of country gentlemen. As far as this immense advantage can be obtained without the sacrifice of justice and reason, well and good; but we would not oppress any order of society, or violate right and wrong, to obtain any population of squires, however dense. It is the grossest of all absurdities to say the present state of the law is absurd and unjust but it must not be altered because the alteration would drive gentlemen out of the country! If gentlemen cannot breathe fresh air without injustice, let them putrefy in Cranborne Alley. Make just laws, and let squires live and die where they please.

The evidence collected in the House of Commons respecting the Game Laws is so striking and so decisive against the gentlemen of the trigger, that their only resource is to represent it as not worthy of belief. But why not worthy of belief? It is not stated what part of it is incredible. Is it the plenty of game in London for sale? the unfrequency of convictions? the occasional but frequent excess of supply above demand in an article supplied by stealing? or its destruction when the sale is not without risk and the price extremely low? or the readiness of grandees to turn the excess of their game into fish or poultry? All these circumstances appear to us so natural and so likely, that we should, without any evidence, have had little doubt of their existence. There are a few absurdities in the evidence of one of the poulterers; but, with this exception, we see no reason whatever for impugning the credibility and exactness of the mass of testimony prepared by the Committee.

It is utterly impossible to teach the common people to respect property in animals bred the possessor knows not where—which he cannot recognize by any mark, which may leave him the next moment, which are kept, not for his profit, but for his amusement. Opinion never will be in favour of such property: if the *animus furandi* exists, the propensity will be gratified by poaching. It is in vain to increase the severity of the protecting laws. They make the case weaker, instead of stronger; and are more resisted and worse executed, exactly in proportion as they are contrary to public opinion: the case of the game laws is a memorable lesson upon the philosophy of legislation. If a certain degree of punishment does not cure the offence, it is supposed, by the Bankes School, that there is nothing to be done but to multiply this punishment by two, and then again and again, till the object is accomplished. The efficient maximum of punishment, however, is not what the Legislature chooses to enact, *but what the great mass of mankind think the maximum ought to be.* The moment the punishment passes this Rubicon it becomes less and less instead of greater and greater. Juries and Magistrates will not commit—informers* are afraid of public indignation— poachers will not submit to be sent to Botany Bay without a battle—blood is shed for pheasants—the public attention is called to this preposterous state of the law—and even ministers (whom nothing pesters so much as the interests of humanity) are at last compelled to come forward and do what is right. Apply this to the game laws. It was before penal to sell game: within these few years it has been made penal to buy it. From the scandalous cruelty of the law, night poachers are transported for seven years. And yet, never was so much game sold or such a spirit of ferocious resistance excited to the laws. One fourth of all the commitments in Great Britain are for offences against the game laws. There is a general feeling that some alteration must take place—a feeling not only among Reviewers, who never see nor eat game,

---

* There is a remarkable instance of this in the new Turnpike Act. The penalty for taking more than the legal number of outside passengers is £10 per head, if the coachman is in part or wholly the owner. This will rarely be levied, because it is too much. A penalty of £100 would produce perfect impunity. The maximum of practical severity would have been about £5. Any magistrate would cheerfully levy this sum; while doubling it will produce reluctance in the Judge, resistance in the culprit, and unwillingness in the informer.

but among the double-barrelled, shot-belted members of the House of Commons, who are either alarmed or disgusted by the vice and misery which their cruel laws and childish passion for amusement are spreading among the lower orders of mankind.

It is said: 'In spite of all the game sold, there is game enough left; let the laws therefore remain as they are.' And so it was said formerly: 'There is sugar enough; let the slave trade remain as it is.' But at what expense of human happiness is this quantity of game or of sugar, and this state of poacher law and slave law, to remain! The first object of a good government is not that rich men should have their pleasures in perfection, but that all orders of men should be good and happy; and if crowded covies and chuckling cock-pheasants are only to be procured by encouraging the common people in vice, and leading them into cruel and disproportionate punishment, it is the duty of the government to restrain the cruelties which the country members, in reward for their assiduous loyalty, have been allowed to introduce into the game laws.

The plan of the new bill (long since anticipated, in all its provisions, by the acute author of the pamphlet before us) is that the public at large should be supplied by persons licensed by magistrates, and that all qualified persons should be permitted to sell their game to these licensed distributors; and there seems a fair chance that such a plan would succeed. The questions are, would sufficient game come into the hands of the licensed salesman? would the licensed salesman confine himself to the purchase of game from qualified persons? would buyers of game purchase elsewhere than from the licensed salesman? would the poacher be understood by the honest dealer? would game remain in the same plenty as before? It is understood that the game laws are to remain as they are; with this only difference, that the qualified man can sell to the licensed man, and the licentiate to the public.

It seems probable to us, that vast quantities of game would, after a little time, find their way into the hands of licensed poulterers. Great people are very often half eaten up by their establishments. The quantity of game killed in a large shooting party is very great; to eat it is impossible, and to dispose of it in presents very troublesome. The preservation of game is very expensive, and when it could be bought it would be no more a compliment to send it as a present than it would be to send geese and fowls. If game were sold, very large shooting establishments might be made to pay their own expenses. The shame is made by the law; there is a disgrace in being detected and fined. If that barrier were removed, superfluous partridges would go to the poulterers as readily as superfluous venison does to the venison butcher, or as a gentleman sells the corn and mutton off his farm which he cannot consume. For these reasons, we do not doubt that the shops of licensed poulterers would be full of game in the season; and this part of the argument, we think, the arch-enemy, Sir John Shelley, himself would concede to us.

The next question is, from whence they would procure it. A licence for selling game, granted by country magistrates, would, from their jealousy upon these subjects, be granted only to persons of some respectability and property. The purchase of game from unqualified persons would of course be guarded against by very heavy penalties, both personal and pecuniary; and these penalties would be inflicted, because opinion would go with them. 'Here is a respectable tradesman,' it would be said, 'who might have bought as much game as he pleased in a lawful manner, but who, in order to increase his profits by buying it a little cheaper, has encouraged a poacher to steal it.' Public opinion, therefore, would certainly be in favour of a very strong punishment; and a licensed vendor of game, who exposed himself to these risks, would expose himself to the loss of liberty, property, character, and licence. The persons interested to put a stop to such a practice would not be the paid agents of Government, as in cases of smuggling; but all the gentlemen of the country, the customers of the tradesman for fish, poultry, or whatever else he dealt in, would have an interest in putting down the practice. In all probability, the practice would become disreputable, like the purchase of stolen poultry; and this would be a stronger barrier than the strongest laws. There would of course be some exceptions to this statement. A few shabby people would, for the chance of gaining sixpence, incur the risk of ruin and disgrace; but it is probable that the general practice would be otherwise.

For the same reasons, the consumers of game would rather give a little more for it to a licensed poulterer than expose themselves to severe penalties by purchasing from poachers. The great mass of London consumers are supplied now, not from shabby people in whom they can have no confidence, not from hawkers and porters, but from respectable tradesmen, in whose probity they have the most perfect confidence. Men will brave the law for pheasants, but not for sixpence or a shilling; and the law itself is much more difficult to be braved when it allows pheasants to be brought at some price than when it endeavours to render them utterly inaccessible to wealth. All the licensed salesmen, too, would have a direct interest in stopping the contraband trade of game. They would lose no character in doing so; their informations would be reasonable and respectable. . ... At present the poacher is in the same situation as the smuggler would be if rum and brandy could not be purchased of any fair trader. The great check to the profits of the smuggler are, that if you want his commodities, and will pay a higher price, you may have them elsewhere without risk or disgrace. But forbid the purchase of these luxuries at any price, shut up the shop of the brandy merchant, and you render the trade of the smuggler of incalculable value. The object of the intended bill is to raise up precisely the same competition to the trade of the poacher by giving the public an opportunity of buying lawfully and honestly the tempting articles in which he now deals exclusively.

§

For these reasons we think the experiment of legalizing the sale of game ought to be tried. The game laws have been carried to a pitch of oppression which is a disgrace to the country. The prisons are half filled with peasants, shut up for the irregular slaughter of rabbits and birds—a sufficient reason for killing a weasel but not for imprisoning a man. Something should be done; it is disgraceful to a Government to stand by and see such enormous evils without interference. It is true they are not connected with the struggles of party; but still, the happiness of the common people, whatever gentlemen may say, ought every now and then to be considered.

FEMALE EDUCATION

A GREAT deal has been said of the original difference of capacity between men and women; as if women were more quick, and men more judicious—as if women were more remarkable for delicacy of association, and men for stronger powers of attention. All this, we confess, appears to us very fanciful. That there is a difference in the understandings of the men and the women we every day meet with, everybody, we suppose, must perceive; but there is none surely which may not be accounted for by the difference of circumstances in which they have been placed, without referring to any conjectural difference of original conformation of mind. As long as boys and girls run about in the dirt, and trundle hoops together, they are both precisely alike. If you catch up one half of these creatures and train them to a particular set of actions and opinions, and the other half to a perfectly opposite set, of course their understandings will differ, as one or the other sort of occupations has called this or that talent into action. There is surely no occasion to go into any deeper or more abstruse reasoning in order to explain so very simple a phenomenon. Taking it, then, for granted, that nature has been as bountiful of understanding to one sex as the other, it is incumbent on us to consider what are the principal objections commonly made against the communication of a greater share of knowledge to women than commonly falls to their lot at present: for though it may be doubted whether women should learn all that men learn, the immense disparity which now exists between their knowledge we should hardly think could admit of any rational defence. It is not easy to imagine that there can be any just cause why a woman of forty should be more ignorant than a boy of twelve years of age. If there be any good at all in female ignorance, this (to use a very colloquial phrase) is surely too much of a good thing.

Something in this question must depend, no doubt, upon the

leisure which either sex enjoys for the cultivation of their understandings; and we cannot help thinking that women have fully
as much, if not more, idle time upon their hands, than men.
Women are excluded from all the serious business of the world;
men are lawyers, physicians, clergymen, apothecaries, and justices
of the peace—sources of exertion which consume a great deal
more time than producing and suckling children; so that, if the
thing is a thing that ought to be done, if the attainments of
literature are objects really worthy the attention of females, they
cannot plead the want of leisure as an excuse for indolence and
neglect. The lawyer who passes his day in exasperating the
bickerings of Roe and Doe is certainly as much engaged as his
lady who has the whole of the morning before her to correct
the children and pay the bills. The apothecary who rushes from
an act of phlebotomy in the western parts of the town to insinuate
a bolus in the east is surely as completely absorbed as that
fortunate female who is darning the garment or preparing the
repast of her Æsculapius at home; and, in every degree and
situation of life, it seems that men must necessarily be exposed
to more serious demands upon their time and attention than
can possibly be the case with respect to the other sex. We are
speaking always of the fair demands which ought to be made
upon the time and attention of women; for, as the matter now
stands, the time of women is considered as worth nothing at all.
Daughters are kept to occupations in sewing, patching, mantua-
making, and mending, by which it is impossible they can earn
tenpence a day. The intellectual improvement of women is
considered to be of such subordinate importance that twenty
pounds paid for needlework would give to a whole family leisure
to acquire a fund of real knowledge. They are kept with nimble
fingers and vacant understandings, till the season for improvement is utterly passed away and all chance of forming more
important habits completely lost. We do not therefore say that
women have more leisure than men if it be necessary they should
lead the life of artisans; but we make this assertion only upon
the supposition that it is of some importance women should be
instructed; and that many ordinary occupations, for which a
little money will find a better substitute, should be sacrificed to
this consideration.

We bar, in this discussion, any objection which proceeds from the mere novelty of teaching women more than they are already taught. It may be useless that their education should be improved or it may be pernicious; and these are the fair grounds on which the question may be argued. But those who cannot bring their minds to consider such an unusual extension of knowledge without connecting with it some sensation of the ludicrous should remember that in the progress from absolute ignorance there is a period when cultivation of the mind is new to every rank and description of persons. A century ago who would have believed that country gentlemen could be brought to read and spell with the ease and accuracy which we now so frequently remark, or [have] supposed that they could be carried up even to the elements of ancient and modern history? Nothing is more common, or more stupid, than to take the actual for the possible; to believe that all which is, is all which can be; first to laugh at every proposed deviation from practice as impossible, then, when it is carried into effect, to be astonished that it did not take place before.

It is said that the effect of knowledge is to make women pedantic and affected, and that nothing can be more offensive than to see a woman stepping out of the natural modesty of her sex to make an ostentatious display of her literary attainments. This may be true enough, but the answer is so trite and obvious that we are almost ashamed to make it. All affectation and display proceed from the supposition of possessing something better than the rest of the world possesses. Nobody is vain of possessing two legs and two arms, because that is the precise quantity of either sort of limb which everybody possesses. Who ever heard a lady boast that she understood French?—for no other reason, that we know of, but because everybody in these days does understand French; and though there may be some disgrace in being ignorant of that language, there is little or no merit in its acquisition. Diffuse knowledge generally among women, and you will at once cure the conceit which knowledge occasions while it is rare. Vanity and conceit we shall of course witness in men and women as long as the world endures: but by multiplying the attainments upon which these feelings are founded, you increase the difficulty of indulging them, and render them much more tolerable, by making them the proofs of a much higher merit. When learning ceases to be uncommon among women, learned women will cease to be affected.

H

A great many of the lesser and more obscure duties of life necessarily devolve upon the female sex. The arrangement of all household matters, and the care of children in their early infancy, must of course depend upon them. Now there is a very general notion that the moment you put the education of women upon a better footing than it is at present, at that moment there will be an end of all domestic economy, and that if you once suffer women to eat of the tree of knowledge the rest of the family will very soon be reduced to the same kind of aërial and unsatisfactory diet. These, and all such opinions, are referable to one great and common cause of error;—that man does everything and that nature does nothing, and that everything we see is referable to positive institution rather than to original feeling. Can anything, for example, be more perfectly absurd than to suppose that the care and perpetual solicitude which a mother feels for her children depends upon her ignorance of Greek and Mathematics, and that she would desert an infant for a quadratic equation? We seem to imagine that we can break in pieces the solemn institution of nature by the little laws of a boarding-school, and that the existence of the human race depends upon teaching women a little more or a little less; that Cimmerian ignorance can aid parental affection, or the circle of arts and sciences produce its destruction. In the same manner, we forget the principles upon which the love of order, arrangement, and all the arts of economy depend. They depend not upon ignorance nor idleness, but upon the poverty, confusion, and ruin which would ensue from neglecting them. Add to these principles the love of what is beautiful and magnificent, and the vanity of display, and there can surely be no reasonable doubt but that the order and economy of private life is amply secured from the perilous inroads of knowledge.

We would fain know, too, if knowledge is to produce such baneful effects upon the material and the household virtues, why this influence has not already been felt? Women are much better educated now than they were a century ago; but they are by no means less remarkable for attention to the arrangements of their household, or less inclined to discharge the offices of parental affection. It would be very easy to show that the same objection has been made at all times to every improvement in the education of both sexes, and all ranks, and been as uniformly and com-

pletely refuted by experience. A great part of the objections made
to the education of women are rather objections made to human
nature than to the female sex: for it is surely true that knowledge,
where it produces any bad effects at all, does as much mischief
to one sex as to the other, and gives birth to fully as much
arrogance, inattention to common affairs, and eccentricity among
men, as it does among women. But it by no means follows that
you get rid of vanity and self-conceit because you get rid of
learning. Self-complacency can never want an excuse; and the
best way to make it more tolerable, and more useful, is to give
to it as high and as dignified an object as possible. But, at all
events, it is unfair to bring forward against a part of the world
an objection which is equally powerful against the whole. When
foolish women think they have any distinction, they are apt to
be proud of it; so are foolish men. But we appeal to anyone who
has lived with cultivated persons of either sex, whether he has
not witnessed as much pedantry, as much wrongheadedness, as
much arrogance, and certainly a great deal more rudeness,
produced by learning in men than in women: therefore we should
make the accusation general, or dismiss it altogether; though,
with respect to pedantry, the learned are certainly a little
unfortunate that so very emphatic a word, which is occasionally
applicable to all men embarked eagerly in any pursuit, should
be reserved exclusively for them: for, as pedantry is an ostentatious obtrusion of knowledge, in which those who hear us
cannot sympathize, it is a fault of which soldiers, sailors, sports-
men, gamesters, cultivators, and all men engaged in a particular
occupation, are quite as guilty as scholars; but they have the
good fortune to have the vice only of pedantry,—while scholars
have both the vice and the name for it too.

Some persons are apt to contrast the acquisition of important
knowledge with what they call simple pleasures; and deem it
more becoming that a woman should educate flowers, make
friendships with birds, and pick up plants, than enter into more
difficult and fatiguing studies. If a woman has no taste and genius
for higher occupations, let her engage in these to be sure, rather
than remain destitute of any pursuit. But why are we necessarily
to doom a girl, whatever be her taste or her capacity, to one
unvaried line of petty and frivolous occupation? If she is full of
strong sense and elevated curiosity, can there be any reason why

she should be diluted and enfeebled down to a mere culler of simples and fancier of birds?—why books of history and reasoning are to be torn out of her hand, and why she is to be sent, like a butterfly, to hover over the idle flowers of the field? Such amusements are innocent to those whom they can occupy; but they are not innocent to those who have too powerful understandings to be occupied by them. Light broths and fruits are innocent food only to weak or to infant stomachs; but they are poison to that organ in its perfect and mature state. But the great charm appears to be in the word *simplicity*—simple pleasures! If by a simple pleasure is meant an innocent pleasure, the observation is best answered by showing that the pleasure which results from the acquisition of important knowledge is quite as innocent as any pleasure whatever; but if by a simple pleasure is meant one the cause of which can be easily analysed, or which does not last long, or which in itself is very faint, then simple pleasures seem to be very nearly synonymous with small pleasures; and if the simplicity were to be a little increased, the pleasure would vanish altogether.

As it is impossible that every man should have industry or activity sufficient to avail himself of the advantages of education, it is natural that men who are ignorant themselves should view with some degree of jealousy and alarm any proposal for improving the education of women. But such men may depend upon it, however the system of female education may be exalted, that there will never be wanting a due proportion of failures; and that after parents, guardians, and preceptors have done all in their power to make everybody wise, there will still be a plentiful supply of women who have taken special care to remain otherwise; and they may rest assured, if the utter extinction of ignorance and folly is the evil they dread, that their interests will always be effectually protected, in spite of every exertion to the contrary.

We must in candour allow, that those women who begin, will have something more to overcome than may probably hereafter be the case. We cannot deny the jealousy which exists among pompous and foolish men respecting the education of women. There is a class of pedants who would be cut short in the estimation of the world a whole cubit if it were generally known that a young lady of eighteen could be taught to decline the tenses of the middle voice or acquaint herself with the Æolic varieties of that celebrated language. Then women have, of course, all ignorant men for enemies to their instruction, who being bound (as they think), in point of sex, to know more, are not well pleased in point of fact to know less. But, among men of sense and liberal politeness, a woman who has successfully cultivated her mind without diminishing the gentleness and propriety of her manners is always sure to meet with a respect and attention bordering upon enthusiasm.

There is in either sex a strong and permanent disposition to appear agreeable to the other: and this is the fair answer to those who are fond of supposing that a higher degree of knowledge would make women rather the rivals than the companions of men. Presupposing such a desire to please, it seems much more probable that a common pursuit should be a fresh source of interest than a cause of contention. Indeed, to suppose that any mode of education can create a general jealousy and rivalry between the sexes is so very ridiculous, that it requires only to be stated in order to be refuted. The same desire of pleasing secures all that delicacy and reserve which are of such inestimable value to women. We are quite astonished, in hearing men converse on such subjects, to find them attributing such beautiful effects to ignorance. It would appear, from the tenor of such objections, that ignorance had been the great civilizer of the world. Women are delicate and refined only because they are ignorant;—they manage their household, only because they are ignorant;—they attend to their children, only because they know no better. Now, we must really confess we have all our lives been so ignorant as not to know the value of ignorance. We have always attributed the modesty and the refined manners of women to their being well taught in moral and religious duty, to the hazardous situation in which they are placed, to that perpetual vigilance which it is their duty to exercise over thought, word, and action, and to that cultivation of the mild virtues which those who cultivate the stern and magnanimous virtues expect at their hands. After all, let it be remembered, we are not saying there are no objections to the diffusion of knowledge among the female sex. We would not hazard such a proposition respecting anything; but we are saying that upon the whole it is the best method of employing time; and that there are fewer objections to it than to any other method. There are, perhaps, 50,000 females in Great Britain who are exempted by circumstances from all necessary labour; but every human being must do something with their existence, and the pursuit of knowledge is, upon the whole, the most innocent, the most dignified, and the most useful method of filling up that idleness of which there is always so large a portion in nations far advanced in civilization. Let any man reflect, too, upon the solitary situation in which women are placed—the ill-treatment to which they are sometimes exposed and which they must endure in silence and without the power of complaining—and he must feel convinced that the happiness of a woman will be materially increased in proportion as education has given to her the habit and the means of drawing her resources from herself.

There are a few common phrases in circulation, respecting the duties of women, to which we wish to pay some degree of attention, because they are rather inimical to those opinions which we have advanced on this subject. Indeed, independently of this, there is nothing which requires more vigilance than the current phrases of the day, of which there are always some resorted to in every dispute, and from the sovereign authority of which it is often vain to make any appeal. 'The true theatre for a woman is the sick chamber'—'Nothing so honourable to a woman as not to be spoken of at all'. These two phrases, the delight of *Noodledom*, are grown into commonplaces upon the subject; and are not unfrequently employed to extinguish that love of knowledge in women which, in our humble opinion, it is of so much importance to cherish. Nothing, certainly, is so ornamental and delightful in women as the benevolent affections; but time cannot be filled up, and life employed, with high and impassioned virtues. Some of these feelings are of rare occurrence —all of short duration—or nature would sink under them. A scene of distress and anguish is an occasion where the finest qualities of the female mind may be displayed; but it is a monstrous exaggeration to tell women that they are born only for scenes of distress and anguish. Nurse father, mother, sister and brother, if they want it;—it would be a violation of the plainest duties to neglect them. But, when we are talking of the common occupations of life, do not let us mistake the accidents for the occupations;—when we are arguing how the twenty-three hours

of the day are to be filled up, it is idle to tell us of those feelings
and agitations above the level of common existence, which may
employ the remaining hour. Compassion, and every other virtue,
are the great objects we all ought to have in view; but no man
(and no woman) can fill up the twenty-four hours by acts of
virtue. But one is a lawyer, and the other a ploughman, and the
third a merchant; and then, acts of goodness, and intervals of
compassion and fine feeling, are scattered up and down the
common occupations of life. We know women are to be compassionate; but they cannot be compassionate from eight o'clock
in the morning till twelve at night—and what are they to do in
the interval? This is the only question we have been putting all
along, and is all that can be meant by literary education.

[1810]

METHODISM

[The title is indiscriminate, and in effect unjust, but far more so now than it was then. Disgusted by the pietistic excesses of religious revivalism, Sydney Smith gives thirty-five flagrant examples from the 'Evangelical and Methodistical magazines for the year 1807 . . . which contain the sentiments of Arminian and Calvinistic methodists and of the *evangelical* clergymen of the Church of England.' He uses the general term Methodism 'to designate these three classes of fanatics, not troubling ourselves to point out the finer shades and nicer discriminations of lunacy, but treating them all as in one general conspiracy against common sense and rational orthodox Christianity'. His extracts, which deserve all the ridicule he invites for them, are mostly concerned with special 'interferences' and 'revelations'. A clergyman drops dead while playing cards. A young man, stung by a bee, utters oaths and imprecations, and is immediately stung again, on the tongue: 'thus can the Lord engage one of the meanest of his creatures in reproving the bold transgressor who dares to take his name in vain'. The wickedness of enjoying music, dancing, and stage-plays is demonstrated, and fear of death and judgment recommended, in a number of edifying anecdotes. Smith has no difficulty in exposing the odious self-complacency of people who call themselves 'the dear friends of the Redeemer'; but the most valuable part of his essay is its final summing-up, which here follows.]

UPON the foregoing facts, and upon the spirit evinced by these extracts, we shall make a few comments.

1. It is obvious that this description of Christians entertain very erroneous and dangerous notions of the present judgments of God. A belief that Providence interferes in all the little actions of our lives refers all merit and demerit to bad and good fortune, and causes the successful man to be always considered as a good man, and the unhappy man as the object of divine vengeance. It furnishes ignorant and designing men with a power which is sure to be abused: the cry of, *a judgment, a*

judgment, it is always easy to make, but not easy to resist. It
encourages the grossest superstitions; for if the Deity rewards
and punishes on every slight occasion, it is quite impossible but
that such a helpless being as man will set himself at work to
discover the will of Heaven in the appearances of outward nature,
and to apply all the phenomena of thunder, lightning, wind,
and every striking appearance to the regulation of his conduct;
as the poor Methodist, when he rode into Piccadilly in a thunder-
storm, and imagined that all the uproar of the elements was a
mere hint to him not to preach at Mr Romaine's chapel. Hence
a great deal of error and a great deal of secret misery. This
doctrine of a theocracy must necessarily place an excessive power
in the hands of the clergy: it applies so instantly and so tremen-
dously to men's hopes and fears, that it must make the priest
omnipotent over the people, as it always has done where it has
been established. It has a great tendency to check human exertions and to prevent the employment of those secondary means
of effecting an object which Providence has placed in our power.
The doctrine of the immediate and perpetual interference of
Divine Providence is not true. If two men travel the same road,
the one to rob, the other to relieve a fellow-creature who is
starving, will any but the most fanatic contend that they do
not both run the same chance of falling over a stone and breaking
their legs? and is it not matter of fact, that the robber often
returns safe and the just man sustains the injury? Have not the
soundest divines of both churches always urged this unequal
distribution of good and evil, in the present state, as one of the
strongest natural arguments for a future state of retribution?
Have not they contended, and well and admirably contended,
that the supposition of such a state is absolutely necessary to
our notion of the justice of God, absolutely necessary to restore
order to that moral confusion which we all observe and deplore
in the present world? The man who places religion upon a false
basis is the greatest enemy to religion. If victory is always to the
just and good, how is the fortune of impious conquerors to be
accounted for? Why do they erect dynasties, and found families
which last for centuries? The reflecting mind whom you have
instructed in this manner, and for present effect only, naturally
comes upon you hereafter with difficulties of this sort; he finds
he has been deceived; and you will soon discover that in breeding

up a fanatic you have unwittingly laid the foundation of an atheist. The honest and the orthodox method is to prepare young people for the world as it actually exists; to tell them that they will often find vice perfectly successful, virtue exposed to a long train of afflictions; that they must bear this patiently, and look to another world for its rectification.

2. The second doctrine which it is necessary to notice among the Methodists, is the doctrine of inward impulse and emotions, which, it is quite plain, must lead, if universally insisted upon and preached among the common people, to every species of folly and enormity. When a human being believes that his internal feelings are the monitions of God, and that these monitions must govern his conduct, and when a great stress is purposely laid upon these inward feelings in all the discourses from the pulpit, it is of course impossible to say to what a pitch of extravagance mankind may not be carried, under the influence of such dangerous doctrines.

3. The Methodists hate pleasure and amusements; no theatre, no cards, no dancing, no punchinello, no dancing dogs, no blind fiddlers;—all the amusements of the rich and of the poor must disappear, wherever these gloomy people get a footing. It is not the abuse of pleasure which they attack, but the interspersion of pleasure, however much it is guided by good sense and moderation. It is not only wicked to hear the licentious plays of Congreve, but wicked to hear Henry the Fifth, or the School for Scandal. It is not only dissipated to run about to all the parties in London and Edinburgh, but dancing is not *fit for a being who is preparing himself for Eternity*. Ennui, wretchedness, melancholy, groans and sighs, are the offerings which these unhappy men make to a Deity who has covered the earth with gay colours and scented it with rich perfumes, and shown us, by the plan and order of his works, that he has given to man something better than a bare existence and scattered over his creation a thousand superfluous joys which are totally unnecessary to the mere support of life.

4. The Methodists lay very little stress upon practical righteousness. They do not say to their people: Do not be deceitful, do not be idle, get rid of your bad passions. Or at least (if they do say these things) they say them very seldom. Not that they preach faith without works; for if they told the people that they might rob and murder with impunity, the civil magistrate must be

compelled to interfere with such doctrine; but they say a great deal about faith and very little about works. What are commonly called the mysterious parts of our religion are brought into the foreground, much more than the doctrines which lead to practice; —and this among the lowest of the community.

The Methodists have hitherto been accused of dissenting from the Church of England. This, as far as relates to mere subscription to articles, is not true; but they differ in their choice of the articles upon which they dilate and expand, and to which they appear to give a preference, from the stress which they place upon them. There is nothing heretical in saying that God *sometimes* intervenes with his special providence; but these people differ from the Established Church in the degree in which they insist upon this doctrine. In the hands of a man of sense and education it is a safe doctrine; in the management of the Methodists, we have seen how ridiculous and degrading it becomes. In the same manner, a clergyman of the Church of England would not do his duty if he did not insist upon the necessity of faith as well as of good works; but, as he believes that it is much more easy to give credit to doctrines than to live well, he labours most in those points where human nature is the *most* liable to prove defective. Because he does so, he is accused of giving up the articles of his faith, by men who have their partialities also in doctrine, but partialities not founded upon the same sound discretion and knowledge of human nature.

5. The Methodists are always desirous of making men more religious than it is possible, from the constitution of human nature, to make them. If they could succeed as much as they wish to succeed, there would be at once an end of delving and spinning, and of every exertion of human industry. Men must eat, and drink, and work; and if you wish to fix upon them high and elevated notions, as the *ordinary* furniture of their minds, you do these two things;—you drive men of warm temperaments mad, and you introduce, in the rest of the world, a low and shocking familiarity with words and images which every real friend to religion would wish to keep sacred. *The friends of the dear Redeemer who are in the habit of visiting the Isle of Thanet*—(as in the extract we have quoted)—Is it possible that this mixture of the most awful with the most familiar images, so common among Methodists now and with the enthusiasts in the time of

Cromwell, must not, in the end, divest religion of all the deep
and solemn impressions which it is calculated to produce? In
a man of common imagination (as we have before observed) the
terror and the feeling which it first excited must necessarily be
soon separated, but where the fervour of impression is long
preserved piety ends in Bedlam. Accordingly there is not a mad-
house in England where a considerable part of the patients have
not been driven to insanity by the extravagance of these people.
We cannot enter such places without seeing a number of honest
artisans, covered with blankets, and calling themselves angels
and apostles, who, if they had remained contented with the
instruction of men of learning and education, would still have
been sound masters of their own trade, sober Christians, and
useful members of society.

6. It is impossible not to observe how directly all the doctrine
of the Methodists is calculated to gain power among the poor
and ignorant. To say that the Deity governs this world by general
rules and that we must wait for another and a final scene of
existence before vice meets with its merited punishment and
virtue with its merited reward, to preach this up daily, would
not add a single votary to the Tabernacle nor sell a Number of
the Methodistical Magazine; but to publish an account of a man
who was cured of scrofula by a single sermon, of Providence
destroying the innkeeper at Garstang for appointing a cock-fight
near the Tabernacle, this promptness of judgment and immediate
execution is so much like human justice, and so much better
adapted to vulgar capacities, that the system is at once admitted
as soon as any one can be found who is impudent or ignorant
enough to teach it; and, being once admitted, it produces too
strong an effect upon the passions to be easily relinquished. The
case is the same with the doctrine of inward impulse, or, as they
term it, experience. If you preach up to ploughmen and artisans
that every singular feeling which comes across them is a visitation
of the Divine Spirit, can there be any difficulty, *under* the influence
of this nonsense, in converting these simple creatures into active
and mysterious fools, and making them your slaves for life? It
is not possible to raise up any dangerous enthusiasm by telling
men to be just, and good, and charitable; but keep this part of
Christianity out of sight, and talk long and enthusiastically, before
ignorant people, of the mysteries of our religion, and you will

not fail to attract a crowd of followers: verily the Tabernacle loveth not that which is simple, intelligible, and leadeth to good sound practice.

Having endeavoured to point out the spirit which pervades these people, we shall say a few words upon the causes, the effects, and the cure of this calamity. The fanaticism so prevalent in the present day is one of those evils from which society is never wholly exempt, but which bursts out at different periods, with peculiar violence, and sometimes overwhelms everything in its course. The last eruption took place about a century and a half ago and destroyed both Church and Throne with its tremendous force. Though irresistible, it was short; enthusiasm spent its force; the usual reaction took place; and England was deluged with ribaldry and indecency because it had been worried with fanatical restrictions. By degrees, however, it was found out that orthodoxy and loyalty might be secured by other methods than licentious conduct and immodest conversation. The public morals improved; and there appeared as much good sense and moderation upon the subject of religion as ever can be expected from mankind in large masses. Still, however, the mischief which the Puritans had done was not forgotten; a general suspicion prevailed of the dangers of religious enthusiasm; and the fanatical preacher wanted his accustomed power among a people recently recovered from a religious war, and guarded by songs, proverbs, popular stories, and the general tide of humour and opinion, against all excesses of that nature. About the middle of the last century, however, the character of the genuine fanatic was a good deal forgotten, and the memory of the civil wars worn away; the field was clear for extravagance in piety; and causes which must always produce an immense influence upon the mind of man were left to their own unimpeded operations. Religion is so noble and powerful a consideration—it is so buoyant and so insubmergible—that it may be made, by fanatics, to carry with it any degree of error and of perilous absurdity. In this instance Messrs Whitfield and Wesley happened to begin. They were men of considerable talents; they observed the common decorums of life; they did not run naked into the streets, or pretend to the prophetical character; and therefore they were not committed to Newgate. They preached with great energy to weak people; who first stared, then listened, then believed, then felt the inward feeling of grace, and became as foolish as their teachers could possibly wish them to be. In short, folly ran its ancient course, and human nature evinced itself to be what it always has been under similar circumstances. The great and permanent cause, therefore, of the increase of Methodism, is the cause which has given birth to fanaticism in all ages,—*the facility of mingling human errors with the fundamental truths of religion.* The formerly imperfect residence of the clergy may, perhaps, in some trifling degree, have aided this source of Methodism. But unless a man of education, and a gentleman, could stoop to such disingenuous arts as the Methodist preachers,—unless he hears heavenly music all of a sudden, and enjoys *sweet experiences,*—it is quite impossible that he can contend against such artists as these. More active than they are at present the clergy might perhaps be; but the calmness and moderation of an Establishment can never possibly be a match for sectarian activity. If the common people are *ennui'd* with the fine acting of Mrs Siddons, they go to Sadler's Wells. The subject is too serious for ludicrous comparisons: but the Tabernacle really is to the Church, what Sadler's Wells is to the Drama. There, popularity is gained by vaulting and tumbling; by low arts which the regular clergy are not too idle to have recourse to, but too dignified;—their institutions are chaste and severe,—they endeavour to do that which, *upon the whole, and for a great number of years,* will be found to be the most admirable and the most useful: it is no part of their plan to descend to small artifices for the sake of present popularity and effect. The religion of the common people under the government of the Church may remain as it is for ever;—enthusiasm must be progressive, or it will expire.

It is probable that the dreadful scenes which have lately been acted in the world, and the dangers to which we are exposed, have increased the numbers of the Methodists. To what degree will Methodism extend in this country? This question is not easy to answer. That it has rapidly increased within these few years we have no manner of doubt, and we confess we cannot see what is likely to impede its progress. The party which it has formed in the Legislature and the artful neutrality with which they give respectability to their small number, the talents of some of this party and the unimpeached excellence of their characters, all make it probable that fanaticism will increase rather than diminish. The Methodists have made an alarming inroad into the Church, and they are attacking the Army and Navy. The principality of Wales, and the East-India Company, they have already acquired. All mines and subterraneous places belong to them; they creep into hospitals and small schools, and so work their way upwards. It is the custom of the religious neutrals to beg all the little livings, particularly in the north of England, from the minister for the time being; and from these fixed points they make incursions upon the happiness and common sense of the vicinage. We most sincerely deprecate such an event; but it will excite in us no manner of surprise if a period arrives when the churches of the sober and orthodox part of the English clergy are completely deserted by the middling and lower classes of the community. We do not prophesy any such event, but we contend that it is not impossible—hardly improbable. If such, in future, should be the situation of this country, it is impossible to say what political animosities may not be ingrafted upon this marked and dangerous division of mankind into the *godly* and the *ungodly*. At all events, we are quite sure that happiness will be destroyed, reason degraded, sound religion banished from the world; and that when fanaticism becomes too foolish and too prurient to be endured (as is at last sure to be the case), it will be succeeded by a long period of the grossest immorality, atheism, and debauchery.

We are not sure that this evil admits of any cure, or of any considerable palliation. We most sincerely hope that the government of this country will never be guilty of such indiscretion as to tamper with the Toleration Act, or to attempt to put down these follies by the intervention of the law. If experience has taught us anything, it is the absurdity of controlling men's notions of eternity by acts of Parliament. Something may perhaps be done, in the way of ridicule, towards turning the popular opinion. It may be as well to extend the privileges of the dissenters to the members of the Church of England; for, as the law now stands, any man who dissents from the established church may open a place of worship where he pleases. No orthodox clergyman can do so without the consent of the parson of the parish, who always refuses because he does not choose to have his monopoly disturbed, and refuses in parishes where there are not accommodations for one half of the persons who wish to frequent the

Church of England, and in instances where he knows that the chapels from which he excludes the established worship will be immediately occupied by sectaries. It may be as well to encourage in the early education of the clergy . . . a better and more animated method of preaching; and it may be necessary, hereafter, if the evil gets to a great height, to relax the articles of the English church, and to admit a greater variety of Christians within the pale. The greatest and best of all remedies is perhaps the education of the poor;—we are astonished that the Established Church in England is not awake to this means of arresting the progress of Methodism. Of course, none of these things will be done; nor is it *clear*, if they were done, that they would do *much* good. Whatever happens, we are for common sense and orthodoxy. Insolence, servile politics, and the spirit of persecution, we condemn and attack, whenever we observe them;—but to the learning, the moderation, and the rational piety of the Establishment, we most earnestly wish a decided victory over the nonsense, the melancholy, and the madness, of the tabernacle.

God send that our wishes be not in vain.

[1808]

PERSECUTING BISHOPS

IT is a great point in any question to clear away encumbrances and to make a naked circle about the object in dispute, so that there may be a clear view of it on every side. In pursuance of this disencumbering process we shall first acquit the Bishop* of all wrong intentions. He has a very bad opinion of the practical effects of high Calvinistic doctrines upon the common people, and he thinks it his duty to exclude those clergymen who profess them from his diocese. There is no moral wrong in this. He has accordingly devised no fewer than *eighty-seven* interrogatories, by which he thinks he can detect the smallest taint of Calvinism that may lurk in the creed of the candidate; and in this also, whatever we may think of his reasoning, we suppose his purpose to be blameless. He believes, finally, that he has legally the power so to interrogate and exclude; and in this perhaps he is not mistaken. His intentions, then, are good, and his conduct, perhaps, not amenable to the law. All this we admit in his favour: but against him we must maintain that his conduct upon the points in dispute has been singularly injudicious, extremely harsh, and, in its effects (though not in its intentions), very oppressive and vexatious to the Clergy.

We have no sort of intention to avail ourselves of an anonymous publication to say unkind, uncivil, or disrespectful things to a man of rank, learning, and character—we hope to be guilty of no such impropriety; but we cannot believe we are doing wrong in ranging ourselves on the weaker side, in the cause of propriety and justice. The Mitre protects its wearer from indignity; but it does not secure impunity.

It is a strong presumption that a man is wrong, when all his friends, whose habits naturally lead them to coincide with him, think him wrong. If a man were to indulge in taking medicine till the apothecary, the druggist, and the physician, all called upon him to abandon his philocathartic propensities—if he were

[* Herbert Marsh, Bishop of Peterborough.]

to gratify his convivial habits till the landlord demurred and the waiter shook his head—we should naturally imagine that advice so wholly disinterested was not given before it was wanted, and that it merited some little attention and respect. Now, though the Bench of Bishops certainly love power, and love the Church, as well as the Bishop of Peterborough, yet not one defended him —not one rose to say, 'I have done, or I would do, the same thing'. It was impossible to be present at the last debate on this question without perceiving that his Lordship stood alone—and this in a very gregarious profession that habitually combines and butts against an opponent with a very extended front. If a lawyer is wounded, the rest of the profession pursue him, and put him to death. If a churchman is hurt, the others gather round for his protection, stamp with their feet, push with their horns, and demolish the dissenter who did the mischief.

The Bishop has at least done a very unusual thing in his Eighty-seven Questions. The two Archbishops, and we believe every other Bishop, and all the Irish hierarchy, admit curates into their dioceses without any such precautions. The necessity of such severe and scrupulous inquisition, in short, has been apparent to nobody but the Bishop of Peterborough; and the authorities by which he seeks to justify it are anything but satisfactory. His Lordship states that forty years ago he was himself examined by written interrogatories, and that he is not the only Bishop who has done it; but he mentions no names; and it was hardly worth while to state such extremely slight precedents for so strong a deviation from the common practice of the Church.

The Bishop who rejects a curate upon the Eighty-seven Questions is necessarily and inevitably opposed to the Bishop who ordained him. The Bishop of Gloucester ordains a young man of twenty-three years of age, not thinking it necessary to put to him these interrogatories, or putting them, perhaps, and approving answers diametrically opposite to those that are required by the Bishop of Peterborough. The young clergyman then comes to the last-mentioned Bishop; and the Bishop, after *putting him to the Question*, says, 'You are unfit for a clergyman',—though, ten days before, the Bishop of Gloucester has made him one! It is bad enough for ladies to pull caps, but still worse for Bishops to pull mitres. Nothing can be more mischievous or indecent than such scenes; and no man of common prudence or know-

ledge of the world but must see that they ought immediately
to be put a stop to. If a man is a captain in the army in one part
of England, he is a captain in all. The general who commands
north of the Tweed does not say, You shall never appear in my
district, or exercise the functions of an officer, if you do not
answer eighty-seven questions on the art of war, according to
my notions. The same officer who commands a ship of the line
in the Mediterranean, is considered as equal to the same office
in the North Seas. The sixth commandment is suspended, by
one medical diploma, from the north of England to the south.
But by this new system of interrogation a man may be admitted
into orders at Barnet, rejected at Stevenage, readmitted at
Brogden, kicked out as a Calvinist at Witham Common, and
hailed as an ardent Arminian on his arrival at York.

It matters nothing to say that sacred things must not be compared with profane. In their importance, we allow, they cannot;
but in their order and discipline they may be so far compared
as to say, that the discrepancy and contention which would be
disgraceful and pernicious in worldly affairs should, in common
prudence, be avoided in the affairs of religion. Mr Greenough
has made a map of England according to its geological varieties
—blue for the chalk, green for the clay, red for the sand, and
so forth. Under this system of Bishop Marsh, we must petition
for the assistance of the geologist in the fabrication of an ecclesiastical map. All the Arminian districts must be purple. Green
for one theological extremity—sky-blue for another—as many
colours as there are Bishops—as many shades of these colours
as there are Archdeacons—a tailor's pattern card—the picture
of vanity, fashion, and caprice!

The Bishop seems surprised at the resistance he meets with;
and yet, to what purpose has he read ecclesiastical history if he
expects to meet with anything but the most determined opposition? Does he think that every sturdy supralapsarian bullock
whom he tries to sacrifice to the Genius of Orthodoxy will not
kick, and push, and toss; that he will not, if he *can*, shake the
axe from his neck, and hurl his mitred butcher into the air?
His Lordship has undertaken a task of which he little knows the
labour or the end. We know these men fully as well as the
Bishop; he has not a chance of success against them. If one
motion in Parliament will not do, they will have twenty. They

will ravage, roar, and rush, till the very chaplains, and the Masters and Misses Peterborough, request his Lordship to desist. He is raising up a storm in the English Church of which he has not the slightest conception, and which will end, as it ought to end, in his Lordship's disgrace and defeat.

The longer we live the more we are convinced of the justice of the old saying, that an *ounce of mother wit is worth a pound of clergy*; that discretion, gentle manners, common sense, and good nature, are, in men of high ecclesiastical station, of far greater importance than the greatest skill in discriminating between sublapsarian and supralapsarian doctrines. Bishop Marsh should remember that all men wearing the mitre work by character as well as doctrine; that a tender regard to men's rights and feelings, a desire to avoid sacred squabbles, a fondness for quiet, and an ardent wish to make everybody happy, would be of far more value to the Church of England than all his learning and vigilance of inquisition. The Irish Tithes will probably fall next session of Parliament; the common people are regularly receding from the Church of England—baptizing, burying, and confirming for themselves. Under such circumstances, what would the worst enemy of the English Church require?—a bitter, bustling, theological Bishop, accused by his clergy of tyranny and oppression—the cause of daily petitions and daily debates in the House of Commons—the idoneous vehicle of abuse against the Establishment—a stalking-horse to bad men for the introduction of revolutionary opinions, mischievous ridicule, and irreligious feelings. Such will be the advantages which Bishop Marsh will secure for the English Establishment in the ensuing session. It is inconceivable how such a prelate shakes all the upper works of the Church and ripens it for dissolution and decay. Six such Bishops, multiplied by eighty-seven, and working with five hundred and twenty-two questions, would fetch everything to the ground in less than six months. But what if it pleased Divine Providence to afflict every prelate with the spirit of putting eighty-seven queries, and the two Archbishops with the spirit of putting twice as many, and the Bishop of Sodor and Man with the spirit of putting only forty-three queries? There would then be a grand total of two thousand three hundred and thirty-five interrogations flying about the English Church; and sorely vexed would the land be with Question and Answer.

We will suppose this learned Prelate, without meanness or undue regard to his worldly interests, to feel that fair desire of rising in his profession which any man in any profession may feel without disgrace. Does he forget that his character in the ministerial circles will soon become that of a violent impracticable man, whom it is impossible to place in the highest situations, who has been trusted with too much already and must be trusted with no more? Ministers have something else to do with their time, and with the time of Parliament, than to waste them in debating squabbles between Bishops and their clergy. They naturally wish, and on the whole reasonably expect, that everything should go on silently and quietly in the Church. They have no objection to a learned Bishop; but they deprecate one atom more of learning than is compatible with moderation, good sense, and the soundest discretion. It must be the grossest ignorance of the world to suppose that the Cabinet has any pleasure in watching Calvinists.

The Bishop not only puts the questions, but he actually assigns the limits within which they are to be answered. Spaces are left in the paper of interrogations, to which limits the answer is to be confined;—two inches to original sin; an inch and a half to justification; three-quarters to predestination; and to free-will only a quarter of an inch. But if his Lordship gives them an inch they will take an ell. His Lordship is himself a theological writer, and by no means remarkable for his conciseness. To deny space to his brother theologians, who are writing on the most difficult subjects, not from choice but necessity, not for fame but for bread, and to award rejection as the penalty of prolixity, does appear to us no slight deviation from Christian gentleness.

§

We are aware that the Bishop of Peterborough, in his speech, disclaims the object of excluding the Calvinists by this system of interrogation. We shall take no other notice of his disavowal than expressing our sincere regret that he ever made it; but the question is not at all altered by the intention of the interrogator. Whether he aims at the Calvinists only, or includes them with other heterodox respondents, the fact is, they *are* included in the proscription and excluded from the Church, the practical effect of the practice being that men are driven out of the Church who have as much right to exercise the duties of clergymen as the Bishop himself. If heterodox opinions are the great objects of the Bishop's apprehensions, he has his Ecclesiastical Courts, where regular process may bring the offender to punishment, and from whence there is an appeal to higher courts. This would be the fair thing to do. The Curate and the Bishop would be brought into the light of day and subjected to the wholesome restraint of public opinion.

His Lordship boasts that he has excluded only two curates. So the Emperor of Hayti boasted that he had only cut off two persons' heads for disagreeable behaviour at his table. In spite of the paucity of the visitors executed, the example operated as a considerable impediment to conversation; and the intensity of the punishment was found to be a full compensation for its rarity. How many persons have been deprived of curacies which they might have enjoyed but for the tenour of these interrogatories? How many respectable clergymen have been deprived of the assistance of curates connected with them by blood, friendship, or doctrine, and compelled to choose persons for no other qualification than that they could pass through the eye of the Bishop's needle? Violent measures are not to be judged of merely by the number of times they have been resorted to, but by the terror, misery, and restraint which the severity is likely to have produced.

We never met with any style so entirely clear of all redundant and vicious ornament as that which the ecclesiastical Lord of Peterborough has adopted towards his clergy. It, in fact, may be reduced to these few words—'Reverend Sir, I shall do what I please. Peterborough'. Even in the House of Lords he speaks what we must call very plain language. Among other things, he says that the allegations of the petitions are *false*. Now as every Bishop is, besides his other qualities, a gentleman, and as the word *false* is used only by laymen who mean to hazard their lives by the expression, and as it cannot be supposed that foul language is ever used because it can be used with personal impunity, his Lordship must therefore be intended to mean not *false*, but *mistaken*—not a wilful deviation from truth, but an accidental and unintended departure from it.

His Lordship talks of the drudgery of wading through ten

pages of answers to his eighty-seven questions. Who has occasioned this drudgery but the person who means to be so much more active, useful, and important, than all other Bishops, by proposing questions which nobody has thought to be necessary but himself? But to be intolerably strict and harsh to a poor curate who is trying to earn a morsel of hard bread, and then to complain of the drudgery of reading his answers, is much like knocking a man down with a bludgeon and then abusing him for splashing you with his blood and pestering you with his groans. It is quite monstrous that a man who inflicts eighty-seven new questions in Theology upon his fellow-creatures should talk of the drudgery of reading their answers. . . .

[1822]

SPRING GUNS AND MAN-TRAPS

WHEN Lord Dacre (then Mr Brand) brought into the House of Commons his bill for the amendment of the Game Laws, a system of greater mercy and humanity was in vain recommended to that popular branch of the Legislature. The interests of humanity, and the interests of the lord of the manor, were not, however, opposed to each other; nor any attempt made to deny the superior importance of the last. No such bold or alarming topics were agitated; but it was contended that if laws were less ferocious there would be more partridges; if the lower orders of mankind were not torn from their families and banished to Botany Bay, hares and pheasants would be increased in number, or, at least, not diminished. It is not however till after long experience that mankind ever think of recurring to humane experiments for effecting their objects. The rulers who ride the people never think of coaxing and patting till they have worn out the lashes of their whips and broken the rowels of their spurs. The legislators of the trigger replied, that two laws had lately passed which would answer their purpose of preserving game: the one an act for transporting men found with arms in their hands for the purposes of killing game in the night, the other an act for rendering the buyers of the game equally guilty with the seller and for involving both in the same penalty. Three seasons have elapsed since the last of these laws was passed; and we appeal to the experience of all the great towns in England whether the difficulty of procuring game is in the slightest degree increased?—whether hares, partridges, and pheasants are not purchased with as much facility as before the passing of this act?—whether the price of such unlawful commodities is even in the slightest degree increased? Let the Assize and Sessions' Calendars bear witness whether the law for transporting poachers has not had the most direct tendency to encourage brutal assaults and ferocious murders. There is hardly now a jail-delivery in which some gamekeeper has not murdered

a poacher, or some poacher a gamekeeper. If the question concerned the payment of five pounds, a poacher would hardly risk
his life rather than be taken; but when he is to go to Botany
Bay for seven years, he summons together his brother poachers—
they get brave from rum, numbers, and despair—and a bloody
battle ensues.

Another method by which it is attempted to defeat the depre-
dations of the poacher is by setting spring guns to murder any
person who comes within their reach; and it is to this last new
feature in the *supposed* Game Laws, to which, on the present
occasion, we intend principally to confine our notice.

We utterly disclaim all hostility to the Game Laws in general.
Game ought to belong to those who feed it. All the landowners
in England are fairly entitled to all the game in England. These
laws are constructed upon a basis of substantial justice; but there
is a great deal of absurdity and tyranny mingled with them, and
a perpetual and vehement desire on the part of the country
gentlemen to push the provisions of these laws up to the highest
point of tyrannical severity.

'Is it lawful to put to death by a spring gun, or any other
machine, an unqualified person trespassing upon your woods or
fields in pursuit of game, and who has received due notice of
your intention, and of the risk to which he is exposed?' This,
we think, is stating the question as fairly as can be stated. We
purposely exclude gardens, orchards, and all contiguity to the
dwelling-house. We exclude, also, all felonious intention on the
part of the deceased. The object of his expedition shall be proved
to be game, and the notice he received of his danger shall be
allowed to be as complete as possible. It must also be part of
the case, that the spring gun was placed there for the express
purpose of defending the game, by killing or wounding the
poacher, or spreading terror, or doing anything that a reasonable
man ought to know would happen from such a proceeding.

Suppose any gentleman were to give notice that all other
persons must abstain from his manors; that he himself and his
servants paraded the woods and fields with loaded pistols and
blunderbuses and would shoot anybody who fired at a partridge;
and suppose he were to keep his word, and shoot through the
head some rash trespasser who defied this bravado and was
determined to have his sport:—is there any doubt that he would

be guilty of murder? We suppose no resistance on the part of the trespasser, but that, the moment he passes the line of demarcation with his dogs and gun, he is shot dead by the proprietor of the land from behind a tree. If this is not murder, what is murder? We will make the case a little better for the homicide squire. It shall be night; the poacher, an unqualified person, steps over the line of demarcation with his nets and snares, and is instantly shot through the head by the pistol of the proprietor. We have no doubt that this would be murder—that it ought to be considered as murder and punished as murder. We think this so clear that it would be a waste of time to argue it. There is no kind of resistance on the part of the deceased; no attempt to run away; he is not even challenged: but instantly shot dead by the proprietor of the wood, for no other crime than *the intention* of killing game unlawfully. We do not suppose that any man possessed of the elements of law and common sense would deny this to be a case of murder, let the previous notice to the deceased have been as perfect as it could be. It is true, a trespasser in a park may be killed; but then it is when he will not render himself to the keepers, upon a hue and cry to stand to the king's peace. But deer are property, game is not; and this power of slaying deer-stealers is by the 21st Edward I, *de Malefactoribus in Parcis*, and by 3rd and 4th William and Mary, c. 10. So rioters may be killed, house-burners, ravishers, felons refusing to be arrested, felons escaping, felons breaking gaol, men resisting a civil process—may all be put to death. All these cases of justifiable homicide are laid down and admitted in our books. But who ever heard that to pistol a poacher was justifiable homicide? It has long been decided that it is unlawful to kill a dog who is pursuing game in a manor. 'To decide the contrary,' says Lord Ellenborough, 'would outrage reason and sense.' (Vere *v.* Lord Cawdor and King, 11 *East*, 386.) Pointers have always been treated by the legislature with great delicacy and consideration. To '*wish to be a dog and to bay the moon*' is not quite so mad a wish as the poet thought it.

If these things are so, what is the difference between the act of firing yourself, and placing an engine which does the same thing? In the one case, your hand pulls the trigger; in the other, it places the wire which communicates with the trigger and causes the death of the trespasser. There is the same intention of slaying in both cases; there is precisely the same human agency in both cases; only the steps are rather more numerous in the latter case. As to the bad effects of allowing proprietors of game to put trespassers to death at once, or to set guns that will do it, we can have no hesitation in saying that the first method, of giving the power of life and death to esquires, would be by far the most humane. For . . . a live armigeral spring gun would distinguish an accidental trespasser from a real poacher—a woman or a boy from a man—perhaps might spare a friend or an acquaintance—or a father of a family with ten children— or a small freeholder who voted for Administration. But this new rural artillery must destroy, without mercy and selection, every one who approaches it.

In the case of Ilot *versus* Wilks Esq, the four judges, Abbot, Bailey, Holroyd, and Best, gave their opinions *seriatim* on points connected with this question. In this case, as reported in Chetwynd's edition of Burn's Justice, 1820, vol. ii. p. 500, Abbot C. J. observes as follows: 'I cannot say that repeated and increasing acts of aggression may not reasonably call for increased means of defence and protection. I believe that many of the persons who cause engines of this description to be placed in their grounds, do not do so with an intention to injure any person, but really believe that the publication of notices will prevent any person from sustaining an injury; and that no person having the notice given him will be weak and foolish enough to expose himself to the perilous consequences of his trespass. Many persons who place such engines in their grounds, do so for the purpose of preventing, by means of terror, injury to their property, rather than from any motive of doing malicious injury.'

'Increased means of defence and protection,' but increased (his Lordship should remember) from the payment of five pounds to instant death—and instant death inflicted, not by the arm of the law but by the arm of the proprietor;—could the Lord Chief Justice of the King's Bench intend to say, that the impossibility of putting an end to poaching by other means would justify the infliction of death upon the offender? Is he so ignorant of the philosophy of punishing as to imagine he has nothing to do but to give ten stripes instead of two, a hundred instead of ten, and a thousand if a hundred will not do? to substitute the prison for pecuniary fines and the gallows instead of the gaol? It is impossible so enlightened a Judge can forget that the sympathies of mankind must be consulted, that it would be wrong to break a person upon the wheel for stealing a penny loaf, and that gradations in punishments must be carefully accommodated to gradations in crime; that if poaching is punished more than mankind in general think it ought to be punished, the fault will either escape with impunity, or the delinquent be driven to desperation; that if poaching and murder are punished equally, every poacher will be an assassin. Besides, too, if the principle is right in the unlimited and unqualified manner in which the Chief Justice puts it—if defence goes on increasing with aggression, the Legislature at least must determine upon their equal pace. If an act of Parliament made it a capital offence to poach upon a manor, as it is to commit a burglary in a dwelling-house, it might then be as lawful to shoot a person for trespassing upon your manor as it is to kill a thief for breaking into your house. But the real question is—and so in sound reasoning his Lordship should have put it—'If the law at this moment determines the aggression to be in such a state that it merits only a pecuniary fine after summons and proof, has any sporadic squire the right to say that it shall be punished with death, before any summons and without any proof?'

It appears to us, too, very singular, to say, that many persons who cause engines of this description to be placed in their ground do not do so with an intention of injuring any person, but really believe that the publication of notices will prevent any person from sustaining an injury, and that no person, having the notice given him, will be weak and foolish enough to expose himself to the perilous consequences of his trespass. But if this is the real belief of the engineer, if he thinks the mere notice will keep people away, then he must think it a mere inutility that the guns should be placed at all: if he thinks that many will be deterred, and a few come, then he must mean to shoot those few. He who believes his gun will never be called upon to do its duty need set no gun, and trust to rumour of their being set, or being loaded, for his protection. Against the gun and the powder we have no complaint; they are perfectly fair and admissible: our quarrel is with the bullets. He who sets a *loaded* gun means it should go off when it is touched. But what signifies the mere empty wish that there may be no mischief, when I perform an action which my common sense tells me may produce the worst mischief? If I hear a great noise in the street, and fire a bullet to keep people quiet, I may not perhaps have intended to kill; I may have wished to have produced quiet by mere terror, and I may have expressed a strong hope that my object has been effected without the destruction of human life. Still I have done that which every man of sound intellect knows is likely to kill; and if any one falls from my act, I am guilty of murder. 'Further' (says Lord Coke), 'if there be an evil intent, though that intent extendeth not to death, it is murder. Thus, if a man, knowing that many people are in the street, throw a stone over the wall, intending only to frighten them, or to give them a little hurt, and thereupon one is killed—this is murder— for he had an ill intent; though that intent extended not to death, and though he knew not the party slain.' (3 *Inst*. 57.) If a man is not mad, he must be presumed to foresee common consequences if he puts a bullet into a spring gun—he must be supposed to foresee that it will kill any poacher who touches the wire—and to that consequence he must stand. We do not suppose all preservers of game to be so bloodily inclined that they would prefer the death of a poacher to his staying away. Their object is to preserve game; they have no objection to preserve the lives of their fellow-creatures also, if both can exist at the same time; if not, the least worthy of God's creatures must fall— the rustic without a soul,—not the Christian partridge—not the immortal pheasant—not the rational woodcock, or the accountable hare.

The Chief Justice quotes the instance of glass and spikes fixed upon walls. He cannot mean to infer from this, because the law connives at the infliction of such small punishments for the protection of property, that it does allow, or ought to allow, proprietors to proceed to the punishment of death. Small means of annoying trespassers may be consistently admitted by the law, though more severe ones are forbidden and ought to be forbidden, unless it follows that what is good in any degree is good in the highest degree. You may correct a servant boy with a switch, but if you bruise him sorely you are liable to be indicted, if you kill him you are hanged. A blacksmith corrected his servant with a bar of iron: the boy died, and the blacksmith was executed. (Grey's Case, *Kel*. 64, 65.) A woman kicked and stamped on the belly of her child—she was found guilty of murder. (1 *East*, P.C. 261.) *Si immoderate suo jure utatur, tunc reus homicidii sit.* There is, besides, this additional difference in the two cases put by the Chief Justice, that no publication of notices can be so plain, in the case of the guns, as the sight of the glass or the spikes; for a trespasser may not believe in the notice which he receives, or he may think he shall see the gun and so avoid it, or that he may have the good luck to avoid it if he does not see it; whereas, of the presence of the glass or the spikes he can have no doubt, and he has no hope of placing his hand in any spot where they are not. In the one case he cuts his fingers upon full and perfect notice, the notice of his own senses; in the other case, he loses his life after a notice which he may disbelieve, and by an engine which he may hope to escape.

Mr Justice Bailey observes, in the same case, that it is not an indictable offence to set spring guns. Perhaps not; it is not an indictable offence to go about with a loaded pistol, intending to shoot anybody who grins at you; but if you do it you are hanged. Many inchoate acts are innocent, the consummation of which is a capital offence.

This is not a case where the motto applies of *Volenti non fit injuria.* The man does not will to be hurt, but he wills to get the game, and with that rash confidence natural to many characters believes he shall avoid the evil and gain the good. On the contrary, it is a case which exactly arranges itself under the maxim, *Quando aliquid prohibetur ex directo, prohibetur et per obliquum.* Give what notice he may, the proprietor cannot lawfully shoot a trespasser (who neither runs nor resists) with a loaded pistol. He cannot do it *ex directo*; how then can he do it *per obliquum*, by arranging on the ground the pistol which commits the murder?

Mr Justice Best delivers the following opinion. His Lordship concluded as follows: 'This case has been discussed at the bar, as if these engines were exclusively resorted to for the protection of game; but I consider them as lawfully applicable to the protection of every species of property against unlawful trespassers. But if even they might not lawfully be used for the protection of game, I, for one, should be extremely glad to adopt such means, if they were found sufficient for that purpose; because I think it a great object that gentlemen should have a temptation to reside in the country, amongst their neighbours and tenantry, whose interests must be materially advanced by such a circumstance. The links of society are thereby better preserved, and the mutual advantage and dependence of the higher and lower classes of society, existing between each other, more beneficially maintained. We have seen, in a neighbouring country, the baneful consequences of the non-residence of the landed gentry; and in an ingenious work, lately published by a foreigner, we learn the fatal effects of a like system on the Continent. By preserving game, gentlemen are tempted to reside in the country; and, considering that the diversion of the field is the only one of which they can partake on their estates, I am of opinion that, for the purpose I have stated, it is of essential importance that this species of property should be inviolably protected.'

If this speech of Mr Justice Best is correctly reported, it follows that a man may put his fellow-creatures to death for any infringement of his property—for picking the sloes and blackberries off his hedges—for breaking a few dead sticks out of them by night or by day, with resistance or without resistance, with warning or without warning;—a strange method this of keeping up the links of society and maintaining the dependence of the lower upon the higher classes. It certainly is of importance that gentlemen should reside on their estates in the country, but not that gentlemen with such opinions as these should reside. The more they are absent from the country the less strain will there be upon those links to which the learned Judge alludes, the more firm that dependence upon which he places so just a value. In the case of Dean *versus* Clayton, Bart., the Court of Common Pleas were equally divided upon the lawfulness of killing a dog coursing a hare by means of a concealed dog-spear. We confess that we cannot see the least difference between transfixing with a spear, or placing a spear so that it will transfix; and therefore if Vere *versus* Lord Cawdor and King is good law the action could have been maintained in Dean *versus* Clayton; but the solemn consideration concerning the life of the pointer is highly creditable to all the judges. They none of them say that it is lawful to put a trespassing pointer to death under any circumstances, or that they themselves would be glad to do it; they all seem duly impressed with the recollection that they are deciding the fate of an animal faithfully ministerial to the pleasures of the upper classes of society: there is an awful desire to do their duty, and a dread of any rash and intemperate decision. Seriously speaking, we can hardly believe this report of Mr Justice Best's speech to be correct; yet we take it from a book which guides the practice of nine tenths of all the magistrates of England. Does a Judge—a cool, calm man, in whose hands are the issues of life and death, from whom so many miserable trembling human beings await their destiny—does he tell us, and tell us in a court of justice, that he places such little value on the life of man that he himself would plot the destruction of his fellow-creatures for the preservation of a few hares and partridges? 'Nothing which falls from me' (says Mr Justice Bailey) 'shall have a tendency to encourage the practice.'—'I consider them' (says Mr Justice Best) 'as lawfully applicable to the protection of every species of property; but even if they might not lawfully be used for the protection of game, *I for one should be extremely glad to adopt them*,* if they were found sufficient for that purpose.' Can any man doubt to which of these two magistrates he would rather entrust a decision on his life, his liberty, and his possessions? We should be very sorry to misrepresent Mr Justice Best, and will give to his disavowal of such sentiments, if he does disavow them, all the publicity in our power; but we have cited his very words conscientiously and correctly, as they are given in the Law Report. We have no doubt he meant to do his duty; we blame not his motives, but his feelings and his reasoning.

Let it be observed that, in the whole of this case, we have put every circumstance in favour of the murderer. We have supposed it to be in the night-time; but a man may be shot in the day by a spring gun.† We have supposed the deceased to be a poacher; but he may be a very innocent man, who has missed his way—

---

* [The judge himself, in a speech from the bench, indignantly denied having said: 'even if they might not lawfully be used . . . I should be extremely glad to adopt them.' His main position, however, had not been misrepresented in Chetwynd's inaccurate report. He did defend the setting of spring guns, only insisting that 'the fullest notice possible should be given'. Sydney Smith's answer to that point, elaborated in a later article, is to the effect that giving notice of an intention to murder does not make it any the less murder. 'If a man were to blow a trumpet all over the country, and say that he would shoot any man who asked him how he did, would he acquire a right to do so by such notice?']

† Large damages have been given for wounds inflicted by spring guns set in a garden in the day time, where the party wounded had no notice.

an unfortunate botanist, or a lover. We have supposed notice; but it is a very possible event that the dead man may have been utterly ignorant of the notice. This instrument, so highly approved of by Mr Justice Best—this knitter together of the different orders of society—is levelled promiscuously against the guilty or the innocent, the ignorant and the informed. No man who sets such an infernal machine believes that it can reason or discriminate; it is made to murder all alike, and it does murder all alike.

Blackstone says that the law of England, like that of every other well-regulated community, is tender of the public peace and careful of the lives of the subjects; 'that it will not suffer with impunity any crime to be prevented by death, *unless the same, if committed, would also be punished by death*'. (*Commentaries*, vol. iv, p. 182.) 'The law sets so high a value upon the life of a man, that it always intends some misbehaviour in the person who takes it away, unless by the command, or express permission of the law.'—'And as to the necessity which excuses a man who kills another *se defendendo*, Lord Bacon calls even that *necessitas culpabilis*.' (*Commentaries*, vol. iv, p. 187.) So far this Luminary of the law.—But the very amusements of the rich are, in the estimation of Mr Justice Best, of so great importance, that the poor are to be exposed to sudden death who interfere with them. There are other persons of the same opinion with this magistrate respecting the pleasures of the rich. In the last Session of Parliament a bill was passed, entitled 'An Act for the summary Punishment, in certain Cases, of Persons wilfully or maliciously damaging, or committing Trespasses on, public or private Property.' *Anno primo*—(a bad specimen of what is to happen)— *Georgii IV. Regis*, cap. 56. In this act it is provided, that 'if any person shall wilfully, *or* maliciously, commit any damage, injury, or spoil, upon any building, fence, hedge, gate, stile, guide-post, mile-stone, tree, wood, underwood, orchard, garden, nursery-ground, crops, vegetables, plants, land, or other matter or thing growing or being thereon, or to or upon real or personal property of any nature or kind soever, he may be immediately seized by anybody, without a warrant, taken before a magistrate, and fined (according to the mischief he has done) to the extent of £5; or, in default of payment, may be committed to the jail for three months'. And at the end comes a clause, exempting from the operation of this act *all mischief done in hunting, and by shooters who*

K

are qualified. This is surely the most impudent piece of legislation that ever crept into the statute-book; and, coupled with Mr Justice Best's declaration, constitutes the following affectionate relation between the different orders of society. Says the higher link to the lower, 'If you meddle with my game, I will immediately murder you;—if you commit the slightest injury upon my real or personal property, I will take you before a magistrate, and fine you five pounds. I am in Parliament, and you are not; and I have just brought in an act of Parliament for that purpose. But so important is it to you that my pleasures should not be interrupted, that I have exempted myself and friends from the operation of this act; and we claim the right (without allowing you any such summary remedy) of riding over your fences, hedges, gates, stiles, guide-posts, mile-stones, woods, underwoods, orchards, gardens, nursery-grounds, crops, vegetables, plants, lands, or other matters or things growing or being thereupon— including your children and yourselves, if you do not get out of the way.' Is there, upon earth, such a mockery of justice as an act of Parliament, pretending to protect property, sending a poor hedge-breaker to gaol, and specially exempting from its operation the accusing and the judging squire, who, at the tail of the hounds, have that morning, perhaps, ruined as much wheat and seeds as would purchase fuel a whole year for a whole village? . . .

It is expected by some persons that the severe operation of these engines will put an end to the trade of a poacher. This has always been predicated of every fresh operation of severity, that it was to put an end to poaching. But if this argument is good for one thing, it is good for another. Let the first pickpocket who is taken be hung alive by the ribs, and let him be a fortnight in wasting to death. Let us seize a little grammar boy who is robbing orchards, tie his arms and legs, throw over him a delicate puff-paste, and bake him in a bun-pan in an oven. If poaching can be extirpated by intensity of punishment, why not all other crimes? If racks and gibbets and tenterhooks are the best method of bringing back the golden age, why do we refrain from so easy a receipt for abolishing every species of wickedness? The best way of answering a bad argument is not to stop it, but to let it go on in its course till it leaps over the boundaries of common sense. There is a little book called *Beccaria on Crimes and Punish-*

ments, which we strongly recommend to the attention of Mr Justice Best. He who has not read it is neither fit to make laws nor to administer them when made.

As to the idea of abolishing poaching altogether, we will believe that poaching is abolished when it is found impossible to buy game; or when they have risen so greatly in price that none but people of fortune can buy them. But we are convinced this never can and never will happen. All the traps and guns in the world will never prevent the wealth of the merchant and manufacturer from commanding the game of the landed gentleman. You may, in the pursuit of this visionary purpose, render the common people savage, ferocious, and vindictive; you may disgrace your laws by enormous punishments, and the national character by these new secret assassinations; but you will never separate the wealthy glutton from his pheasant. The best way is, to take what you want, and to sell the rest fairly and openly. This is the real spring gun and steel trap which will annihilate, not the unlawful trader, but the unlawful trade.

There is a sort of horror in thinking of a whole land filled with lurking engines of death—machinations against human life under every green tree—traps and guns in every dusky dell and bosky bourn—the *ferae natura*, the lords of manors eyeing their peasantry as so many butts and marks, and panting to hear the click of the trap and to see the flash of the gun. How any human being educated in liberal knowledge and Christian feeling can doom to certain destruction a poor wretch tempted by the sight of animals that naturally appear to him to belong to one person as well as another, we are at a loss to conceive. We cannot imagine how he could live in the same village, and see the widows and orphans of the man whose blood he had shed for such a trifle. We consider a person who could do this to be deficient in the very elements of mortals—to want that sacred regard to human life which is one of the cornerstones of civil society. If he sacrifices the life of man for his mere pleasures, he would do so, if he dared, for the lowest and least of his passions. He may be defended, perhaps, by the abominable injustice of the Game Laws, though we think and hope he is not. But there rests upon his head, and there is marked in his account, the deep and indelible sin of *blood-guiltiness*.

[1821]

PUBLIC SCHOOLS

IN arguing any large or general question it is of infinite importance to attend to the first feelings which the mention of the topic has a tendency to excite, and the name of a public school brings with it immediately the idea of brilliant classical attainments: but upon the importance of these studies we are not now offering any opinion. The only points for consideration are, whether boys are put in the way of becoming good and wise men by these schools, and whether they actually gather there those attainments which it pleases mankind, for the time being, to consider as valuable and to decorate by the name of learning.

By a public school we mean an endowed place of education of old standing to which the sons of gentlemen resort in considerable numbers and where they continue to reside from eight or nine to eighteen years of age. We do not give this as a definition which would have satisfied Porphyry or Duns Scotus, but as one sufficiently accurate for our purpose. The characteristic features of these schools are their antiquity, the numbers, and the ages of the young people who are educated at them. We beg leave, however, to premise that we have not the slightest intention of insinuating anything to the disparagement of the present discipline or present rulers of these schools as compared with other times and other men: we have no reason whatever to doubt that they are as ably governed at this, as they have been at any preceding period. Whatever objections we may have to these institutions, they are to faults not depending upon present administration, but upon original construction.*

---

* A public school is thought to be the best cure for the insolence of youthful aristocracy. This insolence, however, is not a little increased by the homage of masters, and would soon meet with its natural check in the world. There can be no occasion to bring five hundred boys together to teach to a young nobleman that proper demeanour which he would learn so much better from the first English gentleman whom he might think proper to insult.

At a public school (for such is the system established by immemorial custom) every boy is alternately tyrant and slave. The power which the elder part of these communities exercises over the younger is exceedingly great, very difficult to be controlled, and accompanied, not unfrequently, with cruelty and caprice. It is the common law of the place that the young should be implicitly obedient to the elder boys; and this obedience resembles more the submission of a slave to his master, or of a sailor to his captain, than the common and natural deference which would always be shown by one boy to another a few years older than himself. Now, this system we cannot help considering as an evil,—because it inflicts upon boys, for two or three years of their lives, many painful hardships and much unpleasant servitude. These sufferings might perhaps be of some use in military schools; but to give a boy the habit of enduring privations to which he will never again be called upon to submit, to inure him to pains which he will never again feel, and to subject him to the privation of comforts with which he will always in future abound, is surely not a very useful and valuable severity in education. It is not the life in miniature which he is to lead hereafter, nor does it bear any relation to it. He will never again be subjected to so much insolence and caprice, nor ever, in all human probability, called upon to make so many sacrifices. The servile obedience which it reaches might be useful to a menial domestic, or the habits of enterprise which it encourages prove of importance to a military partisan; but we cannot see what bearing it has upon the calm, regular, civil life, which the sons of gentlemen, destined to opulent idleness or to any of the three learned professions, are destined to lead. Such a system makes many boys very miserable, and produces those bad effects upon the temper and disposition which unjust suffering always does produce; but what good it does, we are much at a loss to conceive. Reasonable obedience is extremely useful in forming the disposition. Submission to tyranny lays the foundation of hatred, suspicion, cunning, and a variety of odious passions. We are convinced that those young people will turn out to be the best men who have been guarded most effectually in their childhood from every species of useless vexation, and experienced in the greatest degree the blessings of a wise and rational indulgence. But even if these effects upon future character are not produced, still, four or five years in childhood make a very considerable period of human existence, and it is by no means a trifling consideration whether they are passed happily or unhappily. The wretchedness of school tyranny is trifling enough to a man who only contemplates it, in ease of body and tranquillity of mind, through the medium of twenty intervening years; but it is quite as real, and quite as acute, while it lasts, as any of the sufferings of mature life: and the utility of these sufferings, or the price paid in compensation for them, should be clearly made out to a conscientious parent, before he consents to expose his children to them.

This system also gives to the elder boys an absurd and pernicious opinion of their own importance, which is often with difficulty effaced by a considerable commerce with the world. The *head* of a public school is generally a very conceited young man, utterly ignorant of his own dimensions, and losing all that habit of conciliation towards others, and that anxiety for self-improvement, which result from the natural modesty of youth. Nor is this conceit very easily and speedily gotten rid of;—we have seen (if we mistake not) public-school importance lasting through the half of after-life, strutting in lawn, swelling in ermine, and displaying itself, both ridiculously and offensively, in the haunts and business of bearded men.

There is a manliness in the athletic exercises of public schools which is as seductive to the imagination as it is utterly unimportant in itself. Of what importance is it in after-life whether a boy can play well or ill at cricket, or row a boat with the skill and precision of a water-man? If our young lords and esquires were hereafter to wrestle together in public, or the gentlemen of the Bar to exhibit Olympic games in Hilary Term, the glory attached to these exercises at public schools would be rational and important. But of what use is the body of an athlete when we have good laws over our heads, or when a pistol, a postchaise, or a porter can be hired for a few shillings? A gentleman does nothing but ride or walk; and yet such a ridiculous stress is laid upon the manliness of the exercises customary at public schools—exercises in which the greatest blockheads commonly excel the most—which often render habits of idleness inveterate, and often lead to foolish expense and dissipation at a more advanced period of life.

One of the supposed advantages of a public school is the greater knowledge of the world which a boy is considered to derive from those situations; but if by a knowledge of the world is meant a knowledge of the forms and manners which are found to be the most pleasing and useful in the world, a boy from a public school is almost always extremely deficient in these particulars; and his sister, who has remained at home at the apron-strings of her mother, is very much his superior in the science of manners. It is probably true that a boy at a public school has made more observations on human character, because he has had more opportunities of observing than have been enjoyed by young persons educated either at home or at private schools: but this little advance gained at a public school is so soon overtaken at college or in the world, that to have made it is of the least possible consequence and utterly undeserving of any risk incurred in the acquisition. Is it any injury to a man of thirty or thirty-five years of age—to a learned serjeant or venerable dean—that at eighteen they did not know so much of the world as some other boys of the same standing? They have probably escaped the arrogant character so often attendant upon this trifling superiority; nor is there much chance that they have ever fallen into the common and youthful error of mistaking a premature initiation into vice for a knowledge of the ways of mankind: and, in addition to these salutary exemptions, a winter in London brings it all to a level, and offers to every novice the advantages which are supposed to be derived from this prococity of confidence and polish.

According to the general prejudice in favour of public schools, it would be thought quite as absurd and superfluous to enumerate the illustrious characters who have been bred at our three great seminaries of this description, as it would be to descant upon the illustrious characters who have passed in and out of London over our three great bridges. Almost every conspicuous person is supposed to have been educated at public schools; and there are scarcely any means (as it is imagined) of making an actual comparison; and yet, great as the rage is, and long has been, for public schools, it is very remarkable that the most eminent men in every art and science have not been educated in public schools; and this is true even if we include in the term of public schools not only Eton, Winchester, and Westminster, but the

Charterhouse, St Paul's School, Merchant Taylors', Rugby, and every school in England at all conducted upon the plan of the three first. The great schools of Scotland we do not call public schools, because in these the mixture of domestic life gives to them a widely different character. Spenser, Pope, Shakespeare, Butler, Rochester, Spratt, Parnell, Garth, Congreve, Gay, Swift, Thomson, Shenstone, Akenside, Goldsmith, Samuel Johnson, Beaumont and Fletcher, Ben Jonson, Sir Philip Sidney, Savage, Arbuthnot, and Burns, among the poets, were not educated in the system of English schools. Sir Isaac Newton, Maclaurin, Wallis, Hamstead, Saundreson, Simpson, and Napier, among men of science, were not educated in public schools. The three best historians that the English language has produced, Clarendon, Hume, and Robertson, were not educated at public schools. Public schools have done little in England for the fine arts—as in the examples of Inigo Jones, Vanbrugh, Reynolds, Gainsborough, Garrick, etc. The great medical writers and discoverers in Great Britain, Harvey, Cheselden, Hunter, Jenner, Meade, Brown, and Cullen, were not educated at public schools. Of the great writers on morals and metaphysics, it was not the system of public schools which produced Bacon, Shaftesbury, Hobbes, Berkeley, Butler, Hume, Hartley, or Dugald Stewart. . . . [Here follow 45 other celebrated names]. . . . If it be urged that public schools have only assumed their present character within this last century or half century, and that what are now called public schools partook before this period of the nature of private schools, there must then be added to our lists the names of Milton, Dryden, Addison, etc., etc., and it will follow, that the English have done almost all that they have done in the arts and sciences without the aid of that system of education to which they are now so much attached. Ample as this catalogue of celebrated names already is, it would be easy to double it; yet as it stands it is obviously sufficient to show the great eminence may be attained in any line of fame without the aid of public schools. Some more striking inferences might perhaps be drawn from it, but we content ourselves with the simple fact.

The most important peculiarity in the constitution of a public school is its numbers, which are so great, that a close inspection of the master into the studies and conduct of each individual is quite impossible. . . . Upon this system, a boy is left almost entirely to himself, to impress upon his own mind, as well as he can, the distant advantages of knowledge, and to withstand, from his own innate resolution, the examples and the seductions of idleness. A firm character survives this brave neglect, and very exalted talents may sometimes remedy it by subsequent diligence; but schools are not made for a few youths of pre-eminent talents and strong characters; such prizes can, of course, be drawn but by a very few parents. The best school is that which is best accommodated to the greatest variety of characters and which embraces the greatest number of cases. It cannot be the main object of education to render the splendid more splendid, and to lavish care upon those who would almost thrive without any care at all. A public school does this effectually; but it commonly leaves the idle almost as idle, and the dull almost as dull, as it found them. It disdains the tedious cultivation of those middling talents of which, only, the great mass of human beings are possessed. When a strong desire of improvement exists it is encouraged, but no pains are taken to inspire it. A boy is cast in among five or six hundred other boys, and is left to form his own character;—if his love of knowledge survives this severe trial, it in general carries him very far: and, upon the same principle, a savage who grows up to manhood is in general well made and free from all bodily defects, not because the severities of such a state are favourable to animal life but because they are so much the reverse that none but the strongest can survive them. A few boys are incorrigibly idle, and a few incorrigibly eager for knowledge; but the great mass are in a state of doubt and fluctuation, and they come to school for the express purpose, not of being left to themselves—for that could be done anywhere—but that their wavering tastes and propensities should be decided by the intervention of a master. In a forest, or public school for oaks and elms, the trees are left to themselves; the strong plants live and the weak ones die: the towering oak that remains is admired, the saplings that perish around it are cast into the flames and forgotten. But it is not surely to the vegetable struggle of a forest, or the hasty glance of a forester, that a botanist would commit a favourite plant; he would naturally seek for it a situation of less hazard and a cultivator whose limited occupations would enable him to give to it a reasonable share of his time and attention. The very meaning of education seems to us to be, that the old should teach the young, and the wise direct the weak; that a man who professes to instruct, should get among his pupils, study their characters, gain their affections, and form their inclinations and aversions. In a public school, the numbers render this impossible; it is impossible that sufficient time should be found for this useful and affectionate interference. Boys, therefore, are left to their own crude conceptions and ill-formed propensities; and this neglect is called a spirited and manly education. . . .

It is contended, by the friends to public schools, that every person, before he comes to man's estate, must run through a certain career of dissipation, and that if that career is, by means of a private education, deferred to a more advanced period of life it will only be begun with greater eagerness and pursued into more blamable excess. The time must, of course, come, when every man must be his own master, when his conduct can be no longer regulated by the watchful superintendence of another but must be guided by his own discretion. Emancipation must come at last, and we admit that the object to be aimed at is that such emancipation should be gradual and not premature. Upon this very invidious point of the discussion we rather wish to avoid offering any opinion. The manners of great schools vary considerably from time to time, and what may have been true many years ago is very possibly not true at the present period. In this instance, every parent must be governed by his own observations and means of information. If the licence which prevails at public schools is only a fair increase of liberty, proportionate to advancing age and calculated to prevent the bad effects of a sudden transition from tutelary thraldom to perfect self-government, it is certainly a good rather than an evil. If, on the contrary, there exists in these places of education a system of premature debauchery, and if they only prevent men from being corrupted by the world by corrupting them before their entry into the world, they can then only be looked upon as evils of the greatest magnitude, however they may be sanctioned by opinion or rendered familiar to us by habit.

The vital and essential part of a school is the master, but at a public school no boy, or at the best only a very few, can see enough of him to derive any considerable benefit from his character, manners, and information. It is certainly of eminent use, particularly to a young man of rank, that he should have lived among boys; but it is only so when they are all moderately watched by some superior understanding. The morality of boys is generally very imperfect, their notions of honour extremely mistaken, and their objects of ambition frequently very absurd. The probability then is, that the kind of discipline they exercise over each other will produce (when left to itself) a great deal of mischief; and yet this is the discipline to which every child at a public school is, not only necessarily exposed, but principally confined. Our objection (we again repeat) is not to the interference of boys in the formation of the character of boys; their character, we are persuaded, will be very imperfectly formed without their assistance; but our objection is to that almost exclusive agency which they exercise in public schools.

After having said so much in opposition to the general prejudice in favour of public schools, we may be expected to state what species of school we think preferable to them. . . . That education seems to us to be the best which mingles a domestic with a school life, and which gives to a youth the advantage which is to be derived from the learning of a master, and the emulation which results from the society of other boys, together with the affectionate vigilance which he must experience in the house of his parents. But where this species of education, from peculiarity of circumstances or situation, is not attainable, we are disposed to think a society of twenty or thirty boys, under the guidance of a learned man, and above all of a man of good sense, to be a seminary the best adapted for the education of youth. The numbers are sufficient to excite a considerable degree of emulation, to give to a boy some insight into the diversities of the human character, and to subject him to the observation and control of his superiors. It by no means follows that a judicious man should always interfere with his authority and advice because he has always the means; he may connive at many things which he cannot approve, and suffer some little failures to proceed to a certain extent, which, if indulged in wider limits, would be attended with irretrievable mischief: he will be aware that his object is to fit his pupil for the world, that constant control is a very bad preparation for complete emancipation from all control, that it is not bad policy to expose a young man, under the eye of superior wisdom, to some of those dangers which will assail him hereafter in greater number and in greater strength when he has only his own resources to depend upon. A private education conducted upon these principles is not calculated to gratify quickly the vanity of a parent who is blest with a child of strong character and pre-eminent abilities: to be the first scholar of an obscure master, at an obscure place, is no very splendid distinction; nor does it afford that opportunity, of which so many parents are desirous, of forming great connections for their children: but if the object be to induce the young to love knowledge and virtue, we are inclined to suspect, that, for the average of human talents and characters, these are the situations in which such tastes will be the most effectually formed.

[1810]

THE SUPPRESSION OF VICE

A SOCIETY that holds out as its object the suppression of vice must at first sight conciliate the favour of every respectable person; and he who objects to an institution calculated apparently to do so much good is bound to give very clear and satisfactory reasons for his dissent from so popular an opinion. We certainly have, for a long time, had doubts of its utility; and now think ourselves called upon to state the grounds of our distrust.

Though it were clear that individual informers are useful auxiliaries to the administration of the laws, it would by no means follow that these informers should be allowed to combine, to form themselves into a body, to make a public purse, and to prosecute under a common name. An informer—whether he is paid by the week, like the agents of this society, or by the crime, as in common cases—is in general a man of a very indifferent character. So much fraud and deception are necessary for carrying on his trade, it is so odious to his fellow subjects, that no man of respectability will ever undertake it. It is evidently impossible to make such a character otherwise than odious. A man who receives weekly pay for prying into the transgressions of mankind, and bringing them to consequent punishment, will always be hated by mankind; and the office must fall to the lot of some man of desperate fortunes and ambiguous character. The multiplication, therefore, of such officers, and the extensive patronage of such characters, may, by the management of large and opulent societies, become an evil nearly as great as the evils they would suppress. The alarm which a private and disguised accuser occasions in a neighbourhood is known to be prodigious, not only to the guilty, but to those who may be at once innocent, and ignorant, and timid. The destruction of social confidence is another evil, the consequence of information. An informer gets access to my house or family, worms my secret out of me, and then betrays me to the magistrate. Now all these evils may be tolerated in a small degree, while in a greater degree they would be perfectly intolerable. Thirty or forty informers roaming about the metropolis may frighten the mass of offenders a little, and do some good: ten thousand informers would either create an insurrection, or totally destroy the confidence and cheerfulness of private life. Whatever may be said, therefore, of the single and insulated informer, it is quite a new question when we come to a corporation of informers supported by large contributions. The one may be a good, the other a very serious evil; the one legal, the other wholly out of the contemplation of law,—which often, and very wisely, allows individuals to do what it forbids to many individuals assembled.

If once combination is allowed for the suppression of vice, where are its limits to be? Its capital may as well consist of £100,000 *per annum*, as of a thousand: its numbers may increase from a thousand subscribers, which this society, it seems, had reached in its second year, to twenty thousand: and in that case what accused person of an inferior condition of life would have the temerity to stand against such a society? Their mandates would very soon be law, and there is no compliance into which they might not frighten the common people and the lower orders of tradesmen. The idea of a society of gentlemen calling themselves an Association for the Suppression of Vice would alarm any small offender, to a degree that would make him prefer any submission to any resistance. He would consider the very fact of being accused by them as almost sufficient to ruin him.

An individual accuser accuses at his own expense; and the risk he runs is a good security that the subject will not be harassed by needless accusations,—a security which, of course, he cannot have against such a society as this, to whom pecuniary loss is an object of such little consequence. It must never be forgotten, that this is not a society for *punishing* people who have been found to transgress the law, but for *accusing* persons of transgressing the law; and that before trial the accused person is to be considered as innocent, and is to have every fair chance of establishing his innocence. He must be no common defendant, however, who does not contend against such a society with very fearful odds;—the best counsel engaged for his opponents,—great practice in the particular court and particular species of cause,— witnesses thoroughly hackneyed in a court of justice,—and an unlimited command of money. It by no means follows that the legislature in allowing individuals to be informers meant to subject the accused person to the superior weight and power of such societies. The very influence of names must have a considerable weight with the jury. Lord Dartmouth, Lord Radstock, and the Bishop of Durham, *versus* a Whitechapel butcher or a publican! Is this a fair contest before a jury? It is not so even in London; and what must it be in the country, where a society for the suppression of vice may consist of all the principal persons in the neighbourhood? These societies are now established in York, in Reading, and in many other large towns. Wherever this is the case, it is far from improbable that the same persons, at the Quarter or Town Sessions, may be both judges and accusers; and still more fatally so, if the offence is tried by a special jury. This is already most notoriously the case in societies for the preservation of game. They prosecute a poacher;—the jury is special; and the poor wretch is found guilty by the very same persons who have accused him.

If it is lawful for respectable men to combine for the purpose of turning informers, it is lawful for the lowest and most despicable race of informers to do the same thing; and then it is quite clear that every species of wickedness and extortion would be the consequence. We are rather surprised that no society of perjured attorneys and fraudulent bankrupts has risen up in this metropolis for the suppression of vice. A chairman, deputy-chairman, subscriptions, and an annual sermon, would give great dignity to their proceedings; and they would soon begin to take some rank in the world.

It is true that it is the duty of grand juries to inform against vice; but the law knows the probable number of grand jurymen. the times of their meeting, and the description of persons of whom they consist. Of voluntary societies it can know nothing,— their numbers, their wealth, or the character of their members. It may therefore trust to a grand jury what it would by no means trust to an unknown combination. A vast distinction is to be made, too, between official duties and voluntary duties. The first are commonly carried on with calmness and moderation; the latter often characterized, in their execution, by rash and intemperate zeal.

The present society receives no members but those who are

of the Church of England. As we are now arguing the question generally, we have a right to make any supposition. It is equally free, therefore, upon general principles, for a society of sectarians to combine and exclude members of the Church of England; and the suppression of vice may thus come in aid of Methodism, Jacobinism, or of any set of principles, however perilous, either to Church or State. The present Society may perhaps consist of persons whose sentiments on these points are rational and respectable. Combinations, however, of this sort may give birth to something far different; and such a supposition is the fair way of trying the question.

We doubt if there be not some mischief in averting the fears and hopes of the people from the known and constituted authorities of the country to those self-created powers;—a Society that punishes in the Strand, another which rewards at Lloyd's Coffee-house! If these things get to any great height they throw an air of insignificance over those branches of the government to whom these cares properly devolve and whose authority is by these means assisted, till it is superseded. It is supposed that a project must necessarily be good because it is intended for the aid of law and government. At this rate, there should be a society in aid of the government, for procuring intelligence from foreign parts, with accredited agents all over Europe. There should be a voluntary transport board and a gratuitous victualling office. There should be a duplicate, in short, of every department of the State,—the one appointed by the King, and the other by itself. There should be a real Lord Glenbervie, in the woods and forests,—and with him a monster, a voluntary Lord Glenbervie, serving without pay, and guiding *gratis*, with secret counsel, the axe of his prototype. If it be asked, who are the constituted authorities who are legally appointed to watch over morals, and whose functions the Society usurp? our answer is, that there are in England about 12,000 clergy, not unhandsomely paid, for persuading the people, and about 4,000 justices, 30 grand juries, and 40,000 constables whose duty and whose inclination it is to compel them to do right. Under such circumstances, a voluntary moral society does indeed seem to be the purest result of volition; for there certainly is not the smallest particle of necessity mingled with its existence.

It is hardly possible that a society for the suppression of vice can ever be kept within the bounds of good sense and moderation. If there are many members who have really become so from a feeling of duty, there will necessarily be some who enter the Society to hide a bad character, and others whose object it is to recommend themselves to their betters by a sedulous and bustling inquisition into the immoralities of the public. The loudest and noisiest suppressors will always carry it against the more prudent part of the community; the most violent will be considered as the most moral; and those who see the absurdity will, from the fear of being thought to encourage vice, be reluctant to oppose it.

It is of great importance to keep public opinion on the side of virtue. To their authorized and legal correctors, mankind are, on common occasions, ready enough to submit; but there is something in the self-erection of a voluntary magistracy which creates so much disgust, that it almost renders vice popular, and puts the offence at a premium. We have no doubt but that the immediate effect of a voluntary combination for the suppression of vice is an involuntary combination in favour of the vices to be suppressed; and this is a very serious drawback from any good of which such societies may be the occasion; for the state of morals, at any one period, depends much more upon opinion than law; and to bring odious and disgusting auxiliaries to the aid of virtue is to do the utmost possible good to the cause of vice. We regret that mankind are as they are; and we sincerely wish that the species at large were as completely devoid of every vice and infirmity as the President, Vice-President, and Committee of the Suppressing Society; but, till they are thus regenerated, it is of the greatest consequence to teach them virtue and religion in a manner which will not make them hate both the one and the other. The greatest delicacy is required in the application of violence to moral and religious sentiment. We forget that the object is, not to produce the outward compliance, but to raise up the inward feeling which secures the outward compliance. You may drag men into church by main force, and prosecute them for buying a pot of beer, and cut them off from the enjoyment of a leg of mutton; and you may do all this till you make the common people hate Sunday, and the clergy, and religion, and everything which relates to such subjects. There are many crimes, indeed, where persuasion cannot

L

be waited for, and where the untaught feelings of all men go along with the violence of the law. A robber and a murderer must be knocked on the head like mad dogs; but we have no great opinion of the possibility of indicting men into piety or of calling in the Quarter Sessions to the aid of religion. You may produce outward conformity by these means; but you are so far from producing (the only thing worth producing) the inward feeling, that you incur a great risk of giving birth to a totally opposite sentiment.

The violent modes of making men good, just alluded to, have been resorted to at periods when the science of legislation was not so well understood as it is now, or when the manners of the age have been peculiarly gloomy or fanatical. The improved knowledge, and the improved temper of later times, push such laws into the background and silently repeal them. A suppressing Society, hunting everywhere for penalty and information, has a direct tendency to revive ancient ignorance and fanaticism, and to re-enact laws which, if ever they ought to have existed at all, were certainly calculated for a very different style of manners and a very different degree of information. To compel men to go to church under a penalty appears to us to be absolutely absurd. The bitterest enemy of religion will necessarily be that person who is driven to a compliance with its outward ceremonies by informers and justices of the peace. In the same manner, any constable who hears another swear an oath has a right to seize him and carry him before a magistrate, where he is to be fined so much for each execration. It is impossible to carry such laws in execution, and it is lucky that it is impossible, for their execution would create an infinitely greater evil than it attempted to remedy. The common sense and common feeling of mankind, if left to themselves, would silently repeal such laws; and it is one of the evils of these societies that they render absurdity eternal and ignorance indestructible. Do not let us be misunderstood: upon the subject to be accomplished, there can be but one opinion;—it is only upon the means employed, that there can be the slightest difference of sentiment. To go to church is a duty of the greatest possible importance, and on the blasphemy and vulgarity of swearing there can be but one opinion. But such duties are not the objects of legislation; they must be left to the general state of public sentiment; which sentiment must be influenced by example, by the exertions of the pulpit and the press, and, above all, by education. The fear of God can never be taught by constables, nor the pleasures of religion be learnt from a common informer.

Beginning with the best intentions in the world, such societies must in all probability degenerate into a receptacle for every species of tittle-tattle, impertinence, and malice. Men whose trade is rat-catching love to catch rats; the bug-destroyer seizes on his bug with delight; and the suppressor is gratified by finding his vice. The last soon becomes a mere tradesman like the others; none of them moralize or lament that their respective evils should exist in a world. The public feeling is swallowed up in the pursuit of a daily occupation and in the display of a technical skill. Here, then, is a society of men who invite accusation, who receive it (almost unknown to themselves) with pleasure, and who, if they hate dulness and inoccupation, can have very little pleasure in the innocence of their fellow creatures. The natural consequence of all this is, that (besides that portion of rumour which every member contributes at the weekly meeting) their table must be covered with anonymous lies against the characters of individuals. Every servant discharged from his master's service, every villain who hates the man he has injured, every cowardly assassin of character, now knows where his accusations will be received and where they cannot fail to produce some portion of the mischievous effects which he wishes. The very first step of such a Society should be to declare in the plainest manner that they would never receive any anonymous accusation. This would be the only security to the public that they were not degrading themselves into a receptacle for malice and falsehood. Such a declaration would inspire some species of confidence and make us believe that their object was neither the love of power nor the gratification of uncharitable feelings. The Society for the Suppression, however, have done no such thing. They request, indeed, the signature of the informers whom they invite; but they do not (as they ought) make that signature an indispensable condition.

Nothing has disgusted us so much in the proceedings of this Society as the control which they exercise over the amusements of the poor. One of the specious titles under which this legal meanness is gratified is *Prevention of Cruelty to Animals*.

Of cruelty to animals, let the reader take the following specimens:—

Running an iron hook in the intestines of an animal; presenting this first animal to another as his food; and then pulling this second creature up, and suspending him by the barb in his stomach.

Riding a horse till he drops, in order to see an innocent animal torn to pieces by dogs.

Keeping a poor animal upright for many weeks, to communicate a peculiar hardness to his flesh.

Making deep incisions into the flesh of another animal while living, in order to make the muscles more firm.

Immersing another animal, while living, in hot water.

Now we do fairly admit that such abominable cruelties as these are worthy the interference of the law: and that the Society should have punished them cannot be matter of surprise to any feeling mind.—But stop, gentle reader! these cruelties are the cruelties of the Suppressing Committee, not of the poor. You must not think of punishing these.—The first of these cruelties passes under the pretty name of *angling*, and therefore there can be no harm in it, the more particularly as the President himself has one of the best preserved trout streams in England. The next is hunting; and, as many of the Vice-Presidents and of the Committee hunt, it is not possible there can be any cruelty in hunting.* The next is a process for making *brawn*—a dish never tasted by the poor, and therefore not to be disturbed by indictment. The fourth is the mode of *crimping* cod; and the fifth, of boiling lobsters; all high-life cruelties, with which a justice of the peace has no business to meddle. The real thing which calls forth the sympathies, and harrows up the soul, is to see a number of boisterous artisans baiting a bull or a bear; not a savage hare,

* 'How reasonable creatures' (says the Society), 'can enjoy a pastime which is the cause of such suffering to brute animals, or how they can consider themselves entitled, for their own amusement, to stimulate those animals, by means of the antipathies which Providence has thought proper to place between them, to worry and tear and often to destroy each other, it is difficult to conceive. So inhuman a practice, by a retribution peculiarly just, tends obviously to render the human character brutal and ferocious,' etc. etc. (*Address*, pp. 71, 72). We take it for granted that the reader sees clearly that no part of this description can possibly apply to the case of *hunting*.

or a carnivorous stag,—but a poor, innocent, timid bear;—not pursued by magistrates and deputy lieutenants and men of education, but by those who must necessarily seek their relaxation in noise and tumultuous merriment,—by men whose feelings are blunted and whose understanding is wholly devoid of refinement. The Society detail, with symptoms of great complacency, their detection of a bear-baiting in Blackboy Alley, Chick Lane, and the prosecution of the offenders before a magistrate. It appears to us that nothing can be more partial and unjust than this kind of proceedings. A man of ten thousand a year may worry a fox as much as he pleases,—may encourage the breed of a mischievous animal on purpose to worry it; and a poor labourer is carried before a magistrate for paying sixpence to see an exhibition of courage between a dog and a bear! Any cruelty may be practised to gorge the stomachs of the rich,—none to enliven the holidays of the poor. We venerate those feelings which really protect creatures susceptible of pain and incapable of complaint. But heaven-born pity, nowadays, calls for the income-tax and the court guide; and ascertains the rank and fortune of the tormentor before she weeps for the pain of the sufferer. It is astonishing how the natural feelings of mankind are distorted by false theories. Nothing can be more mischievous than to say that the pain inflicted by the dog of a man of quality is not (when the strength of the two animals is the same) equal to that produced by the cur of a butcher. Haller, in his Pathology, expressly says, *that the animal bitten knows no difference in the quality of the biting animal's master*; and it is now the universal opinion, among all enlightened men, that the misery of the brawner would be very little diminished if he could be made sensible that he was to be eaten up only by persons of the first fashion. The contrary supposition seems to us to be absolute nonsense; it is the desertion of the true *Baconian* philosophy and the substitution of a mere unsupported conjecture in its place. The trespass, however, which calls forth all the energies of a suppresser is the sound of a fiddle. That the common people are really enjoying themselves is now beyond all doubt: and away rush Secretary, President, and Committee, to clap the cotillon into the Compter, and to bring back the life of the poor to its regular standard of decorous gloom. The gambling houses of St James's remain untouched. The peer ruins himself and his family with impunity;

while the Irish labourer is privately whipped for not making a
better use of the excellent moral and religious education which
he has received in the days of his youth!

It is not true, as urged by the Society, that the vices of the
poor are carried on in houses of public resort, and those of the
rich in their own houses. The Society cannot be ignorant of the
innumerable gambling houses resorted to by men of fashion. Is
there one they have suppressed, or attempted to suppress? Can
anything be more despicable than such distinctions as these?
Those who make them seem to have for other persons' vices all
the rigour of the ancient Puritans—without a particle of their
honesty or their courage. To suppose that any society will ever
attack the vices of people of fashion is wholly out of the question.
If the Society consisted of tradesmen, they would infallibly be
turned off by the vicious customers whose pleasures they interrupted: and what gentleman so fond of suppressing as to interfere
with the vices of good company and inform against persons who
were really genteel? He knows very well that the consequence
of such interference would be a complete exclusion from elegant
society; that the upper classes could not and would not endure
it; and that he must immediately lose his rank in the world if
his zeal subjected fashionable offenders to the slightest inconvenience from the law. Nothing therefore remains but to rage
against the Sunday dinners of the poor, and to prevent a brick-
layer's labourer from losing on the seventh day that beard which
has been augmenting the other six. We see at the head of this
Society the names of several noblemen, and of other persons
moving in the fashionable world. Is it possible they can be
ignorant of the innumerable offences against the law of morality
which are committed by their own acquaintance and connections?
Is there one single instance where they have directed the attention
of the Society to this higher species of suppression, and sacrificed
men of consideration to that zeal for virtue which watches so
acutely over the vices of the poor? It would give us very little
pleasure to see a duchess sent to the Poultry Compter; but if we
saw the Society flying at such high game we should at least say
they were honest and courageous, whatever judgment we might
form of their good sense. At present they should denominate
themselves a Society for suppressing the vices of persons whose
income does not exceed £500 *per annum*; and then, to put all

classes upon an equal footing, there must be another society of barbers, butchers, and bakers, to return to the higher classes that moral character by which they are so highly benefited.

To show how impossible it is to keep such societies within any kind of bounds, we shall quote a passage respecting circulating libraries, from their Proceedings: 'Your Committee have good reasons for believing, that the circulation of their notices among the printsellers, warning them against the sale or exhibition of indecent representations, has produced, and continues to produce, the best effects. But they have to lament that the extended establishments of circulating libraries, however useful they may be, in a variety of respects, to the easy and general diffusion of knowledge, are extremely injurious to morals and religion, by the indiscriminate admission which they give to works of a prurient and immoral nature. It is a toilsome task to any virtuous and enlightened mind, to wade through the catalogues of these collections, and much more to select such books from them as have only an apparent bad tendency. But your Committee being convinced that their attention ought to be directed to those institutions which possess such powerful and numerous means of poisoning the minds of young persons, and especially of the female youth, have therefore begun to make some endeavours towards their better regulation.' In the same spirit we see them writing to a country magistrate in Devonshire, respecting a wake advertised in the public papers. Nothing can be more presumptuous than such conduct, or produce, in the minds of impartial men, a more decisive impression against the Society.

The natural answer from the members of the Society (the only answer they have ever made to the enemies of their institution) will be that we are lovers of vice, desirous of promoting indecency, of destroying the Sabbath, and of leaving mankind to the unrestrained gratification of their passions. We have only very calmly to reply that we are neither so stupid nor so wicked as not to concur in every scheme which has for its object the preservation of rational religion and sound morality; but the scheme must be well concerted, and those who are to carry it into execution must deserve our confidence, from their talents and their character. Upon religion and morals depends the happiness of mankind; but the fortune of knaves and the power of fools is sometimes made to rest on the same apparent basis; and we will never (if we can help it) allow a rogue to get rich, or a blockhead to get powerful, under the sanction of these awful words. We do not by any means intend to apply these contemptuous epithets to the Society for the Suppression. That there are among their numbers some very odious hypocrites, is not impossible; that many men who believe they come there from the love of virtue, do really join the Society from the love of power, we do not doubt: but we see no reason to doubt that the great mass of subscribers consists of persons who have very sincere intentions of doing good. That they have, in some instances, done a great deal of good, we admit with the greatest pleasure. We believe that in the hands of truly honest, intrepid, and above all, discreet men, such a society might become a valuable institution, improve in some degree the public morals, and increase the public happiness. So many qualities, however, are required to carry it on well, —the temptations to absurdity and impertinence are so very great,—that we ever despair of seeing our wishes upon this subject realized. In the present instance our object has been to suppress the arrogance of suppressers,—to keep them within due bounds,—to show them that to do good requires a little more talent and reflection than they are aware of,—and, above all, to impress upon them that true zeal for virtue knows no distinction between the rich and the poor; and that the cowardly and the mean can never be the true friends of morality and the promoters of human happiness. If they attend to these rough doctrines, they will ever find in the writers of this Journal their warmest admirers and their most sincere advocates and friends.

[1809]

PRISONS AND PRISONER'S
COUNSEL

[On the proper treatment of prisoners Smith contributed four long articles to the REVIEW. The following extracts are from two of them. It is easy enough, now, to see that he had certain blind spots. He was afraid lest the efforts of 'good and amiable people', which in general he heartily supported, should have the effect of reducing the 'terror' of punishment. Some of his own proposals reflect this anxiety. The Society for the Improvement of Prison Discipline regarded a reduction in the number of recommitments as evidence that their work was prospering. Against this view Smith contended that 'the real and only test of a good prison system is the diminution of offences by the terror of the punishment'. To this end he recommended 'the treadwheel, or the capstan, or some species of labour where the labourer could not see the result of his toil, where it was as monotonous, irksome, and dull as possible'. Such proposals are no longer defensible, but Smith honestly believed them to be for the ultimate benefit of the prisoner himself. That he had the prisoner's interests genuinely at heart our extracts show. The first of them belongs to 1821, the others to 1826.]

THERE are in every county in England large public schools maintained at the expense of the county, for the encouragement of profligacy and vice, and for providing a proper succession of housebreakers, profligates, and thieves. They are schools, too, conducted without the smallest degree of partiality or favour, there being no man (however mean his birth or obscure his situation) who may not easily procure admission to them. The moment any young person evinces the slightest propensity for these pursuits he is provided with food, clothing, and lodging, and put to his studies under the most accomplished thieves and cut-throats the county can supply. There is not, to be sure, a formal arrangement of lectures, after the manner of our universities; but the petty larcenous stripling, being left destitute of every species of employment and locked up with accomplished villains as idle as himself, listens to their pleasant narrative of successful crimes, and pants for the hour of freedom, that he may begin the same bold and interesting career.

This is a perfectly true picture of the prison establishments of many counties in England, and was so, till very lately, of almost all; and the effects so completely answered the design, that in the year 1818 there were committed to the gaols of the United Kingdom more than one hundred and seven thousand persons— a number supposed to be greater than that of all the commitments in the other kingdoms of Europe put together.

The bodily treatment of prisoners has been greatly improved since the time of Howard. There is still, however, much to do; and the attention of good and humane people has been lately called to their state of moral discipline. It is inconceivable to what a spirit of party this has given birth;—all the fat and sleek people—the enjoyers—the mumpsimus, and 'well as we are' people, are perfectly outrageous at being compelled to do their duty and to sacrifice time and money to the lower orders of mankind. Their first resource was to deny all the facts which were brought forward for the purposes of amendment; and the alderman's sarcasm of the Turkey carpet in gaols was banded from one hardhearted and fat-witted gentleman to another: but the advocates of prison-improvement are men in earnest—not playing at religion, but of deep feeling and of indefatigable industry in charitable pursuits. Mr Buxton went in company with men of the most irreproachable veracity; and found in the heart of the metropolis, and in a prison of which the very Turkey carpet alderman was an official visitor, scenes of horror, filth, and cruelty, which would have disgraced even the interior of a slave-ship.

This dislike of innovation proceeds sometimes from the disgust excited by false humanity, canting hypocrisy, and silly enthusiasm. It proceeds also from a stupid and indiscriminate horror of change, whether of evil for good, or good for evil. There is also much party spirit in these matters. A good deal of these humane projects and institutions originate from Dissenters. The plunderers of the public, the jobbers, and those who sell themselves to some great man who sells himself to a greater, all scent from afar the danger of political change, are sensible that the correction of one abuse may lead to that of another, feel uneasy at any visible operation of public spirit and justice, hate and tremble at a man who exposes and rectifies abuses from a sense of duty, and think if such things are suffered to be that their candle-ends and cheese-parings are no longer safe: and these sagacious persons, it must be said for them, are not very wrong in this feeling. Providence, which has denied to them all that is great and good, has given them a fine tact for the preservation of their plunder: their real enemy is the spirit of inquiry, the dislike of wrong, the love of right, and the courage and diligence which are the concomitants of these virtues. When once this spirit is up, it may be as well directed to one abuse as another. To say you must not torture a prisoner with bad air and bad food, and to say you must not tax me without my consent or that of my representative, are both emanations of the same principle, occurring to the same sort of understanding, congenial to the same disposition, published, protected, and enforced by the same qualities. This it is that really excites the horror against Mrs Fry, Mr Gurney, Mr Bennet, and Mr Buxton. Alarmists such as we have described have no particular wish that prisons should be dirty, gaolers cruel, or prisoners wretched; they care little about such matters either way; but all their malice and meanness is called up into action when they see secrets brought to light and abuses giving way before the diffusion of intelligence and the aroused feelings of justice and compassion. As for us, we have neither love of change nor fear of it, but a love of what is just and wise, as far as we are able to find it out.

§

There have been two capital errors in the criminal codes of feudal Europe, from which a great variety of mistakes and injustice have proceeded: the one, a disposition to confound accusation with guilt; the other, to mistake a defence of prisoners accused by the Crown, for disloyalty and disaffection to the Crown; and from these errors our own code has been slowly and gradually recovering, by all those struggles and exertions which it always costs to remove *folly sanctioned by antiquity*. In the early periods of our history, the accused person could call no evidence:—then, for a long time, his evidence against the King could not be examined upon oath; consequently, he might as well have produced none, as all the evidence against him was upon oath. Till the reign of Anne, no one accused of felony could produce witnesses upon oath; and the old practice was vindicated, in opposition to the new one, introduced under the statute of that day, on the grounds of humanity and tenderness to the prisoner! because, as his witnesses were not restricted by an oath, they were at liberty to indulge in simple falsehood as much as they pleased;—so argued the blessed defenders of nonsense in those days. Then it was ruled to be indecent and improper that counsel should be employed against the Crown, and therefore, the prisoner accused of treason could have no counsel. In like manner a party accused of felony could have no counsel to assist him in the trial. Counsel might indeed stay in the court, but apart from the prisoner, with whom they could have no communication. They were not allowed to put any question or to suggest any doubtful point of law; but if the prisoner (likely to be a weak unlettered man) could himself suggest any doubt in matter of law, the Court determined first if the question of law should be entertained, and then assigned counsel to argue it. In those times, too, the jury were punishable if they gave a false verdict against the King, but were *not* punishable if they gave a false verdict against the prisoner. The preamble of the Act of 1696 runs thus:— 'Whereas it is expedient that persons charged with high treason should make a full and sufficient defence.' Might it not be altered to *persons charged with any species or degree of crime?* All these errors have given way to the force of truth, and to the power of common sense and common humanity—the Attorney and Solicitor General, for the time being, always protesting against each alteration, and regularly and officially prophesying the utter destruction of the whole jurisprudence of Great Britain. There is no man now alive, perhaps, so utterly foolish as to propose that prisoners should be prevented from producing evidence upon oath and being heard by their counsel in cases of high treason; and yet it cost a struggle for *seven* sessions to get this measure through the two houses of Parliament. But mankind are much like the children they beget—they always make wry faces at what is to do them good, and it is necessary sometimes to hold the nose, and force the medicine down the throat. They enjoy the health and vigour consequent upon the medicine, but cuff the doctor and sputter at his stuff!

A most absurd argument was advanced in the honourable House, that the practice of employing counsel would be such an expense to the prisoner!—just as if anything was so expensive as being hanged! What a fine topic for the ordinary! 'You are going' (says that exquisite divine) 'to be hanged tomorrow, it is true, but consider what a sum you have saved! Mr Scarlett or Mr Brougham might certainly have presented arguments to the jury which would have insured your acquittal; but do you forget that gentlemen of their eminence must be recompensed by large fees, and that if your life had been saved you would actually have been out of pocket above £20? You will now die with the consciousness of having obeyed the dictates of a wise economy, and with a grateful reverence for the laws of your country, which prevents you from running into such unbounded expense—so let us now go to prayers.'

It is ludicrous enough to recollect, when the employment of counsel is objected to on account of the expense to the prisoner, that the same merciful law which, to save the prisoner's money, has *denied* him counsel and produced his conviction, seizes upon all his savings the moment he is convicted.

Of all false and foolish *dicta*, the most trite and the most absurd is that which asserts that the Judge is counsel for the prisoner. We do not hesitate to say that this is merely an unmeaning phrase, invented to defend a pernicious abuse. The Judge *cannot* be counsel for the prisoner, *ought not* to be counsel for the prisoner, never *is* counsel for the prisoner. To force an ignorant man into a court of justice, and to tell him that the Judge is his counsel, appears to us quite as foolish as to set a hungry man down to his meals and to tell him that the table was his dinner. In the first place, a counsel should always have private and previous communication with the prisoner, which the Judge, of course, cannot have. The prisoner reveals to his counsel how far he is guilty, or he is not; states to him all the circumstances of his case—and might often enable his advocate, if his advocate were allowed to speak, to explain a long string of circumstantial evidence in a manner favourable to the innocence of his client. Of all these advantages, the Judge, if he had every disposition to befriend the prisoner, is of course deprived. Something occurs to the prisoner in the course of the cause; he suggests it in a whisper to his counsel, doubtful if it is a wise point to urge or not. His counsel thinks it of importance, and would urge it if his mouth were not shut. Can a prisoner have this secret communication with a judge, and take his advice, whether or not he, the Judge, shall mention it to the jury? The counsel has (after all the evidence has been given) a bad opinion of his client's case; but he suppresses that opinion, and it is his duty to do so. He is not to decide; that is the province of the jury; and in spite of his own opinion his client may be innocent. He is brought there (or would be brought there if the privilege of speech were allowed) for the express purpose of saying all that could be said on one side of the question. He is a weight in *one* scale, and some one else holds the balance. This is the way in which the truth is elicited in civil, and would be in criminal, cases. But does *the Judge* ever assume the appearance of believing a prisoner to be innocent whom he thinks to be guilty? If the prisoner advances inconclusive or weak arguments, does not the Judge say they are weak and inconclusive, and does he not often sum up against his own client? How then is he counsel for the prisoner? If the counsel for the prisoner were to see a strong point which the counsel for the prosecution had missed, would he supply the deficiency of his antagonist and urge what had been neglected to be urged? But is it not the imperious duty of the Judge to do so? How then can these two functionaries stand in the same relation to the prisoner? In fact, the only meaning of the phrase is this, that the Judge will not suffer any undue advantage to be taken of the ignorance and helplessness of the prisoner, that he will point out any evidence or circumstance in his favour and see that equal justice is done to both parties. But in this sense he is as much the counsel of the prosecutor as of the prisoner. This is all the Judge can do, or even pretends to do; but he can have no previous communication with the prisoner; he can have no confidential communication in court with the prisoner before he sums up; he cannot fling the whole weight of his understanding into the opposite scale against the counsel for the prosecution, and produce that collision of faculties which, in all other cases but those of felony, is supposed to be the happiest method of arriving at truth. Baron Garrow, in his charge to the grand jury at Exeter on the 16th of August 1824, thus expressed his opinion of a Judge being counsel for the prisoner:—'It has been said, and truly said, that in criminal courts, Judges were counsel for the prisoners. So undoubtedly they were, as far as they could to prevent undue prejudice, to guard against improper influence being excited against prisoners; but it was impossible for them to go farther than this; for they could not suggest the course of defence prisoners ought to pursue; for Judges only saw the depositions so short a time before the accused appeared at the bar of their country that it was quite impossible for them to act fully in that capacity.' The learned Baron might have added that it would be more correct to call the Judge counsel for the prosecution; for his only previous instructions were the depositions for the prosecution, from which, in the absence of counsel, he examined the evidence against the prisoner. On the prisoner's behalf he had no instructions at all.

Can anything, then, be more flagrantly and scandalously unjust, than, in a long case of circumstantial evidence, to refuse to a prisoner the benefit of counsel? A footmark, a word, a sound, a tool dropped, all gave birth to the most ingenious inferences; and the counsel for the prosecution is so far from being blamable for entering into all these things that they are all essential to the detection of guilt, and they are all links of a long and intricate chain: but if a close examination into, and a logical statement of, all these circumstances be necessary for the establishment of guilt, is not the same closeness of reasoning and the same logical statement necessary for the establishment of innocence? If justice cannot be done to society without the intervention of a practised and ingenious mind who may connect all these links together and make them clear to the apprehension of a jury, *can* justice be done to the prisoner unless similar practice and similar ingenuity are employed to detect the flaws of the chain and to point out the disconnection of the circumstances?

Is there any one gentleman in the House of Commons who, in yielding his vote to this paltry and perilous fallacy of the Judge being counsel for the prisoner, does not feel that were he himself a criminal he would prefer almost any counsel at the bar to the tender mercies of the Judge? How strange that any man who could make his election would eagerly and diligently surrender this exquisite privilege, and addict himself to the perilous practice of giving fees to counsel! Nor let us forget, in considering

Judges as counsel for the prisoner, that there have been such men as Chief Justice Jeffries, Mr Justice Page, and Mr Justice Alybone, and that in bad times such men may reappear. 'If you do not allow me counsel, my Lords (says Lord Lovat), it is impossible for me to make any defence, by reason of my infirmity. I do not see, I do not hear. I come up to the bar at the hazard of my life. I have fainted several times; I have been up so early, ever since four o'clock this morning. I therefore ask for assistance; and if you do not allow me counsel, or such aid as is necessary, it will be impossible for me to make any defence at all.' Though Lord Lovat's guilt was evident, yet the managers of the impeachment felt so strongly the injustice which was done, that, by the hands of Sir W. Young, the chief manager, a bill was brought into Parliament to allow counsel to persons impeached by that House, which was not previously the case; so that the evil is already done away with, in a great measure, to persons of rank: it so happens in legislation, when a gentleman suffers, public attention is awakened to the evils of laws. Every man who makes laws says, 'This may be my case', but it requires the repeated efforts of humane men, or, as Mr North calls them, dilettanti philosophers, to awaken the attention of law-makers to evils from which they are themselves exempt. We do not say this to make the leaders of mankind unpopular, but to rouse their earnest attention in cases where the poor only are concerned, and where neither good nor evil can happen to themselves.

A great stress is laid upon the moderation of the opening counsel; that is, he does not conjure the farmers in the jury-box, by the love which they bear to their children—he does not declaim upon blood-guiltiness—he does not describe the death of Abel by Cain, the first murderer—he does not describe scattered brains, ghastly wounds, pale features, and hair clotted with gore—he does not do a thousand things which are not in English taste and which it would be very foolish and very vulgar to do. We readily allow all this. But yet, if it be a cause of importance, it is essentially necessary to our counsellor's reputation that this man should be hung! And accordingly, with a very calm voice and composed manner, and with many expressions of candour, he sets himself to comment astutely upon the circumstances. Distant events are immediately connected; meaning is given to insignificant facts; new motives are ascribed to innocent actions; farmer gives way after farmer in the jury-box; and a rope of eloquence is woven round the prisoner's neck! Every one is delighted with the talents of the advocate; and because there has been no noise, no violent action, and no consequent perspiration, he is praised for his candour and forbearance, and the lenity of our laws is the theme of universal approbation. In the meantime, the speech-maker and the prisoner know better.

We should be glad to know of any one nation in the world, taxed by kings, or even imagined by poets (except the English), who have refused to prisoners the benefit of counsel. Why is the voice of humanity heard everywhere else, and disregarded here? In Scotland, the accused have not only counsel to speak for them, but a copy of the indictment and a list of the witnesses. In France, in the Netherlands, in the whole of Europe, counsel are allotted as a matter of course. Everywhere else but here, accusation is considered as unfavourable to the exercise of human faculties. It is admitted to be that crisis in which, above all others, an unhappy man wants the aid of eloquence, wisdom, and coolness. In France, the Napoleon Code has provided not only that counsel should be allowed to the prisoner, but that, as with us in Scotland, his counsel should have the last word.

It is a most affecting moment in a court of justice, when the evidence has all been heard, and the Judge asks the prisoner what he has to say in his defence. The prisoner, who has (by great exertions, perhaps, of his friends) saved up money enough to procure counsel, says to the Judge, 'that he leaves his defence to his counsel'. We have often blushed for English humanity to hear the reply: 'Your counsel cannot speak for you, you must speak for yourself.' And this is the reply given to a poor girl of eighteen—to a foreigner—to a deaf man—to a stammerer—to the sick—to the feeble—to the old—to the most abject and ignorant of human beings! It is a reply, we must say, at which common sense and common feeling revolt:—for it is full of brutal cruelty and of base inattention of those who make laws to the happiness of those for whom laws were made. We wonder that any juryman can convict under such a shocking violation of all natural justice. The iron age of Clovis and Clottaire can produce no more atrocious violation of every good feeling and every good principle. Can a sick man find strength and nerves to speak

M

before a large assembly?—can an ignorant man find words?—
can a low man find confidence? Is not he afraid of becoming
an object of ridicule?—can he believe that his expressions will
be understood? How often have we seen a poor wretch struggling
against the agonies of his spirit and the rudeness of his conceptions, and his awe of better-dressed men and better-taught
men, and the shame which the accusation has brought upon his
head, and the sight of his parents and children gazing at him
in the Court, for the last time perhaps, and after a long absence!
The mariner sinking in the wave does not want a helping hand
more than does this poor wretch. But help is denied to all! Age
cannot have it, nor ignorance, nor the modesty of women! One
hard uncharitable rule silences the defenders of the wretched,
in the worst of human evils; and, at the bitterest of human
moments, mercy is blotted out from the ways of men!

§

But (it is asked) what practical injustice is done?—what
practical evil is there in the present system? The great object
of all law is that the guilty should be punished, and that the
innocent should be acquitted. A very great majority of prisoners,
we admit, are guilty—and so clearly guilty that we believe they
would be found guilty under any system; but among the number
of those who are tried, *some* are innocent, and the chance of
establishing their innocence is very much diminished by the
privation of counsel. In the course of twenty or thirty years,
among the whole mass of English prisoners, we believe *many* are
found guilty who are innocent, and who would not have been
found guilty if an able and intelligent man had watched over
their interest and represented their case. If this happen only to
two or three every year, it is quite a sufficient reason why the
law should be altered. That such cases exist we firmly believe;
and this is the practical evil—perceptible to men of sense and
reflection, but not likely to become the subject of general petition.
To ask why there are not petitions, why the evil is not more
noticed, is mere parliamentary froth and ministerial juggling.
Gentlemen are rarely hung. If they were so, there would be
petitions without end for counsel. The creatures exposed to the
cruelties and injustice of the law are dumb creatures, who feel

the evil without being able to express their feeling. Besides, the question is not whether the evil is found out, but whether the evil exist. Whoever thinks it is an evil should vote against it, whether the sufferer from the injustice discover it to be an injustice or whether he suffer in ignorant silence. When the bill was enacted which allowed counsel for treason there was not a petition from one end of England to the other. Can there be a more shocking answer from the Ministerial Bench than to say, For real evil we care nothing—only for detected evil? We will set about curing any wrong which affects our popularity and power: but as to any other evil, we wait till the people find it out, and in the meantime commit such evils to the care of Mr George Lamb and of Sir James Mackintosh. We are sure so good a man as Mr Peel can never feel in this manner.

Howard devoted himself to his country. It was a noble example. Let two gentlemen on the Ministerial side of the House (we only ask for two) commit some crimes which will render their execution a matter of painful necessity. Let them feel, and report to the House, all the injustice and inconvenience of having neither a copy of the indictment, nor a list of witnesses, nor counsel to defend them. We will venture to say that the evidence of two such persons would do more for the improvement of the criminal law than all the orations of Mr Lamb or the lucubrations of Beccaria. Such evidence would save time and bring the question to an issue. It is a great duty, and ought to be fulfilled—and, in ancient Rome, would have been fulfilled.

§

This is justice, when a prisoner has ample means of compelling the attendance of his witnesses; when his written accusation is put into his hand, and he has time to study it; when he knows in what manner his guilt is to be proved, and when he has a man of practised understanding to state his facts and prefer his arguments. Then criminal justice may march on boldly. The Judge has no stain of blood on his ermine, and the phrases which English people are so fond of lavishing upon the humanity of their laws will have a real foundation. At present this part of the law is a mere relic of the barbarous injustice by which accusation in the early part of our jurisprudence was always confounded with guilt. The greater part of these abuses have been brushed away, as this cannot fail soon to be. In the meantime it is defended (as every other abuse has been defended) by men who think it their duty to defend everything which *is*, and to dread everything which *is not*. We are told that the Judge does what he does not do, and ought not to do. The most pernicious effects are anticipated, in trials of felony, from that which is found to produce the most perfect justice in civil causes and in cases of treason and misdemeanour: we are called upon to continue a practice without example in any other country and are required by lawyers to consider that custom as humane which every one who is not a lawyer pronounces to be most cruel and unjust—and which has not been brought forward to general notice, only because its bad effects are confined to the last and lowest of mankind.*

* All this nonsense is now put an end to. Counsel is allowed to the prisoner and they are permitted to speak in his defence.

LETTERS

ON

THE SUBJECT

OF

THE CATHOLICS

TO

MY BROTHER ABRAHAM

WHO

LIVES IN THE COUNTRY

BY PETER PLYMLEY

[1807–1808]

[The *Letters of Peter Plymley*, here reprinted in full, began to appear singly, towards the end of 1807. In March of that year Lord Grenville's 'ministry of all the talents' had resigned, rather than submit to George the Third's demand that they should explicitly pledge themselves not in any circumstances to introduce measures for the relief of Roman Catholics or even offer him advice on the subject. This piece of royal insolence was his answer to their mild proposal that Catholics should be allowed to serve as officers in the army. There followed the 'No Popery' election and the return of a large majority pledged to injustice on this question. The most numerous personal allusions in the letters are to Spencer Perceval, Chancellor of the Exchequer, and George Canning, Foreign Secretary. They are mentioned either by name, or obliquely, in terms of their activities. Thus it is necessary for a reader to know that Perceval had a villa at Hampstead, held the sinecure office of Surveyor of the Meltings and Clerk of the Irons, nearly became Chancellor of the Duchy of Lancaster, and secured the passing of the Jesuits' Bark Bill to deprive the French of quinine. He became Prime Minister in 1809 and died in 1812. Canning, whom Sydney Smith calls 'a pert London joker', was a celebrated wit, a frequent contributor to the weekly ANTI-JACOBIN, the author of *The Needy Knife-grinder*, and a cunning politician. Minor characters in the letters are Mulgrave, First Lord of the Admiralty; Lord Howick (afterwards Earl Grey), Foreign Secretary in Grenville's ministry, and a personal friend of Smith's; Lord Sidmouth (Henry Addington), savage opponent of Catholic emancipation and parliamentary reform; William Huskisson, Secretary to the Treasury, a supporter of Catholic emancipation; William Wilberforce, the anti-slavery man and leader of a nonconformist sect; Lord Hawkesbury (also referred to as Jenkinson), Secretary for War and Colonies; Sturges Bourne, Lord of the Treasury; Eldon, Lord Chancellor; Charles Ellis, friend and follower of Canning; John Letsom, Quaker doctor; 'Cardinal' Troy, Archbishop of Dublin; Thomas Killigrew, Restoration playwright; John Keogh, Irish Catholic leader; George Rose, notorious holder of state sinecures; Lord Melville (Henry Dundas), impeached in 1806, on the initiative of Samuel Whitbread, for misappropriation of public money, but found guilty only of 'negligence'; Hookham Frere, translator of Aristophanes and literary collaborator with Canning; Drs Rees and Kippis, prominent Dissenters; and some others. The nominal head of the administration, till October 1809, was the Duke of Portland, William Bentinck.]

．

I

DEAR ABRAHAM,

A WORTHIER and better man than yourself does not exist; but I have always told you, from the time of our boyhood, that you were a bit of a goose. Your parochial affairs are governed with exemplary order and regularity; you are as powerful in the vestry as Mr Perceval is in the House of Commons,—and, I must say, with much more reason; nor do I know any church where the faces and smock-frocks of the congregation are so clean, or their eyes so uniformly directed to the preacher. There is another point, upon which I will do you ample justice; and that is, that the eyes so directed towards you are wide open; for the rustic has, in general, good principles, though he cannot control his animal habits; and, however loud he may snore, his face is perpetually turned towards the fountain of orthodoxy.

Having done you this act of justice, I shall proceed, according to our ancient intimacy and familiarity, to explain to you my opinions about the Catholics, and to reply to yours.

In the first place, my sweet Abraham, the Pope is not landed— nor are there any curates sent out after him—nor has he been hid at St Albans by the Dowager Lady Spencer—nor dined privately at Holland House—nor been seen near Dropmore. If these fears exist (which I do not believe), they exist only in the mind of the Chancellor of the Exchequer; they emanate from his zeal for the Protestant interest; and, though they reflect the highest honour upon the delicate irritability of his faith, must certainly be considered as more ambiguous proofs of the sanity and vigour of his understanding. By this time, however, the best informed clergy in the neighbourhood of the metropolis are convinced that the rumour is without foundation: and, though the Pope is probably hovering about our coast in a fishing-smack, it is most likely he will fall a prey to the vigilance of our cruisers; and it is certain he has not yet polluted the Protestantism of our soil.

Exactly in the same manner, the story of the wooden gods seized at Charing Cross, by an order from the Foreign Office, turns out to be without the shadow of a foundation: instead of the angels and archangels, mentioned by the informer, nothing was discovered but a wooden image of Lord Mulgrave, going down to Chatham, as a head-piece for the Spanker gun-vessel: it was an exact resemblance of his Lordship in his military uniform; and *therefore* as little like a god as can well be imagined.

Having set your fears at rest, as to the extent of the conspiracy formed against the Protestant religion, I will now come to the argument itself.

You say these men interpret the Scriptures in an unorthodox manner; and that they eat their god.—Very likely. All this may seem very important to you, who live fourteen miles from a market-town, and, from long residence upon your living, are become a kind of holy vegetable; and, in a theological sense, it is highly important. But I want soldiers and sailors for the state; I want to make a greater use than I now can do of a poor country full of men; I want to render the military service popular among the Irish; to check the power of France; to make every possible exertion for the safety of Europe, which in twenty years time will be nothing but a mass of French slaves: and then you, and ten other such boobies as you, call out—'For God's sake, do not think of raising cavalry and infantry in Ireland! . . . They interpret the Epistle to Timothy in a different manner from what we do! . . . They eat a bit of wafer every Sunday, which they call their God!' . . . I wish to my soul they would eat you, and such reasoners as you are. What! when Turk, Jew, Heretic, Infidel, Catholic, Protestant, are all combined against this country; when men of every religious persuasion, and no religious persuasion; when the population of half the globe is up in arms against us; are we to stand examining our generals and armies as a bishop examines a candidate for holy orders? and to suffer no one to bleed for England who does not agree with you about the 2nd of Timothy? You talk about Catholics! If you and your brotherhood have been able to persuade the country into a continuation of this grossest of all absurdities, you have ten times the power which the Catholic clergy ever had in their best days. Louis XIV, when he revoked the Edict of Nantes, never thought of preventing the Protestants from fighting his battles; and gained accordingly some of his most splendid victories by the talents of his Protestant generals. No power in Europe, but yourselves, has ever thought, for these hundred years past, of asking whether a bayonet is Catholic, or Presbyterian, or Lutheran; but whether it is sharp and well-tempered. A bigot delights in public ridicule; for he begins to think he is a martyr. I can promise you the full enjoyment of this pleasure, from one extremity of Europe to the other.

I am as disgusted with the nonsense of the Roman Catholic religion as you can be: and no man who talks such nonsense shall ever tithe the product of the earth, nor meddle with the ecclesiastical establishment in any shape;—but what have I to do with the speculative nonsense of his theology, when the object is to elect the mayor of a county town, or to appoint a colonel of a marching regiment? Will a man discharge the solemn impertinences of the one office with less zeal, or shrink from the bloody boldness of the other with greater timidity, because the blockhead believes in all the Catholic nonsense of the real presence. I am sorry there should be such impious folly in the world, but I should be ten times a greater fool than he is, if I refused, in consequence of his folly, to lead him out against the enemies of the state. Your whole argument is wrong: the state has nothing whatever to do with theological errors which do not violate the common rules of morality and militate against the fair power of the ruler: it leaves all these errors to you, and to such as you. You have every tenth porker in your parish for refuting them; and take care that you are vigilant and logical in the task.

I love the Church as well as you do; but you totally mistake the nature of an establishment when you contend that it ought to be connected with the military and civil career of every individual in the state. It is quite right that there should be one clergyman to every parish interpreting the Scriptures after a particular manner, ruled by a regular hierarchy, and paid with a rich proportion of haycocks and wheatsheafs. When I have laid this foundation for a rational religion in the state—when I have placed ten thousand well-educated men in different parts of the kingdom to preach it up, and compelled everybody to pay them, whether they hear them or not—I have taken such measures as I know must always procure an immense majority in favour of the Established Church; but I can go no farther. I cannot set up a civil inquisition, and say to one, you shall not be a butcher because you are not orthodox; and prohibit another from brewing, and a third from administering the law, and a fourth from defending the country. If common justice did not prohibit me from such a conduct, common sense would. The advantage to be gained by quitting the heresy would make it shameful to abandon it; and men who had once left the Church would continue in such a state of alienation from a point of honour, and transmit that spirit to the latest posterity. This is just the effect your disqualifying laws have produced. They have fed Dr Rees, and Dr Kippis; crowded the congregation of the Old Jewry to suffocation; and enabled every sublapsarian, and super-lapsarian, and semi-pelagian clergyman, to build himself a neat brick chapel, and live with some distant resemblance to the state of a gentleman.

You say the King's coronation oath will not allow him to consent to any relaxation of the Catholic laws.—Why not relax the Catholic laws as well as the laws against Protestant dissenters? If one is contrary to his oath, the other must be so too; for the spirit of the oath is, to defend the Church establishment, which the Quaker and the Presbyterian differ from as much or more than the Catholic; and yet his Majesty has repealed the Cor-poration and Test Act in Ireland, and done more for the Catholics of both kingdoms than had been done for them since the Refor-mation. In 1778, the ministers said nothing about the royal conscience; in 1793 no conscience; in 1804 no conscience; the common feeling of humanity and justice then seem to have had their fullest influence upon the advisers of the Crown: but in 1807--a year, I suppose, eminently fruitful in moral and religious scruples (as some years are fruitful in apples, some in hops)—it is contended by the well-paid John Bowles, and by Mr Perceval (who tried to be well paid), that that is now perjury which we had hitherto called policy and benevolence! Religious liberty has never made such a stride as under the reign of his present Majesty; nor is there any instance in the annals of our history, where so many infamous and damnable laws have been repealed, as those against the Catholics which have been put an end to by him: and then, at the close of this useful policy, his advisers discover that the very measures of concession and indulgence, or (to use my own language) the measures of justice, which he has been pursuing through the whole of his reign, are contrary to the oath he takes at its commencement! That oath binds his Majesty not to consent to any measure contrary to the interest of the Established Church: but who is to judge of the tendency of each particular measure? Not the King alone: it can never be the intention of this law that the King, who listens to the advice of his Parliament upon a road bill, should reject it upon the most important of all measures. Whatever be his own private judgment of the tendency of any ecclesiastical bill, he complies most strictly with his oath, if he is guided in that particular point by the advice of his Parliament, who may be presumed to understand its tendency better than the King, or any other individual. You say, if Parliament had been unanimous in their opinion of the absolute necessity for Lord Howick's bill, and the King had thought it pernicious, he would have been perjured if he had not rejected it. I say, on the contrary, his Majesty would have acted in the most conscientious manner, and have complied most scrupulously with his oath, if he had sacrificed his own opinion to the opinion of the great council of the nation; because the probability was that such opinion was better than his own; and upon the same principle, in common life, you give up your opinion to your physician, your lawyer, and your builder.

You admit this bill did not compel the King to elect Catholic officers, but only gave him the option of doing so if he pleased; but you add, that the King was right in not trusting such dangerous power to himself or his successors. Now, you are either to suppose that the King for the time being has a zeal for the Catholic establishment, or that he has not. If he has not, where is the danger of giving such an option? If you suppose that he may be influenced by such an admiration of the Catholic religion, why did his present Majesty, in the year 1804, consent to that bill which empowered the Crown to station ten thousand Catholic soldiers in any part of the kingdom, and placed them absolutely at the disposal of the Crown? If the King of England for the time being is a good Protestant, there can be no danger in making the Catholic *eligible* to anything: if he is not, no power can possibly be so dangerous as that conveyed by the bill last quoted; to which, in point of peril, Lord Howick's bill is a mere joke. But the real fact is, one bill opened a door to his Majesty's advisers for trick, jobbing, and intrigue; the other did not.

Besides, what folly to talk to me of an oath, which, under all possible circumstances, is to prevent the relaxation of the Catholic laws! for such a solemn appeal to God sets all conditions and contingencies at defiance. Suppose Bonaparte was to retrieve the only very great blunder he has made, and were to succeed, after repeated trials, in making an impression upon Ireland, do you think we should hear any thing of the impediment of a coronation oath? or would the spirit of this country tolerate for an hour such ministers, and such unheard-of nonsense, if the most distant prospect existed of conciliating the Catholics by every species even of the most abject concession? And yet, if your argument is good for any thing, the coronation oath ought to reject, at such a moment, every tendency to conciliation, and to bind Ireland for ever to the crown of France.

I found in your letter the usual remarks about fire, faggot, and bloody Mary. Are you aware, my dear Priest, that there were as many persons put to death for religious opinions under the mild Elizabeth as under the bloody Mary. The reign of the former was, to be sure, ten times as long; but I only mention the fact, merely to show you that something depends upon the age in which men live, as well as on their religious opinions. Three hundred years ago, men burnt and hanged each other for these opinions. Time has softened Catholic as well as Protestant: they both required it; though each perceives only his own improvement, and is blind to that of the other. We are all the creatures of circumstances. I know not a kinder and better man than yourself; but you (if you had lived in those times) would certainly have roasted your Catholic: and I promise you, if the first exciter of this religious mob had been as powerful then as he is now, you would soon have been elevated to the mitre. I do not go the length of saying that the world has suffered as much from Protestant as from Catholic persecution; far from it: but you should remember the Catholics had all the power, when the idea first started up in the world that there could be two modes of faith; and that it was much more natural they should attempt to crush this diversity of opinion by great and cruel efforts, than that the Protestants should rage against those who differed from them, when the very basis of their system was complete freedom in all spiritual matters.

I cannot extend my letter any further at present, but you shall soon hear from me again. You tell me I am a party man. I hope I shall always be so, when I see my country in the hands of a pert London joker and a second-rate lawyer. Of the first, no other good is known than that he makes pretty Latin verses; the second seems to me to have the head of a country parson and the tongue of an Old Bailey lawyer.

If I could see good measures pursued, I care not a farthing who is in power; but I have a passionate love for common justice, and for common sense, and I abhor and despise every man who builds up his political fortune upon their ruin.

God bless you, reverend Abraham, and defend you from the Pope, and all of us from that administration who seek power by opposing a measure which Burke, Pitt, and Fox all considered as absolutely necessary to the existence of the country.

II

DEAR ABRAHAM,

THE Catholic not respect an oath! why not? What upon earth has kept him out of Parliament, or excluded him from all the offices whence he is excluded, but his respect for oaths? There is no law which prohibits a Catholic to sit in Parliament. There could be no such law; because it is impossible to find out what passes in the interior of any man's mind. Suppose it were in contemplation to exclude all men from certain offices who contended for the legality of taking tithes: the only mode of discovering that fervid love of decimation which I know you to possess would be to tender you an oath 'against that damnable doctrine, that it is lawful for a spiritual man to take, abstract, appropriate, subduct, or lead away the tenth calf, sheep, lamb, ox, pigeon, duck, &c. &c. &c.', and every other animal that ever existed, which of course the lawyers would take care to enumerate. Now this oath I am sure you would rather die than take; and so the Catholic is excluded from Parliament because he will not swear that he disbelieves the leading doctrines of his religion!

The Catholic asks you to abolish some oaths which oppress him; your answer is, that he does not respect oaths. Then why subject him to the test of oaths? The oaths keep him out of Parliament; why then, he respects them. Turn which way you will, either your laws are nugatory, or the Catholic is bound by religious obligations as you are: but no eel in the well-sanded fist of a cook-maid, upon the eve of being skinned, ever twisted and writhed as an orthodox parson does when he is compelled by the gripe of reason to admit anything in favour of a Dissenter.

I will not dispute with you whether the Pope be or be not the Scarlet Lady of Babylon. I hope it is not so; because I am afraid it will induce his Majesty's Chancellor of the Exchequer to introduce several severe bills against popery, if that is the case; and though he will have the decency to appoint a previous committee of inquiry as to the fact, the committee will be garbled and the report inflammatory. Leaving this to be settled as he pleases to settle it, I wish to inform you, that, previously to the bill last passed in favour of the Catholics, at the suggestion of Mr Pitt, and for his satisfaction, the opinions of six of the most celebrated of the foreign Catholic universities were taken as to the right of the Pope to interfere in the temporal concerns of any country. The answer cannot possibly leave the shadow of a doubt, even in the mind of Baron Maseres; and Dr Rennel would be compelled to admit it, if three Bishops lay dead at the very moment the question were put to him. To this answer might be added also the solemn declaration and signature of all the Catholics in Great Britain.

I should perfectly agree with you, if the Catholics admitted such a dangerous dispensing power in the hands of the Pope; but they all deny it, and laugh at it, and are ready to abjure it in the most decided manner you can devise. They obey the Pope as the spiritual head of their church; but are you really so foolish as to be imposed upon by mere names? What matters it the seven thousandth part of a farthing who is the spiritual head of any church? Is not Mr Wilberforce at the head of the church of Clapham? Is not Dr Letsom at the head of the Quaker church? Is not the General Assembly at the head of the church of Scotland? How is the government disturbed by these many-headed churches? or in what way is the power of the Crown augmented by this almost nominal dignity?

The King appoints a fast-day once a year, and he makes the Bishops: and if the government would take half the pains to keep the Catholics out of the arms of France that it does to widen Temple Bar, or improve Snow Hill, the King would get into his hands the appointments of the titular Bishops of Ireland. Both Mr C[anning]'s sisters enjoy pensions more than sufficient to place the two greatest dignitaries of the Irish Catholic Church entirely at the disposal of the Crown. Everybody who knows Ireland knows perfectly well that nothing would be easier, with the expenditure of a little money, than to preserve enough of the ostensible appointment in the hands of the Pope to satisfy the scruples of the Catholics, while the real nomination remained with the Crown. But, as I have before said, the moment the very name of Ireland is mentioned, the English seem to bid adieu to common feeling, common prudence, and to common sense, and to act with the barbarity of tyrants and the fatuity of idiots.

Whatever your opinion may be of the follies of the Roman Catholic religion, remember they are the follies of four millions of human beings, increasing rapidly in numbers, wealth, and intelligence, who, if firmly united with this country, would set at defiance the power of France, and if once wrested from their alliance with England, would in three years render its existence as an independent nation absolutely impossible. You speak of danger to the Establishment: I request to know when the Establishment was ever so much in danger as when Hoche was in Bantry Bay, and whether all the books of Bossuet, or the arts of the Jesuits, were half so terrible? Mr Perceval and his parsons forgot all this, in their horror lest twelve or fourteen old women may be converted to holy water and Catholic nonsense. They never see that, while they are saving these venerable ladies from perdition, Ireland may be lost, England broken down, and the Protestant Church, with all its deans, prebendaries, Percevals and Rennels, be swept into the vortex of oblivion.

Do not, I beseech you, ever mention to me again the name of Dr Duigenan. I have been in every corner of Ireland, and have studied its present strength and condition with no common labour. Be assured Ireland does not contain at this moment less than five millions of people. There were returned in the year 1791 to the hearth tax 701,000 houses, and there is no kind of question that there were about 50,000 houses omitted in that return. Taking, however, only the number returned for the tax, and allowing the average of six to a house (a very small average for a potato-fed people), this brings the population to 4,200,000 people in the year 1791: and it can be shown from the clearest evidence (and Mr Newenham in his book shows it), that Ireland for the last fifty years has increased in its population at the rate of 50 or 60,000 per annum; which leaves the present population of Ireland at about five millions, after every possible deduction for *existing circumstances, just and necessary wars, monstrous and unnatural rebellions,* and all other sources of human destruction. Of this population, two out of ten are Protestants; and the half of the Protestant population are Dissenters, and as inimical to the Church as the Catholics themselves. In this state of things, thumbscrews and whipping—admirable engines of policy as they must be considered to be—will not ultimately avail. The Catholics will hang over you; they will watch for the moment; and compel you hereafter to give them ten times as much, against your will, as they would now be contented with if it was voluntarily surrendered. Remember what happened in the American war: when Ireland compelled you to give her everything she asked, and to renounce, in the most explicit manner, your claim of sovereignty over her. God Almighty grant the folly of these present men may not bring on such another crisis of public affairs.

What are your dangers which threaten the Establishment? Reduce this declamation to a point, and let us understand what you mean. The most ample allowance does not calculate that there would be more than twenty members who were Roman Catholics in one house, and ten in the other, if the Catholic emancipation were carried into effect. Do you mean that these thirty members would bring in a bill to take away the tithes from the Protestant and to pay them to the Catholic clergy? Do you mean that a Catholic general would march his army into the House of Commons and purge it of Mr Perceval and Mr Duigenan? or that the theological writers would become all of a sudden more acute and more learned if the present civil incapacities were removed? Do you fear for your tithes, or your doctrines, or your person, or the English Constitution? Every fear, taken separately, is so glaringly absurd, that no man has the folly or the boldness to state it. Every one conceals his ignorance, or his baseness, in a stupid general panic, which, when called on, he is utterly incapable of explaining. Whatever you think of the Catholics, there they are—you cannot get rid of them; your alternative is, to give them a lawful place for stating their grievances, or an unlawful one: if you do not admit them to the House of Commons, they will hold their parliament in Potato-place, Dublin, and be ten times as violent and inflammatory as they would be in Westminster. Nothing would give me such an idea of security as to see twenty or thirty Catholic gentlemen in Parliament, looked upon by all the Catholics as the fair and proper organ of their party. I should have thought it the height of good fortune that such a wish existed on their part, and the very essence of madness and ignorance to reject it. Can you murder the Catholics? Can you neglect them? They are too numerous for both these expedients. What remains to be done is obvious to every human being—but to that man who, instead of being a Methodist preacher, is, for the curse of us and our children, and for the ruin of Troy, and the misery of good old Priam and his sons, become a legislator and a politician.

A distinction, I perceive, is taken, by one of the most feeble nobleman in Great Britain, between persecution and the deprivation of political power; whereas there is no more distinction between these two things than there is between him who makes the distinction and a booby. If I strip off the relic-covered jacket of a Catholic and give him twenty stripes, I persecute. If I say, everybody in the town where you live shall be a candidate for lucrative and honourable offices but you, who are a Catholic, I do not persecute!—What barbarous nonsense is this! as if degradation was not as great an evil as bodily pain or as severe poverty: as if I could not be as great a tyrant by saying, You shall not enjoy—as by saying, You shall suffer. The English, I believe, are as truly religious as any nation in Europe; I know no greater blessing: but it carries with it this evil in its train, that any villain who will bawl out 'The Church is in danger!' may get a place, and a good pension; and that any administration who will do the same thing may bring a set of men into power who, at a moment of stationary and passive piety, would be hooted by the very boys in the streets. But it is not all religion; it is, in great part, that narrow and exclusive spirit which delights to keep the common blessings of sun, and air, and freedom, from other human beings. 'Your religion has always been degraded;

N

you are in the dust, and I will take care you never rise again. I should enjoy less the possession of an earthly good, by every additional person to whom it was extended.' You may not be aware of it yourself, most reverend Abraham, but you deny their freedom to the Catholics upon the same principle that Sarah your wife refuses to give the receipt for a ham or a gooseberry dumpling: she values her receipts, not because they secure to her a certain flavour, but because they remind her that her neighbours want it:—a feeling laughable in a priestess, shameful in a priest; venial when it withholds the blessings of a ham, tyrannical and execrable when it narrows the boon of religious freedom.

You spend a great deal of ink about the character of the present prime minister. Grant you all that you write; I say, I fear he will ruin Ireland, and pursue a line of policy destructive to the true interest of his country: and then you tell me, he is faithful to Mrs Perceval and kind to the Master Percevals! These are, undoubtedly, the first qualifications to be looked to in a time of the most serious public danger; but somehow or another (if public and private virtues must always be incompatible), I should prefer that he destroyed the domestic happiness of Wood or Cockell, owed for the veal of the preceding year, whipped his boys, and saved his country.

The late administration did not do right; they did not build their measures upon the solid basis of facts. They should have caused several Catholics to have been dissected after death by surgeons of either religion; and the report to have been published with accompanying plates. If the viscera, and other organs of life, had been found to be the same as in Protestant bodies; if the provisions of nerves, arteries, cerebrum, and cerebellum, had been the same as we are provided with, or as the Dissenters are now known to possess; then, indeed, they might have met Mr Perceval upon a proud eminence, and convinced the country at large of the strong probability that the Catholics are really human creatures, endowed with the feelings of men and entitled to all their rights. But instead of this wise and prudent measure, Lord Howick, with his usual precipitation, brings forward a bill in their favour, without offering the slightest proof to the country that they were anything more than horses and oxen. The person who shows the lama at the corner of Piccadilly has the precaution

to write up—*Allowed by Sir Joseph Banks to be a real quadruped:*
so his Lordship might have said—*Allowed by the Bench of Bishops
to be real human creatures.* . . . I could write you twenty letters upon
this subject: but I am tired, and so I suppose are you. Our
friendship is now of forty years' standing; you know me to be
a truly religious man; but I shudder to see religion treated like
a cockade, or a pint of beer, and made the instrument of a party.
I love the King, but I love the people as well as the King; and
if I am sorry to see his old age molested, I am much more sorry
to see four millions of Catholics baffled in their just expectations.
If I love Lord Grenville, and Lord Howick, it is because they
love their country: if I abhor ******, it is because I know there
is but one man among them who is not laughing at the enormous
folly and credulity of the country, and that he is an ignorant
and mischievous bigot. As for the light and frivolous jester of
whom it is your misfortune to think so highly, learn, my dear
Abraham, that this political Killigrew, just before the breaking-up
of the last administration, was in actual treaty with them for
a place; and if they had survived twenty-four hours longer, he
would have been now declaiming against the cry of No Popery
instead of inflaming it.—With this practical comment on the
baseness of human nature, I bid you adieu.

III

ALL that I have so often told you, Mr Abraham Plymley, is
now come to pass. The Scythians, in whom you and the neighbouring country gentlemen placed such confidence, are smitten
hip and thigh; their Benningsen put to open shame; their
magazines of train oil intercepted, and we are waking from our
disgraceful drunkenness to all the horrors of Mr Perceval and
Mr Canning.—We shall now see if a nation is to be saved by
schoolboy jokes and doggerel rhymes, by affronting petulance,
and by the tones and gesticulations of Mr Pitt. But these are
not all the auxiliaries on which we have to depend; to these his
colleague will add the strictest attention to the smaller parts of
ecclesiastical government, to hassocks, to psalters, and to sur-
plices; in the last agonies of England, he will bring in a bill to
regulate Easter-offerings; and he will adjust the stipends of

curates*, when the flag of France is unfurled on the hills of Kent. Whatever can be done by very mistaken notions of the piety of a Christian, and by very wretched imitation of the eloquence of Mr Pitt, will be done by these two gentlemen. After all, if they both really were what they both either wished to be or wish to be thought; if the one were an enlightened Christian, who drew from the Gospel the toleration, the charity, and the sweetness which it contains; and if the other really possessed any portion of the great understanding of his Nisus who guarded him from the weapons of the Whigs, I should still doubt if they could save us. But I am sure we are not to be saved by religious hatred, and by religious trifling; by any psalmody, however sweet; or by any persecution, however sharp: I am certain the sounds of Mr Pitt's voice, and the measure of his tones, and the movement of his arms, will do nothing for us; when these tones and movements and voice bring us always declamation without sense or knowledge, and ridicule without good humour or conciliation. Oh, Mr Plymley, Mr Plymley, this never will do. Mrs Abraham Plymley, my sister, will be led away captive by an amorous Gaul; and Joel Plymley, your first-born, will be a French drummer.

Out of sight out of mind seems to be a proverb which applies to enemies as well as friends. Because the French army was no longer seen from the cliffs of Dover; because the sound of cannon was no longer heard by the debauched London bathers on the Sussex coast; because the *Morning Post* no longer fixed the invasion sometimes for Monday, sometimes for Tuesday, some-times (positively for the last time of invading) on Saturday; because all these causes of terror were suspended, you conceived the power of Bonaparte to be at an end, and were setting off for Paris, with Lord Hawkesbury the conqueror.—This is pre-cisely the method in which the English have acted during the whole of the revolutionary war. If Austria or Prussia armed, doctors of divinity immediately printed those passages out of Habakkuk in which the destruction of the Usurper by General Mack and the Duke of Brunswick is so clearly predicted. If Bonaparte halted, there was a mutiny, or a dysentery. If any one of his generals were eaten up by the light troops of Russia, and

---

* The Reverend the Chancellor of the Exchequer has, since this was written, found time in the heat of the session to write a book on the Stipends of Curates.

picked (as their manner is) to the bone, the sanguine spirit of this country displayed itself in all its glory. What scenes of infamy did the Society for the Suppression of Vice lay open to our astonished eyes: tradesmen's daughters dancing, pots of beer carried out between the first and second lesson; and dark and distant rumours of indecent prints. Clouds of Mr Canning's cousins arrived by the waggon; all the contractors left their cards with Mr Rose; and every plunderer of the public crawled out of his hole, like slugs, and grubs, and worms, after a shower of rain.

If my voice could have been heard at the late changes, I should have said, 'Gently; patience; stop a little; the time is not yet come; the mud of Poland will harden, and the bowels of the French grenadiers will recover their tone. When honest good sense and liberality have extricated you out of your present embarrassment, then dismiss them as a matter of course; but you cannot spare them just now; don't be in too great a hurry, or there will be no monarch to flatter, and no country to pillage; only submit for a little time to be respected abroad; overlook the painful absence of the tax-gatherer for a few years; bear up nobly under the increase of freedom and of liberal policy for a little time, and I promise you, at the expiration of that period, you shall be plundered, insulted, disgraced, and restrained to your heart's content. Do not imagine I have any intention of putting servility and canting hypocrisy permanently out of place, or of filling up with courage and sense those offices which naturally devolve upon decorous imbecility and flexible cunning: give us only a little time to keep off the hussars of France, and then the jobbers and jesters shall return to their birthright, and public virtue be called by its own name of fanaticism.'* Such is the advice I would have offered to my infatuated countrymen; but it rained very hard in November, Brother Abraham, and the bowels of our enemies were loosened, and we put our trust in white fluxes and wet mud; and there is nothing now to oppose

---

* This is Mr Canning's term for the detection of public abuses; a term invented by him, and adopted by that simious parasite who is always grinning at his heels. Nature descends down to infinite smallness. Mr Canning has his parasites; and if you take a large buzzing bluebottle fly and look at it in a microscope, you may see twenty or thirty little ugly insects crawling about it, which doubtless think their fly to be the bluest, grandest, merriest, most important animal in the universe, and are convinced the world would be at an end if it ceased to buzz.

to the conqueror of the world but a small table wit and the sallow Surveyor of the Meltings.

You ask me, if I think it possible for this country to survive the recent misfortunes of Europe?—I answer you, without the slightest degree of hesitation: that if Bonaparte lives, and a great deal is not immediately done for the conciliation of the Catholics, it does seem to me absolutely impossible but that we must perish; and take this with you, that we shall perish without exciting the slightest feeling of present or future compassion, but fall amidst the hootings and revilings of Europe, as a nation of blockheads, Methodists, and old women. If there were any great scenery, and heroic feelings, any blaze of ancient virtue, any exalted death, any termination of England that would be ever remembered, ever honoured in that western world where liberty is now retiring, conquest would be more tolerable and ruin more sweet; but it is doubly miserable to become slaves abroad because we would be tyrants at home; to persecute when we are contending against persecution; and to perish because we have raised up worse enemies within, from our own bigotry, than we are exposed to without from the unprincipled ambition of France. It is, indeed, a most silly and afflicting spectacle to rage at such a moment against our own kindred and our own blood; to tell them they cannot be honourable in war because they are conscientious in religion; to stipulate (at the very moment when we should buy their hearts and swords at any price) that they must hold up the right hand in prayer, and not the left; and adore one common God by turning to the east rather than to the west.

What is it the Catholics ask of you? Do not exclude us from the honours and emoluments of the state because we worship God in one way and you worship him in another. In a period of the deepest peace and the fattest prosperity this would be a fair request; it should be granted if Lord Hawkesbury had reached Paris, if Mr Canning's interpreter had threatened the Senate in an opening speech, or Mr Perceval explained to them the improvements he meant to introduce into the Catholic religion; but to deny the Irish this justice now, in the present state of Europe, and in the summer months, just as the season for destroying kingdoms is coming on, is (beloved Abraham), whatever you may think of it, little short of positive insanity.

Here is a frigate attacked by a corsair of immense strength and
size, rigging cut, masts in danger of coming by the board, four
foot water in the hold, men dropping off very fast; in this dreadful
situation how do you think the Captain acts (whose name shall
be Perceval)? He calls all hands upon deck; talks to them of
King, country, glory, sweethearts, gin, French prison, wooden
shoes, Old England, and hearts of oak: they give three cheers,
rush to their guns, and, after a tremendous conflict, succeed in
beating off the enemy. Not a syllable of all this: this is not the
manner in which the honourable Commander goes to work: the
first thing he does is to secure 20 or 30 of his prime sailors who
happen to be Catholics, to clap them in irons, and set over them
a guard of as many Protestants; having taken this admirable
method of defending himself against his infidel opponents, he
goes upon deck, reminds the sailors, in a very bitter harangue,
that they are of different religions; exhorts the Episcopal gunner
not to trust to the Presbyterian quartermaster; issues positive
orders that the Catholics should be fired at upon the first
appearance of discontent; rushes through blood and brains,
examining his men in the Catechism and 39 Articles, and positively forbids every one to sponge or ram who has not taken
the Sacrament according to the Church of England. Was it right
to take out a captain made of excellent British stuff, and to put
in such a man as this? Is not he more like a parson, or a talking
lawyer, than a thoroughbred seaman? And built as she is of
heart of oak, and admirably manned, is it possible with such
a captain to save this ship from going to the bottom?

You have an argument, I perceive, in common with many
others, against the Catholics, that their demands complied with
would only lead to farther exactions, and that it is better to resist
them now, before any thing is conceded, than hereafter, when
it is found that all concessions are in vain. I wish the Chancellor
of the Exchequer, who uses this reasoning to exclude others from
their just rights, had tried its efficacy, not by his understanding,
but by (what are full of much better things) his pockets. Suppose
the person to whom he applied for the Meltings had withstood
every plea of wife and fourteen children, no business, and good
character, and refused him this paltry little office, because he
might hereafter attempt to get hold of the revenues of the Duchy
of Lancaster for life; would not Mr Perceval have contended

eagerly against the injustice of refusing moderate requests because immoderate ones may hereafter be made? Would he not have said (and said truly), Leave such exorbitant attempts as these to the general indignation of the Commons, who will take care to defeat them when they do occur; but do not refuse me the Irons and the Meltings, now, because I may totally lose sight of all moderation hereafter. Leave hereafter to the spirit and the wisdom of hereafter; and do not be niggardly now, from the apprehension that men as wise as you should be profuse in times to come.

You forget, Brother Abraham, that it is a vast art (where quarrels cannot be avoided) to turn the public opinion in your favour and to the prejudice of your enemy; a vast privilege to feel that you are in the right, and to make him feel that he is in the wrong: a privilege which makes you more than a man, and your antagonist less; and often secures victory, by convincing him who contends, that he must submit to injustice if he submits to defeat. Open every rank in the army and the navy to the Catholic; let him purchase at the same price as the Protestant (if either Catholic or Protestant can purchase such refined pleasures) the privilege of hearing Lord Castlereagh speak for three hours; keep his clergy from starving, soften some of the most odious powers of the tything-man, and you will for ever lay this formidable question to rest. But if I am wrong, and you must quarrel at last, quarrel upon just rather than unjust grounds; divide the Catholic and unite the Protestant; be just, and your own exertions will be more formidable and their exertions less formidable; be just, and you will take away from their party all the best and wisest understandings of both persuasions, and knit them firmly to your own cause. 'Thrice is he armed who has his quarrel just'; and ten times as much may he be taxed. In the beginning of any war, however destitute of common sense, every mob will roar and every Lord of the Bedchamber address; but if you are engaged in a war that is to last for years and to require important sacrifices, take care to make the justice of your case so clear and so obvious that it cannot be mistaken by the most illiterate country gentleman who rides the earth. Nothing, in fact, can be so grossly absurd as the argument which says, I will deny justice to you now because I suspect future injustice from you. At this rate you may lock a man up in your stable, and refuse to let him out, because you suspect that he has an intention, at some future period, of robbing your hen-roost. You may horsewhip him at Lady-day because you believe he will affront you at Midsummer. You may commit a greater evil, to guard against a less which is merely contingent and may never happen. You may do what you have done a century ago in Ireland, made the Catholics worse than Helots, because you suspected that they might hereafter aspire to be more than fellow citizens; rendering their sufferings certain from your jealousy, while yours were only doubtful from their ambition; an ambition sure to be excited by the very measures which were taken to prevent it.

The physical strength of the Catholics will not be greater because you give them a share of political power. You may by these means turn rebels into friends; but I do not see how you make rebels more formidable. If they taste of the honey of lawful power, they will love the hive from whence they procure it; if they will struggle with us like men in the same state for civil influence, we are safe. All that I dread is, the physical strength of four millions of men combined with an invading French army. If you are to quarrel at last with this enormous population, still put it off as long as you can; you must gain, and cannot lose, by the delay. The state of Europe cannot be worse; the conviction which the Catholics entertain of your tyranny and injustice cannot be more alarming, nor the opinions of your own people more divided. Time, which produces such effect upon brass and marble, may inspire one Minister with modesty, and another with compassion; every circumstance may be better; some certainly will be so, none can be worse; and after all, the evil may never happen.

You have got hold, I perceive, of all the vulgar English stories respecting the hereditary transmission of forfeited property, and seriously believe that every Catholic beggar wears the terriers of his father's land next his skin, and is only waiting for better times to cut the throat of the Protestant possessor and get drunk in the hall of his ancestors. There is one irresistible answer to this mistake, and that is, that the forfeited lands are purchased indiscriminately by Catholic and Protestant, and that the Catholic purchaser never objects to such a title. Now the land (so purchased by a Catholic) is either his own family estate, or it is not. If it is, you suppose him so desirous of coming into possession that he resorts to the double method of rebellion and purchase; if it is not his own family estate of which he becomes the purchaser, you suppose him first to purchase, then to rebel, in order to defeat the purchase. These things may happen in Ireland; but it is totally impossible they can happen anywhere else. In fact, what land can any man of any sect purchase in Ireland but forfeited property? In all other oppressed countries which I have ever heard of, the rapacity of the conqueror was bounded by the territorial limits in which the objects of his avarice were contained; but Ireland has been actually confiscated twice over, as a cat is twice killed by a wicked parish-boy.

I admit there is a vast luxury in selecting a particular set of Christians, and in worrying them as a boy worries a puppy dog; it is an amusement in which all the young English are brought up from their earliest days. I like the idea of saying to men who use a different hassock from me, that till they change their hassock they shall never be Colonels, Aldermen, or Parliament-men. While I am gratifying my personal insolence respecting religious forms, I fondle myself into an idea that I am religious and that I am doing my duty in the most exemplary (as I certainly am in the most easy) way. But then, my good Abraham, this sport, admirable as it is, is become, with respect to the Catholics, a little dangerous; and if we are not extremely careful in taking the amusement, we shall tumble into the holy water and be drowned. As it seems necessary to your idea of an established Church to have somebody to worry and torment, suppose we were to select for this purpose William Wilberforce, Esq., and the patent Christians of Clapham. We shall by this expedient enjoy the same opportunity for cruelty and injustice, without being exposed to the same risks: we will compel them to abjure vital clergymen by a public test, to deny that the said William Wilberforce has any power of working miracles, touching for barrenness or any other infirmity, or that he is endowed with any preternatural gift whatever. We will swear them to the doctrine of good works, compel them to preach common sense, and to hear it; to frequent Bishops, Deans, and other high Churchmen; and to appear (once in the quarter at the least) at some melodrame, opera, pantomime, or other light scenical representation; in short, we will gratify the love of insolence and power: we will enjoy the old orthodox sport of witnessing

the impotent anger of men compelled to submit to civil degradation, or to sacrifice their notions of truth to ours. And all this
we may do without the slightest risk, because their numbers are
(as yet) not very considerable. Cruelty and injustice must, of
course, exist: but why connect them with danger? Why torture
a bull-dog, when you can get a frog or a rabbit? I am sure my
proposal will meet with the most universal approbation. Do not
be apprehensive of any opposition from ministers. If it is a case
of hatred, we are sure that one man will defend it by the Gospel:
if it abridges human freedom, we know that another will find
precedent for it in the Revolution.

In the name of Heaven, what are we to gain by suffering
Ireland to be rode by that faction which now predominates over
it? Why are we to endanger our own Church and State, not
for 500,000 Episcopalians, but for ten or twelve great Orange
families, who have been sucking the blood of that country for
these hundred years last past? and the folly of the Orangemen
in playing this game themselves is almost as absurd as ours in
playing it for them. They ought to have the sense to see that
their business now is to keep quietly the lands and beeves of
which the fathers of the Catholics were robbed in days of yore;
they must give to their descendants the sop of political power:
by contending with them for names, they will lose realities, and
be compelled to beg their potatoes in a foreign land, abhorred
equally by the English, who have witnessed their oppression, and
by the Catholic Irish, who have smarted under them.

IV

THEN comes Mr Isaac Hawkins Brown (the gentleman who
danced* so badly at the Court of Naples), and asks, if it is not
an anomaly to educate men in another religion than your own?

* In the third year of his present Majesty, and in the 30th of his own
age, Mr Isaac Hawkins Brown, then upon his travels, danced one evening
at the Court of Naples. His dress was a volcano silk with lava buttons. Whether
(as the Neapolitan wits said) he had studied dancing under St Vitus, or
whether David, dancing in a linen vest, was his model, is not known; but
Mr Brown danced with such inconceivable alacrity and vigour, that he threw
the Queen of Naples into convulsions of laughter, which terminated in a
miscarriage, and changed the dynasty of the Neapolitan throne.

It certainly is our duty to get rid of error, and above all of religious error; but this is not to be done *per saltum,* or the measure will miscarry, like the Queen. It may be very easy to dance away the royal embryo of a great kingdom; but Mr Hawkins Brown must look before he leaps, when his object is to crush an opposite sect in religion; false steps aid the one effect as much as they are fatal to the other: it will require not only the lapse of Mr Hawkins Brown, but the lapse of centuries, before the absurdities of the Catholic religion are laughed at as much as they deserve to be; but surely, in the mean time, the Catholic religion is better than none; four millions of Catholics are better than four millions of wild beasts; two hundred priests educated by our own government are better than the same number educated by the man who means to destroy us.

The whole sum now appropriated by Government to the religious education of four millions of Christians is £13,000; a sum about one hundred times as large being appropriated in the same country to about one eighth part of this number of Protestants. When it was proposed to raise this grant from £8,000 to £13,000, its present amount, this sum was objected to by that most indulgent of Christians, Mr Spencer Perceval, as enormous; he himself having secured for his own eating and drinking, and the eating and drinking of the Master and Miss Percevals, the reversionary sum of £21,000 a year of the public money, and having just failed in a desperate and rapacious attempt to secure to himself for life the revenues of the Duchy of Lancaster: and the best of it is, that this Minister, after abusing his predecessors for their impious bounty to the Catholics, has found himself compelled, from the apprehension of immediate danger, to grant the sum in question; thus dissolving his pearl in vinegar, and destroying all the value of the gift by the virulence and reluctance with which it was granted.

I hear from some persons in Parliament, and from others in the sixpenny societies for debate, a great deal about unalterable laws passed at the Revolution. When I hear any man talk of an unalterable law, the only effect it produces upon me is to convince me that he is an unalterable fool. A law passed when there was Germany, Spain, Russia, Sweden, Holland, Portugal, and Turkey; when there was a disputed succession; when four or five hundred acres were won and lost after ten years' hard fighting; when armies were commanded by the sons of kings, and campaigns passed in an interchange of civil letters and ripe fruit; and for these laws, when the whole state of the world is completely changed, we are now, according to my Lord Hawkesbury, to hold ourselves ready to perish. It is no mean misfortune, in times like these, to be forced to say anything about such men as Lord Hawkesbury, and to be reminded that we are governed by them; but, as I am driven to it, I must take the liberty of observing that the wisdom and liberality of my Lord Hawkesbury are of that complexion which always shrinks from the present exercise of these virtues, by praising the splendid examples of them in ages past. If he had lived at such periods, he would have opposed the Revolution by praising the Reformation, and the Reformation by speaking handsomely of the Crusades. He gratifies his natural antipathy to great and courageous measures by playing off the wisdom and courage which have ceased to influence human affairs against that wisdom and courage which living men would employ for present happiness. Besides, it happens unfortunately for the Warden of the Cinque Ports, that to the principal incapacities under which the Irish suffer, they were subjected after that great and glorious Revolution, to which we are indebted for so many blessings and his Lordship for the termination of so many periods. The Catholics were not excluded from the Irish House of Commons, or military commands, before the 3rd and 4th of William and Mary, and the 1st and 2nd of Queen Anne.

If the great mass of the people, environed as they are on every side with Jenkinsons, Percevals, Melvilles, and other perils, were to pray for divine illumination and aid, what more could Providence in its mercy do than send them the example of Scotland? For what a length of years was it attempted to compel the Scotch to change their religion: horse, foot, artillery, and armed Prebendaries, were sent out after the Presbyterian parsons and their congregations. The Percevals of those days called for blood: this call is never made in vain, and blood was shed; but, to the astonishment and horror of the Percevals of those days, they could not introduce the Book of Common Prayer, nor prevent that metaphysical people from going to heaven their true way, instead of our true way. With a little oatmeal for food, and a little sulphur for friction, allaying cutaneous irritation with the one hand, and holding his Calvinistical creed in the other, Sawney ran away to his flinty hills, sung his psalm out of tune his own way, and listened to his sermon of two hours long, amid the rough and imposing melancholy of the tallest thistles. But Sawney brought up his unbreeched offspring in a cordial hatred of his oppressors; and Scotland was as much a part of the weakness of England then, as Ireland is at this moment. The true and the only remedy was applied; the Scotch were suffered to worship God after their own tiresome manner, without pain, penalty, and privation. No lightning descended from heaven; the country was not ruined; the world is not yet come to an end; the dignitaries who foretold all these consequences are utterly forgotten, and Scotland has ever since been an increasing source of strength to Great Britain. In the six hundredth year of our empire over Ireland we are making laws to transport a man if he is found out of his house after eight o'clock at night. That this is necessary, I know too well; but tell me why it is necessary? It is not necessary in Greece, where the Turks are masters.

Are you aware, that there is at this moment an universal clamour throughout the whole of Ireland against the Union? It is now one month since I returned from that country: I have never seen so extraordinary, so alarming, and so rapid a change in the sentiments of any people. Those who disliked the Union before are quite furious against it now; those who doubted, doubt no more: those who were friendly to it have exchanged that friendship for the most rooted aversion; in the midst of all this (which is by far the most alarming symptom), there is the strongest disposition on the part of the Northern Dissenters to unite with the Catholics, irritated by the faithless injustice with which they have been treated. If this combination does take place (mark what I say to you), you will have meetings all over Ireland for the cry of *No Union*; that cry will spread like wildfire and blaze over every opposition; and if this is the case, there is no use in mincing the matter, Ireland is gone, and the death-blow of England is struck; and this event may happen *instantly* —before Mr Canning and Mr Hookham Frere have turned Lord Howick's last speech into doggerel rhyme; before '*the near and dear relations*' have received another quarter of their pension, or Mr Perceval conducted the Curates' Salary Bill safely to a third reading.—If the mind of the English people, cursed as they now are with that madness of religious dissension which has been breathed into them for the purposes of private ambition, can be alarmed by any remembrances, and warned by any events, they should never forget how nearly Ireland was lost to this country during the American war; that it was saved merely by the jealousy of the Protestant Irish towards the Catholics, then a much more insignificant and powerless body than they now are. The Catholic and the Dissenter have since combined together against you. Last war, the winds, those ancient and unsubsidized allies of England; the winds, upon which English ministers depend as much for saving kingdoms as washerwomen do for drying clothes; the winds stood your friends: the French could only get into Ireland in small numbers, and the rebels were defeated. Since then, all the remaining kingdoms of Europe have been destroyed; and the Irish see that their national independence is gone, without having received any single one of those advantages which they were taught to expect from the sacrifice. All good things were to flow from the Union; they have none of them gained anything. Every man's pride is wounded by it; no man's interest is promoted. In the seventh year of that Union, four million Catholics, lured by all kinds of promises to yield up the separate dignity and sovereignty of their country, are forced to squabble with such a man as Mr Spencer Perceval for five thousand pounds with which to educate their children in their own mode of worship; he, the same Mr Spencer, having secured to his own Protestant self a reversionary portion of the public money amounting to four times that sum. A senior Proctor of the University of Oxford, the head of a house, or the examining Chaplain to a Bishop, may believe these things can last: but every man of the world whose understanding has been exercised in the business of life must see (and see with a breaking heart) that they will soon come to a fearful termination.

Our conduct to Ireland, during the whole of this war, has been that of a man who subscribes to hospitals, weeps at charity sermons, carries out broth and blankets to beggars, and then comes home and beats his wife and children. We had compassion for the victims of all other oppression and injustice, except our own. If Switzerland was threatened, away went a Treasury Clerk with a hundred thousand pounds for Switzerland; large bags of money were kept constantly under sailing orders; upon the slightest demonstration towards Naples, down went Sir William Hamilton upon his knees, and begged for the love of St Januarius they would help us off with a little money; all the arts of Machiavel were resorted to, to persuade Europe to borrow; troops were sent off in all directions to save the Catholic and Protestant world; the Pope himself was guarded by a regiment of English dragoons; if the Grand Lama had been at hand, he would have had another; every Catholic clergyman who had the good fortune to be neither English nor Irish was immediately provided with lodging, soap, crucifix, missal, chapel-beads, relics, and holy water; if Turks had landed, Turks would have received an order from the Treasury for coffee, opium, korans, and seraglios. In the midst of all this fury of saving and defending, this crusade for conscience and Christianity, there was an universal agreement among all descriptions of people to continue every species of internal persecution; to deny at home every just right that had been denied before; to pummel poor Dr Abraham Rees and his Dissenters; and to treat the unhappy Catholics of Ireland as if their tongues were mute, their heels cloven, their nature brutal, and designedly subjected by Providence to their Orange masters.

How would my admirable brother, the Rev. Abraham Plymley, like to be marched to a Catholic chapel, to be sprinkled with the sanctified contents of a pump, to hear a number of false quantities in the Latin tongue, and to see a number of persons occupied in making right angles upon the breast and forehead? And if all this would give you so much pain, what right have you to march Catholic soldiers to a place of worship, where there is no aspersion, no rectangular gestures, and where they understand every word they hear, having first, in order to get him to enlist, made a solemn promise to the contrary? Can you wonder, after this, that the Catholic priest stops the recruiting in Ireland, as he is now doing to a most alarming degree?

The late question concerning military rank did not individually affect the lowest persons of the Catholic persuasion; but do you imagine they do not sympathize with the honour and disgrace of their superiors? Do you think that satisfaction and dissatisfaction do not travel down from Lord Fingal to the most potatoless Catholic in Ireland, and that the glory or shame of the sect is not felt by many more than these conditions personally and corporeally affect? Do you suppose that the detection of Sir H. M. and the disappointment of Mr Perceval *in the matter* of the Duchy of Lancaster did not affect every dabbler in public property? Depend upon it, these things were felt through all the gradations of small plunderers, down to him who filches a pound of tobacco from the King's warehouses; while, on the contrary, the acquittal of any noble and official thief would not fail to diffuse the most heartfelt satisfaction over the larcenous and burglarious world. Observe, I do not say because the lower Catholics are affected by what concerns their superiors, that they are not affected by what concerns themselves. There is no disguising the horrid truth, *there must be some relaxation with respect to tithe*: this is the cruel and heartrending price which must be paid for national preservation. I feel how little existence will be worth having if any alteration, however slight, is made in the property of Irish rectors; I am conscious how much such changes must affect the daily and hourly comforts of every Englishman; I shall feel too happy if they leave Europe untouched and are not ultimately fatal to the destinies of America; but I am madly bent upon keeping foreign enemies out of the British empire, and my limited understanding presents me with no other means of effecting my object.

You talk of waiting till another reign before any alteration is made; a proposal full of good sense and good nature if the measure in question were to pull down St James's Palace or to alter Kew Gardens. Will Bonaparte agree to put off his intrigues, and his invasion of Ireland? If so, I will overlook the question of justice, and, finding the danger suspended, agree to the delay. I sincerely hope this reign may last many years, yet the delay of a single session of Parliament may be fatal; but if another year elapses without some serious concession made to the Catholics, I believe, before God, that all future pledges and concessions will be made in vain. I do not think that peace will do you any good under such circumstances: if Bonaparte gives you a respite it will only be to get ready the gallows on which he means to hang you. The Catholic and the Dissenter can unite in peace as well as war. If they do, the gallows is ready; and your executioner, in spite of the most solemn promises, will turn you off the next hour.

With every disposition to please (where to please within fair

O

and rational limits is an high duty), it is impossible for public men to be long silent about the Catholics; pressing evils are not got rid of because they are not talked of. A man may command his family to say nothing more about the stone, and surgical operations; but the ponderous malice still lies upon the nerve, and gets so big that the patient breaks his own law of silence, clamours for the knife, and expires under its late operation. Believe me, you talk folly when you talk of suppressing the Catholic question. I wish to God the case admitted of such a remedy: bad as it is, it does not admit of it. If the wants of the Catholics are not heard in the manly tones of Lord Grenville, or the servile drawl of Lord Castlereagh, they will be heard ere long in the madness of mobs and the conflicts of armed men.

I observe it is now universally the fashion to speak of the first personage in the state as the great obstacle to the measure. In the first place, I am not bound to believe such rumours because I hear them; and in the next place, I object to such language, as unconstitutional. Whoever retains his situation in the ministry, while the incapacities of the Catholics remain, is the advocate for those incapacities; and to him, and to him only, am I to look for responsibility. But waive this question of the Catholics, and put a general case:—How is a minister of this country to act when the conscientious scruples of his Sovereign prevent the execution of a measure deemed by him absolutely necessary to the safety of the country? His conduct is quite clear—he should resign. But what is his successor to do?—Resign. But is the King to be left without ministers, and is he in this manner to be compelled to act against his own conscience? Before I answer this, pray tell me in my turn, what better defence is there against the machinations of a wicked, or the errors of a weak, monarch, than the impossibility of finding a minister who will lend himself to vice and folly? Every English monarch, in such a predicament, would sacrifice his opinions and views to such a clear expression of the public will; and it is one method in which the Constitution aims at bringing about such a sacrifice. You may say, if you please, the ruler of a state is forced to give up his object when the natural love of place and power will tempt no one to assist him in its attainment. This may be force, but it is force without injury and therefore without blame. I am not to be beat out of these obvious reasonings and ancient constitutional provisions by the term conscience. There is no fantasy, however wild, that a man may not persuade himself that he cherishes from motives of conscience; eternal war against impious France, or rebellious America, or Catholic Spain, may in times to come be scruples of conscience. One English monarch may, from scruples of conscience, wish to abolish every trait of religious persecution; another monarch may deem it his absolute and indispensable duty to make a slight provision for Dissenters out of the revenues of the Church of England. So that you see, Brother Abraham, there are cases where it would be the duty of the best and most loyal subjects to oppose the conscientious scruples of their Sovereign, still taking care that their actions were constitutional and their modes respectful. Then you come upon me with personal questions, and say that no such dangers are to be apprehended now under our present gracious Sovereign, of whose good qualities we must be all so well convinced. All these sorts of discussions I beg leave to decline; what I have said upon constitutional topics I mean of course for general, not for particular, application. I agree with you in all the good you have said of the powers that be, and I avail myself of the opportunity of pointing out general dangers to the Constitution, at a moment when we are so completely exempted from their present influence. I cannot finish this letter without expressing my surprise and pleasure at your abuse of the servile addresses poured in upon the Throne; nor can I conceive a greater disgust to a monarch with a true English heart, than to see such a question as that of Catholic Emancipation argued, not with a reference to its justice or importance, but universally considered to be of no farther consequence than as it affects his own private feelings. That these sentiments should be mine, is not wonderful; but how they came to be yours, does, I confess, fill me with surprise. Are you moved by the arrival of the Irish Brigade at Antwerp, and the amorous violence which awaits Mrs Plymley?

V

Dear Abraham,

I never met a parson in my life who did not consider the Corporation and Test Acts as the great bulwarks of the Church; and yet it is now just sixty-four years since bills of indemnity to destroy their penal effects, or in other words, to repeal them, have been passed annually as a matter of course.

Heu vatum ignaræ mentes.

These bulwarks, without which no clergyman thinks he could sleep with his accustomed soundness, have actually not been in existence since any man now living has taken holy orders. Every year the Indemnity Act pardons past breaches of these two laws and prevents any fresh actions of informers from coming to a conclusion before the period for the next indemnity bill arrives; so that these penalties, by which alone the Church remains in existence, have not had one moment's operation for sixty-four years. You will say the legislature, during the whole of this period, has reserved to itself the discretion of suspending or not suspending. But had not the legislature the right of re-enacting, if it was necessary? And now when you have kept the rod over these people (with the most scandalous abuse of all principle) for sixty-four years, and not found it necessary to strike once, is not that the best of all reasons why the rod should be laid aside? You talk to me of a very valuable hedge running across your fields which you would not part with on any account. I go down expecting to find a limit impervious to cattle and highly useful for the preservation of property; but, to my utter astonishment, I find that the hedge was cut down half a century ago and that every year the shoots are clipped the moment they appear above ground: it appears, upon farther inquiry, that the hedge never ought to have existed at all, that it originated in the malice of antiquated quarrels and was cut down because it subjected you to vast inconvenience and broke up your intercourse with a country absolutely necessary to your existence. If the remains of this hedge serve only to keep up an irritation in your neighbours and to remind them of the feuds of former times, good nature and good sense teach you that you ought to grub it up and cast it into the oven. This is the exact state of these two laws; and yet it is made a great argument against concession to the Catholics, that it involves their repeal; which is to say, Do not make me relinquish a folly that will lead to my ruin, because, if you do, I must give up other follies ten times greater than this.

I confess, with all our bulwarks and hedges, it mortifies me to the very quick to contrast with our matchless stupidity and inimitable folly the conduct of Bonaparte upon the subject of religious persecution. At the moment when we are tearing the crucifixes from the necks of the Catholics and washing pious mud from the foreheads of the Hindoos, at that moment this man is assembling the very Jews at Paris and endeavouring to give them stability and importance. I shall never be reconciled to mending shoes in America, but I see it must be my lot, and I will then take a dreadful revenge upon Mr Perceval if I catch him preaching within ten miles of me. I cannot for the soul of me conceive whence this man has gained his notions of Christianity: he has the most evangelical charity for errors in arithmetic and the most inveterate malice against errors in conscience. While he rages against those whom in the true spirit of the Gospel he ought to indulge, he forgets the only instance of severity which that Gospel contains, and leaves the jobbers, and contractors, and money-changers at their seats, without a single stripe.

You cannot imagine, you say, that England will ever be ruined and conquered; and for no other reason that I can find but because it seems so very odd it should be ruined and conquered. Alas! so reasoned, in their time, the Austrian, Russian, and Prussian Plymleys. But the English are brave: so were all these nations. You might get together an hundred thousand men individually brave; but without generals capable of commanding such a machine it would be as useless as a first-rate man of war manned by Oxford clergymen or Parisian shopkeepers. I do not say this to the disparagement of English officers: they have had no means of acquiring experience; but I do say it to create alarm; for we do not appear to me to be half alarmed enough, or to entertain that sense of our danger which leads to the most obvious means of self-defence. As for the spirit of the peasantry in making a gallant defence behind hedge-rows, and through plate-racks and hen-coops, highly as I think of their bravery I do not know any nation in Europe so likely to be struck with the panic as the English, and this from their total unacquaintance with the science of war. Old wheat and beans blazing for twenty miles round, cart mares shot, sows of Lord Somerville's breed running wild over the country, the minister of the parish wounded

solely in his hinder parts, Mrs Plymley in fits: all these scenes
of war an Austrian or a Russian has seen three or four times
over; but it is now three centuries since an English pig has fallen
in a fair battle upon English ground, or a farm-house been rifled,
or a clergyman's wife been subjected to any other proposals of
love than the connubial endearments of her sleek and orthodox
mate. The old edition of Plutarch's Lives, which lies in the corner
of your parlour window, has contributed to work you up to the
most romantic expectations of our Roman behaviour. You are
persuaded that Lord Amherst will defend Kew Bridge like
Cocles; that some maid of honour will break away from her
captivity and swim over the Thames; that the Duke of York
will burn his capitulating hand, and little Mr Sturges Bourne*
give forty years' purchase for Moulsham Hall, while the French
are encamped upon it. I hope we shall witness all this, if the
French do come; but in the mean time I am so enchanted with
the ordinary English behaviour of these invaluable persons, that
earnestly pray no opportunity may be given them for Roman
I valour, and for those very un-Roman pensions which they would
all, of course, take especial care to claim in consequence. But
whatever was our conduct, if every ploughman was as great a
hero as he who was called from his oxen to save Rome from
her enemies, I should still say that at such a crisis you want
the affections of all your subjects in both islands: there is no
spirit which you must alienate, no heart you must avert; every
man must feel he has a country, and that there is an urgent and
pressing cause why he should expose himself to death.

The effects of penal laws, in matters of religion, are never
confined to those limits in which the legislature intended they
should be placed: it is not only that I am excluded from certain
offices and dignities because I am a Catholic, but the exclusion
carries with it a certain stigma, which degrades me in the eyes
of the monopolizing sect, and the very name of my religion
becomes odious. These effects are so very striking in England
that I solemnly believe blue and red baboons to be more popular
here than Catholics and Presbyterians; they are more understood,
and there is a greater disposition to do something for them. When

* There is nothing more objectionable in Plymley's Letters than the abuse
of Mr Sturges Bourne, who is an honourable, able, and excellent person; but
such are the malevolent effects of party spirit.

a country squire hears of an ape, his first feeling is to give it nuts and apples; when he hears of a Dissenter, his immediate impulse is to commit it to the county jail, to shave its head, to alter its customary food, and to have it privately whipped. This is no caricature, but an accurate picture of national feelings as they degrade and endanger us at this very moment. The Irish Catholic gentleman would bear his legal disabilities with greater temper, if these were all he had to bear—if they did not enable every Protestant cheesemonger and tide-waiter to treat him with contempt. He is branded on the forehead with a red-hot iron, and treated like a spiritual felon, because, in the highest of all considerations, he is led by the noblest of all guides, his own disinterested conscience.

Why are nonsense and cruelty a bit the better because they are enacted? If Providence which gives wine and oil had blest us with that tolerant spirit which makes the countenance more pleasant and the heart more glad than these can do, if our Statute Book had never been defiled with such infamous laws, the sepulchral Spencer Perceval would have been hauled through the dirtiest horse-pond in Hampstead had he ventured to propose them. But now persecution is good because it exists; every law which originated in ignorance and malice, and gratifies the passions from whence it sprang, we call the wisdom of our ancestors: when such laws are repealed, they will be cruelty and madness; till they are repealed, they are policy and caution.

I was somewhat amused with the imputation brought against the Catholics by the University of Oxford, that they are enemies to liberty. I immediately turned to my History of England, and marked as an historical error that passage in which it is recorded that in the reign of Queen Anne the famous decree of the University of Oxford respecting passive obedience was ordered by the House of Lords to be burnt by the hands of the common hangmen, as contrary to the liberty of the subject and the law of the land. Nevertheless, I wish, whatever be the modesty of those who impute, that the imputation was a little more true; the Catholic cause would not be quite so desperate with the present Administration. I fear, however, that the hatred to liberty in these poor devoted wretches may ere long appear more doubtful than it is at present to the Vice-Chancellor and his Clergy, inflamed, as they doubtless are, with classical examples of republican virtue, and panting, as they always have been, to reduce the power of the Crown within narrower and safer limits. What mistaken zeal, to attempt to connect one religion with freedom, and another with slavery! Who laid the foundations of English liberty? What was the mixed religion of Switzerland? What has the Protestant religion done for liberty in Denmark, in Sweden, throughout the North of Germany, and in Prussia? The purest religion in the world, in my humble opinion, is the religion of the Church of England: for its preservation (so far as it is exercised without intruding upon the liberties of others) I am ready at this moment to venture my present life, and but through that religion I have no hopes of any other; yet I am not forced to be silly because I am pious, nor will I ever join in eulogiums on my faith which every man of common reading and common sense can so easily refute.

You have either done too much for the Catholics (worthy Abraham), or too little; if you had intended to refuse them political power you should have refused them civil rights. After you had enabled them to acquire property, after you had conceded to them all that you did concede in '78 and '93, the rest is wholly out of your power: you may choose whether you will give the rest in an honourable or a disgraceful mode, but it is utterly out of your power to withhold it.

In the last year, land to the amount of *eight hundred thousand pounds* was purchased by the Catholics in Ireland. Do you think it possible to be-Perceval, and be-Canning, and be-Castlereagh, such a body of men as this out of their common rights, and their common sense? Mr George Canning may laugh and joke at the idea of Protestant bailiffs ravishing Catholic ladies, under the 9th clause of the Sunset Bill; but if some better remedy is not applied to the distractions of Ireland than the jocularity of Mr Canning, they will soon put an end to his pension, and to the pension of those 'near and dear relatives', for whose eating, drinking, washing, and clothing, every man in the United Kingdoms now pays his twopence or threepence a year. You may call these observations coarse, if you please; but I have no idea that the Sophias and Carolines of any man breathing are to eat national veal, to drink public tea, to wear Treasury ribands, and then that we are to be told that it is coarse to animadvert upon this pitiful and eleemosynary splendour. If this is right, why not mention it? If it is wrong, why should not he who enjoys the ease of supporting his sisters in this manner bear the shame of it? Everybody seems hitherto to have spared a man who never spares anybody.

As for the enormous wax candles and superstitious mummeries and painted jackets of the Catholic priests, I fear them not. Tell me that the world will return again under the influence of the small pox; that Lord Castlereagh will hereafter oppose the power of the Court; that Lord Howick and Mr Grattan will do each of them a mean and dishonourable action; that any body who has heard Lord Redesdale speak once will knowingly and willingly hear him again; that Lord Eldon has assented to the fact of two and two making four, without shedding tears or expressing the smallest doubt or scruple; tell me any other thing absurd or incredible, but, for the love of common sense, let me hear no more of the danger to be apprehended from the general diffusion of Popery. It is too absurd to be reasoned upon; every man feels it is nonsense when he hears it stated, and so does every man while he is stating it.

I cannot imagine why the friends to the Church Establishment should entertain such an horror of seeing the doors of Parliament flung open to the Catholics, and view so passively the enjoyment of that right by the Presbyterians and by every other species of Dissenter. In their tenets, in their Church government, in the nature of their endowments, the Dissenters are infinitely more distant from the Church of England than the Catholics are; yet the Dissenters have never been excluded from Parliament. There are 45 members in one House, and 16 in the other, who always are Dissenters. There is no law which would prevent every member of the Lords and Commons from being Dissenters. The Catholics could not bring into Parliament half the number of the Scotch members; and yet one exclusion is of such immense importance, because it has taken place; and the other no human being thinks of, because no one is accustomed to it. I have often thought, if the *wisdom of our ancestors* had excluded all persons with red hair from the House of Commons, of the throes and convulsions it would occasion to restore them to their natural rights. What mobs and riots would it produce! To what infinite abuse and obloquy would the capillary patriot be exposed; what wormwood would distil from Mr Perceval, what froth would drop from

Mr Canning ; how (I will not say *my*, but *our* Lord Hawkesbury, for he belongs to us all)—how our Lord Hawkesbury would work away about the hair of King William and Lord Somers and the authors of the great and glorious Revolution; how Lord Eldon would appeal to the Deity and his own virtues, and to the hair of his children: some would say that red-haired men were superstitious; some would prove they were atheists; they would be petitioned against as the friends of slavery and the advocates for revolt; in short, such a corrupter of the heart and the understanding is the spirit of persecution, that these unfortunate people (conspired against by their fellow subjects of every complexion), if they did not emigrate to countries where hair of another colour was persecuted, would be driven to the falsehood of perukes or the hypocrisy of the Tricosian fluid.

As for the dangers of the Church (in spite of the staggering events which have lately taken place), I have not yet entirely lost my confidence in the power of common sense, and I believe the Church to be in no danger at all; but if it is, that danger is not from the Catholics but from the Methodists, and from that patent Christianity which has been for some time manufacturing at Clapham, to the prejudice of the old and admirable article prepared by the Church. I would counsel my lords the Bishops to keep their eyes upon that holy village and its hallowed vicinity: they will find there a zeal in making converts far superior to anything which exists among the Catholics; a contempt for the great mass of English clergy, much more rooted and profound; and a regular fund to purchase livings for those groaning and garrulous gentlemen whom they denominate (by a standing sarcasm against the regular Church) Gospel preachers and vital clergymen. I am too firm a believer in the general propriety and respectability of the English clergy to believe they have much to fear either from old nonsense or from new; but if the Church must be supposed to be in danger I prefer that nonsense which is grown half venerable from time, the force of which I have already tried and baffled, which at least has some excuse in the dark and ignorant ages in which it originated. The religious enthusiasm manufactured by living men before my own eyes disgusts my understanding as much, influences my imagination not at all, and excites my apprehensions much more.

I may have seemed to you to treat the situation of public

affairs with some degree of levity; but I feel it deeply, and with
nightly and daily anguish; because I know Ireland; I have
known it all my life; I love it, and I foresee the crisis to which
it will soon be exposed. Who can doubt but that Ireland will
experience ultimately from France a treatment to which the
conduct they have experienced from England is the love of a
parent, or a brother? Who can doubt but that five years after
he has got hold of the country, Ireland will be tossed away by
Bonaparte as a present to some one of his ruffian generals, who
will knock the head of Mr Keogh against the head of Cardinal
Troy, shoot twenty of the most noisy blockheads of the Roman
persuasion, wash his pug-dogs in holy water, and confiscate the
salt butter of the Milesian Republic to the last tub? But what
matters this? or who is wise enough in Ireland to heed it? or
when had common sense much influence with my poor dear
Irish? Mr Perceval does not know the Irish; but I know them,
and I know that at every rash and mad hazard, they will break
the Union, revenge their wounded pride and their insulted
religion, and fling themselves into the open arms of France, sure
of dying in the embrace. And now what means have you of
guarding against this coming evil, upon which the future happiness or misery of every Englishman depends? Have you a single
ally in the whole world? Is there a vulnerable point in the French
empire where the astonishing resources of that people can be
attracted and employed? Have you a ministry wise enough to
comprehend the danger, manly enough to believe unpleasant
intelligence, honest enough to state their apprehensions at the
peril of their places? Is there any where the slightest disposition
to join any measure of love, or conciliation, or hope, with that
dreadful bill which the distractions of Ireland have rendered
necessary? At the very moment that the last monarchy in Europe
has fallen, are we not governed by a man of pleasantry and a man
of theology? In the six hundredth year of our empire over Ireland,
have we any memorial of ancient kindness to refer to? any people,
any zeal, any country on which we can depend? Have we any
hope but in the winds of heaven and the tides of the sea? any
prayer to prefer to the Irish but that they should forget and
forgive their oppressors, who, in the very moment that they are
calling upon them for their exertions, solemnly assure them that
the oppression shall still remain?

Abraham, farewell! If I have tired you, remember how often you have tired me and others. I do not think we really differ in politics so much as you suppose; or at least, if we do, that difference is in the means, and not in the end. We both love the Constitution, respect the King, and abhor the French. But though you love the Constitution, you would perpetuate the abuses which have been engrafted upon it; though you respect the King, you would confirm his scruples against the Catholics; though you abhor the French, you would open to them the conquest of Ireland. My method of respecting my Sovereign is by protecting his honour, his empire, and his lasting happiness; I evince my love of the Constitution, by making it the guardian of all men's rights and the source of their freedom; and I prove my abhorrence of the French, by uniting against them the disciples of every Church in the only remaining nation in Europe. As for the men of whom I have been compelled in this age of mediocrity to say so much, they cannot of themselves be worth a moment's consideration, to you, to me, or to any body. In a year after their death they will be forgotten as completely as if they had never been; and are now of no farther importance, than as they are the mere vehicles of carrying into effect the commonplace and mischievous prejudices of the times in which they live.

VI

DEAR ABRAHAM,

WHAT amuses me the most is to hear of the *indulgences* which the Catholics have received, and their exorbitance in not being satisfied with those indulgences: now if you complain to me that a man is obtrusive and shameless in his requests, and that it is impossible to bring him to reason, I must first of all hear the whole of your conduct towards him; for you may have taken from him so much in the first instance, that, in spite of a long series of restitution, a vast latitude for petition may still remain behind.

There is a village (no matter where) in which the inhabitants on one day in the year sit down to a dinner prepared at the common expense: by an extraordinary piece of tyranny (which Lord Hawkesbury would call the wisdom of the village ancestors), the inhabitants of three of the streets, about a hundred years ago, seized upon the inhabitants of the fourth street, bound them hand and foot, laid them upon their backs, and compelled them to look on while the rest were stuffing themselves with beef and beer: the next year, the inhabitants of the persecuted street (though they contributed an equal quota of the expense) were treated precisely in the same manner. The tyranny grew into a custom; and (as the manner of our nature is) it was considered as the most sacred of all duties to keep these poor fellows without their annual dinner: the village was so tenacious of this practice that nothing could induce them to resign it; every enemy to it was looked upon as a disbeliever in Divine Providence, and any nefarious churchwarden who wished to succeed in his election had nothing to do but to represent his antagonist as an abolitionist, in order to frustrate his ambition, endanger his life, and throw the village into a state of the most dreadful commotion. By degrees, however, the obnoxious street grew to be so well peopled, and its inhabitants so firmly united, that their oppressors, more afraid of injustice, were more disposed to be just. At the next dinner they are unbound, the year after allowed to sit upright, then a bit of bread and a glass of water; till at last, after a long series of concessions, they are emboldened to ask, in pretty plain terms, that they may be allowed to sit down at the bottom of the table, and to fill their bellies as well as the rest. Forthwith a general cry of shame and scandal: 'Ten years ago, were you not laid upon your backs? Don't you remember what a great thing you thought it to get a piece of bread? How thankful you were for cheese-parings? Have you forgotten that memorable era, when the Lord of the manor interfered to obtain for you a slice of the public pudding? And now, with an audacity only equalled by your ingratitude, you have the impudence to ask for knives and forks, and to request, in terms too plain to be mistaken, that you may sit down to table with the rest and be indulged even with beef and beer: there are not more than half a dozen dishes which we have reserved for ourselves; the rest has been thrown open to you in the utmost profusion; you have potatoes, and carrots, suet dumplings, sops in the pan, and delicious toast and water, in incredible quantities. Beef, mutton, lamb, pork, and veal are ours; and if you were not the most restless and dissatisfied of human beings, you would never think of aspiring to enjoy them.'

Is not this, my dainty Abraham, the very nonsense and the very insult which is talked to and practised upon the Catholics? You are surprised that men who have tasted of partial justice should ask for perfect justice; that he who has been robbed of coat and cloak will not be contented with the restitution of one of his garments. He would be a very lazy blockhead if he were content, and I (who, though an inhabitant of the village, have preserved, thank God, some sense of justice) most earnestly counsel these half-fed claimants to persevere in their just demands, till they are admitted to a more complete share of a dinner for which they pay as much as the others; and if they see a little attenuated lawyer squabbling at the head of their opponents, let them desire him to empty his pockets, and to pull out all the pieces of duck, fowl, and pudding, which he has filched from the public feast to carry home to his wife and children.

You parade a great deal upon the vast concessions made by this country to the Irish before the Union. I deny that any voluntary concession was ever made by England to Ireland. What did Ireland ever ask that was granted? What did she ever demand that was refused? How did she get her Mutiny Bill— a limited parliament—a repeal of Poyning's Law—a constitution? Not by the concessions of England, but by her fears. When Ireland asked for all these things upon her knees, her petitions were rejected with Percevalism and contempt; when she demanded them with the voice of 60,000 armed men, they were granted with every mark of consternation and dismay. Ask of Lord Auckland the fatal consequences of trifling with such a people as the Irish. He himself was the organ of these refusals. As secretary to the Lord Lieutenant, the insolence and the tyranny of this country passed through his hands. Ask him if he remembers the consequences. Ask him if he has forgotten that memorable evening when he came down booted and mantled to the House of Commons, when he told the House he was about to set off for Ireland that night, and declared before God, if he did not carry with him a compliance with all their demands, Ireland was for ever lost to this country. The present generation have forgotten this; but I have not forgotten it; and I know, hasty and undignified as the submission of England then was, that Lord Auckland was right, that the delay of a single day might very probably have separated the two people for ever. The terms submission and fear are galling terms when applied from the lesser nation to the greater; but it is the plain historical truth, it is the natural consequence of injustice, it is the predicament in which every country places itself which leaves such a mass of hatred and discontent by its side. No empire is powerful enough to endure it; it would exhaust the strength of China, and sink it with all its mandarins and tea-kettles to the bottom of the deep. By refusing them justice, now when you are strong enough to refuse them anything more than justice, you will act over again, with the Catholics, the same scene of mean and precipitate submission which disgraced you before America, and before the volunteers of Ireland. We shall live to hear the Hampstead Protestant pronouncing such extravagant panegyrics upon holy water, and paying such fulsome compliments to the thumbs and offals of departed saints, that parties will change sentiments, and Lord Henry Petty and Sam Whitbread take a spell at No Popery. The wisdom of Mr Fox was alike employed in teaching his country justice when Ireland was weak, and dignity when Ireland was strong. We are fast pacing round the same miserable circle of ruin and imbecility. Alas! where is our guide?

You say that Ireland is a millstone about our necks; that it would be better for us if Ireland were sunk at the bottom of the sea; that the Irish are a nation of irreclaimable savages and barbarians. How often have I heard these sentiments fall from the plump and thoughtless squire, and from the thriving English shopkeeper who has never felt the rod of an Orange master upon his back. Ireland a millstone about your neck! Why is it not a stone of Ajax in your hand? I agree with you most cordially, that, governed as Ireland now is, it would be a vast accession of strength if the waves of the sea were to rise and ingulf her tomorrow. At this moment, opposed as we are to all the world, the annihilation of one of the most fertile islands on the face of the globe, containing five millions of human creatures, would be one of the most solid advantages which could happen to this country. I doubt very much, in spite of all the just abuse which has been lavished upon Bonaparte, whether there is any one of his conquered countries the blotting out of which would be as beneficial to him as the destruction of Ireland would be to us: of countries I speak differing in language from the French, little habituated to their intercourse, and inflamed with all the resentments of a recently conquered people. Why will you attribute the turbulence of our people to any cause but the right—to any cause but your own scandalous oppression? If you tie your horse up to a gate, and beat him cruelly, is he vicious because he kicks you? If you have plagued and worried a mastiff dog for years, is he mad because he flies at you whenever he sees you? Hatred is an active, troublesome passion. Depend upon it, whole nations have always some reason for their hatred. Before you refer the turbulence of the Irish to incurable defects in their character, tell me if you have treated them as friends and equals? Have you protected their commerce? Have you respected their religion? Have you been as anxious for their freedom as your own? Nothing of all this. What then? Why you have confiscated the territorial surface of the country twice over: you have massacred and exported her inhabitants: you have deprived four fifths of them of every civil privilege: you have at every period made her commerce and manufactures slavishly subordinate to your own: and yet the hatred which the Irish bear to you is the result of an original turbulence of character, and of a primitive, obdurate wildness, utterly incapable of civilization. The embroidered inanities and the sixth-form effusions of Mr Canning are really not powerful enough to make me believe this; nor is there any authority on earth (always excepting the Dean of Christ Church) which could make it credible to me. I am sick of Mr Canning. There is not a ha'p'orth of bread to all this sugar and sack. I love not the cretaceous and incredible countenance of his colleague. The only opinion in which I agree with these two gentlemen, is that which they entertain of each other; I am sure that the insolence of Mr Pitt, and the unbalanced accounts of Melville, were far better than the perils of this new ignorance:—

> Nonne fuit satius tristes Amaryllidis iras
> Atque superba pati fastidia—nonne Menalcam,
> Quamvis ille *niger?*

In the midst of the most profound peace, the secret articles of the Treaty of Tilsit, in which the destruction of Ireland is resolved upon, induce you to rob the Danes of their fleet. After the expedition sailed comes the Treaty of Tilsit, containing no article, public or private, alluding to Ireland. The state of the

world, you tell me, justified us in doing this. Just God! do we
think only of the state of the world when there is an opportunity
for robbery, for murder, and for plunder; and do we forget the
state of the world when we are called upon to be wise, and good,
and just? Does the state of the world never remind us, that we
have four millions of subjects whose injuries we ought to atone
for, and whose affections we ought to conciliate? Does the state
of the world never warn us to lay aside our infernal bigotry,
and to arm every man who acknowledges a God and can grasp
a sword? Did it never occur to this administration, that they
might virtuously get hold of a force ten times greater than the
force of the Danish fleet? Was there no other way of protecting
Ireland but by bringing eternal shame upon Great Britain and
by making the earth a den of robbers? See what the men whom
you have supplanted would have done. They would have rendered the invasion of Ireland impossible, by restoring to the
Catholics their long-lost rights: they would have acted in such
a manner that the French would neither have wished for invasion,
nor dared to attempt it: they would have increased the permanent strength of the country while they preserved its reputation unsullied. Nothing of this kind your friends have done,
because they are solemnly pledged to do nothing of this kind;
because to tolerate all religions, and to equalize civil rights to
all sects, is to oppose some of the worst passions of our nature—
to plunder and to oppress is to gratify them all. They wanted
the huzzas of mobs, and they have for ever blasted the fame
of England to obtain them. Were the fleets of Holland, France,
and Spain destroyed by larceny? You resisted the power of 150
sail of the line by sheer courage, and violated every principle
of morals from the dread of 15 hulks, while the expedition itself
cost you three times more than the value of the larcenous matter
brought away. The French trample upon the laws of God and
man, not for old cordage, but for kingdoms, and always take
care to be well paid for their crimes. We contrive, under the
present administration, to unite moral with intellectual deficiency,
and to grow weaker and worse by the same action. If they had
any evidence of the intended hostility of the Danes, why was it
not produced? Why have the nations of Europe been allowed to
feel an indignation against this country beyond the reach of all
subsequent information? Are these times, do you imagine, when

P

we can trifle with a year of universal hatred, dally with the curses of Europe, and then regain a lost character at pleasure, by the parliamentary perspirations of the Foreign Secretary, or the solemn asseverations of the pecuniary Rose? Believe me, Abraham, it is not under such ministers as these that the dexterity of honest Englishmen will ever equal the dexterity of French knaves; it is not in their presence that the serpent of Moses will ever swallow up the serpents of the magicians.

Lord Hawkesbury says that nothing is to be granted to the Catholics from fear. What! not even justice? Why not? There are four millions of disaffected people within twenty miles of your own coast. I fairly confess that the dread which I have of their physical power is with me a very strong motive for listening to their claims. To talk of not acting from fear is mere parliamentary cant. From what motive but fear, I should be glad to know, have all the improvements in our constitution proceeded? I question if any justice has ever been done to large masses of mankind from any other motive. By what other motives can the plunderers of the Baltic suppose nations to be governed in their intercourse *with each other*? If I say, Give this people what they ask because it is just, do you think I should get ten people to listen to me? Would not the lesser of the two Jenkinsons be the first to treat me with contempt? The only true way to make the mass of mankind see the beauty of justice is by showing to them in pretty plain terms the consequences of injustice. If any body of French troops land in Ireland, the whole population of that country will rise against you to a man, and you could not possibly survive such an event three years. Such, from the bottom of my soul, do I believe to be the present state of that country; and so far does it appear to me to be impolitic and unstatesmanlike to concede anything to such a danger, that if the Catholics, in addition to their present just demands, were to petition for the perpetual removal of the said Lord Hawkesbury from his Majesty's councils, I think, whatever might be the effect upon the destinies of Europe, and however it might retard our own individual destruction, that the prayer of the petition should be instantly complied with. Canning's crocodile tears should not move me; the hoops of the maids of honour should not hide him. I would tear him from the banisters of the back stairs, and plunge him in the fishy fumes of the dirtiest of all his Cinque Ports.

VII

Dear Abraham,

In the correspondence which is passing between us you are perpetually alluding to the Foreign Secretary: and in answer to the dangers of Ireland, which I am pressing upon your notice, you have nothing to urge but the confidence which you repose in the discretion and sound sense of this gentleman.* I can only say, that I have listened to him long and often, with the greatest attention; I have used every exertion in my power to take a fair measure of him, and it appears to me impossible to hear him upon any arduous topic without perceiving that he is eminently deficient in those solid and serious qualities upon which, and upon which alone, the confidence of a great country can properly repose. He sweats, and labours, and works for sense, and Mr Ellis seems always to think it is coming, but it does not come; the machine can't draw up what is not to be found in the spring; Providence has made him a light, jesting, paragraph-writing man, and that he will remain to his dying day. When he is jocular he is strong, when he is serious he is like Sampson in a wig: any ordinary person is a match for him: a song, an ironical letter, a burlesque ode, an attack in the Newspaper upon Nicoll's eye, a smart speech of twenty minutes, full of gross misrepresentations and clever turns, excellent language, a spirited manner, lucky quotation, success in provoking dull men, some half information picked up in Pall Mall in the morning: these are your friend's natural weapons; all these things he can do; here I allow him to be truly great: nay, I will be just, and go still farther, if he would confine himself to these things, and consider the *facete* and the playful to be the basis of his character, he would, for that species of man, be universally regarded as a person of a very good understanding; call him a legislator, a reasoner, and the conductor of the affairs of a great nation, and it seems to me as absurd as if a butterfly were to teach bees to make honey.

* The attack upon virtue and morals in the debate upon Copenhagen is brought forward with great ostentation by this gentleman's friends. But is Harlequin less Harlequin because he acts well? I was present: he leaped about, touched facts with his wand, turned yes into no, and no into yes: it was a pantomime well played, but a pantomime; Harlequin deserves higher wages than he did two years ago: is he therefore fit for serious parts?

That he is an extraordinary writer of small poetry, and a diner out of the highest lustre, I do most readily admit. After George Selwyn, and perhaps Tickell, there has been no such man for this half century. The Foreign Secretary is a gentleman, a respectable as well as a highly agreeable man in private life; but you may as well feed me with decayed potatoes as console me for the miseries of Ireland by the resources of his *sense* and his *discretion*. It is only the public situation which this gentleman holds which entitles me or induces me to say so much about him. He is a fly in amber, nobody cares about the fly: the only question is, How the Devil did it get there? Nor do I attack him for the love of glory, but from the love of utility, as a burgomaster hunts a rat in a Dutch dyke, for fear it should flood a province.

The friends of the Catholic question are, I observe, extremely embarrassed in arguing when they come to the loyalty of the Irish Catholics. As for me, I shall go straight forward to my object, and state what I have no manner of doubt, from an intimate knowledge of Ireland, to be the plain truth. Of the great Roman Catholic proprietors, and of the Catholic prelates, there may be a few, and but a few, who would follow the fortunes of England at all events: there is another set of men who, thoroughly detesting this country, have too much property and too much character to lose, not to wait for some very favourable event before they show themselves; but the great mass of Catholic population, upon the slightest appearance of a French force in that country, would rise upon you to a man. It is the most mistaken policy to conceal the plain truth. There is no loyalty among the Catholics: they detest you as their worst oppressors, and they will continue to detest you till you remove the cause of their hatred. It is in your power in six months' time to produce a total revolution of opinions among this people; and in some future letter I will show you that this is clearly the case. At present, see what a dreadful state Ireland is in. The common toast among the low Irish is, the feast of the *passover*. Some allusion to *Bonaparte*, in a play lately acted at Dublin, produced thunders of applause from the pit and the galleries; and a politician should not be inattentive to the public feelings expressed in theatres. Mr Perceval thinks he has disarmed the Irish: he has no more disarmed the Irish than he has resigned a shilling of his own public emoluments. An Irish* peasant fills the barrel of his gun full of tow dipped in oil, butters up the lock, buries it in a bog, and allows the Orange bloodhound to ransack his cottage at pleasure. Be just and kind to the Irish, and you will indeed disarm them; rescue them from the degraded servitude in which they are held by a handful of their own countrymen, and you will add four millions of brave and affectionate men to your strength. Nightly visits, Protestant inspectors, licences to possess a pistol, or a knife and fork, the odious vigour of the *evangelical* Perceval—acts of Parliament, drawn up by some English attorney, to save you from the hatred of four millions of people—the guarding yourselves from universal disaffection by a police; a confidence in the little cunning of Bow Street when you might rest your security upon the eternal basis of the best feelings: this is the meanness and madness to which nations are reduced when they lose sight of the first elements of justice, without which a country can be no more secure than it can be healthy without air. I sicken at such policy and such men. The fact is, the Ministers know nothing about the present state of Ireland; Mr Perceval sees a few clergymen, Lord Castlereagh a few general officers, who take care, of course, to report what is pleasant rather than what is true. As for the joyous and lepid consul, he jokes upon neutral flags and frauds, jokes upon Irish rebels, jokes upon northern, and western, and southern foes, and gives himself no trouble upon any subject: nor is the mediocrity of the idolatrous deputy of the slightest use. Dissolved in grins, he reads no memorials upon the state of Ireland, listens to no reports, asks no questions, and is the

'*Bourn* from whom no traveller returns.'†

The danger of an immediate insurrection is now, I *believe*, blown over. You have so strong an army in Ireland, and the Irish are become so much more cunning from the last insurrection, that you may perhaps be tolerably secure just at present from that evil: but are you secure from the efforts which the French may make to throw a body of troops into Ireland? and do you

---

* No man who is not intimately acquainted with the Irish can tell to what a curious extent this concealment of arms is carried. I have stated the exact mode in which it is done.

† [Sturges Bourne. See reference to him, and author's footnote on page 214.]

consider that event to be difficult and improbable? From Brest
Harbour to Cape St Vincent you have above three thousand
miles of hostile sea coast and twelve or fourteen harbours quite
capable of containing a sufficient force for the powerful invasion
of Ireland. The nearest of these harbours is not two days' sail
from the southern coast of Ireland, with a fair leading wind;
and the farthest not ten. Five ships of the line, for so very short
a passage, might carry five or six thousand troops with cannon
and ammunition; and Ireland presents to their attack southern
coast of more than 500 miles, abounding in deep bays, admirable
harbours, and disaffected inhabitants. Your blockading ships may
be forced to come home for provisions and repairs, or they may
be blown off in a gale of wind and compelled to bear away for
their own coast;—and you will observe, that the very same wind
which locks you up in the British Channel when you are got
there, is evidently favourable for the invasion of Ireland. And
yet this is called Government, and the people huzza Mr Perceval
for continuing to expose his country day after day to such
tremendous perils as these; cursing the men who would have
given up a question in theology to have saved us from such a
risk. The British empire at this moment is in the state of a peach-
blossom—if the wind blows gently from one quarter, it survives,
if furiously from the other, it perishes. A stiff breeze may set in
from the north, the Rochefort squadron will be taken, and the
Minister will be the most holy of men; if it comes from some
other point, Ireland is gone, we curse ourselves as a set of
monastic madmen, and call out for the unavailing satisfaction
of Mr Perceval's head. Such a state of political existence is scarcely
credible; it is the action of a mad young fool standing upon one
foot, and peeping down the crater of Mount Etna, not the conduct of a wise and sober people deciding upon their best and
dearest interests: and in the name, the much-injured name, of
Heaven, what is it all for that we expose ourselves to these
dangers? Is it that we may sell more muslin? Is it that we may
acquire more territory? Is it that we may strengthen what we
have already acquired? No: nothing of all this; but that one set
of Irishmen may torture another set of Irishmen—that Sir Phelim
O'Callaghan may continue to whip Sir Toby M'Tackle, his next
door neighbour, and continue to ravish his Catholic daughters;
and these are the measures which the honest and consistent

Secretary supports; and this is the Secretary whose genius, in the estimation of brother Abraham, is to extinguish the genius of Bonaparte. Pompey was killed by a slave, Goliath smitten by a stripling, Pyrrhus died by the hand of a woman; tremble, thou great Gaul, from whose head an armed Minerva leaps forth in the hour of danger; tremble, thou scourge of God, a pleasant man is come out against thee, and thou shalt be laid low by a joker of jokes, and he shall talk his pleasant talk against thee, and thou shalt be no more!

You tell me, in spite of all this parade of sea coast, Bonaparte has neither ships nor sailors: but this is a mistake. He has not ships and sailors to contest the empire of the seas with Great Britain, but there remains quite sufficient of the navies of France, Spain, Holland, and Denmark, for these short excursions and invasions. Do you think, too, that Bonaparte does not add to his navy every year? Do you suppose, with all Europe at his feet, that he can find any difficulty in obtaining timber, and that money will not procure for him any quantity of naval stores he may want? The mere machine, the empty ship, he can build as well and as quickly as you can; and though he may not find enough of practised sailors to man large fighting fleets—it is not possible to conceive that he can want sailors for such sort of purposes as I have stated. He is at present the despotic monarch of above twenty thousand miles of sea coast, and yet you suppose he cannot procure sailors for the invasion of Ireland. Believe, if you please, that such a fleet met at sea by any number of our ships at all comparable to them in point of force, would be immediately taken, let it be so; I count nothing upon their power of resistance, only upon their power of escaping unobserved. If experience has taught us anything, it is the impossibility of perpetual blockades. The instances are innumerable, during the course of this war, where whole fleets have sailed in and out of harbour in spite of every vigilance used to prevent it. I shall only mention those cases where Ireland is concerned. In December 1796 seven ships of the line, and ten transports, reached Bantry Bay from Brest, without having seen an English ship in their passage. It blew a storm when they were off shore, and therefore England still continues to be an independent kingdom. You will observe that at the very time the French fleet sailed out of Brest Harbour, Admiral Colpoys was cruising off there with a powerful squadron, and still, from the particular circumstances of the weather, found it impossible to prevent the French from coming out. During the time that Admiral Colpoys was cruising off Brest, Admiral Richery, with six ships of the line, passed him, and got safe into the harbour. At the very moment when the French squadron was lying in Bantry Bay, Lord Bridport with his fleet was locked up by a foul wind in the Channel, and for several days could not stir to the assistance of Ireland. Admiral Colpoys, totally unable to find the French fleet, came home. Lord Bridport, at the change of the wind, cruised for them in vain, and they got safe back to Brest without having seen a single one of those floating bulwarks, the possession of which we believe will enable us with impunity to set justice and common sense at defiance. Such is the miserable and preprecarious state of an anemocracy, of a people who put their trust in hurricanes and are governed by wind. In August 1798 three forty-gun frigates landed 1100 men under Humbert, making the passage from Rochelle to Killala without seeing any English ship. In October of the same year four French frigates anchored in Killala Bay with 2000 troops; and though they did not land their troops they returned to France in safety. In the same month a line-of-battle ship, eight stout frigates, and a brig, all full of troops and stores, reached the coast of Ireland and were fortunately, in sight of land, destroyed, after an obstinate engagement, by Sir John Warren.

If you despise the little troop which, in these numerous experiments, did make good its landing, take with you, if you please, this *précis* of its exploits: eleven hundred men, commanded by a soldier raised from the ranks, put to rout a select army of 6000 men, commanded by General Lake, seized their ordnance, ammunition, and stores, advanced 150 miles into a country containing an armed force of 150,000 men, and at last surrendered to the Viceroy, an experienced general, gravely and cautiously advancing at the head of all his chivalry and of an immense army to oppose him. You must excuse these details about Ireland, but it appears to me to be of all other subjects the most important. If we conciliate Ireland, we can do nothing amiss; if we do not, we can do nothing well. If Ireland was friendly, we might equally set at defiance the talents of Bonaparte and the blunders of his rival Mr Canning; we could then support the ruinous and silly bustle of our useless expeditions, and the almost incredible ignorance of our commercial orders in council. Let the present administration give up but this one point, and there is nothing which I would not consent to grant them. Mr Perceval shall have full liberty to insult the tomb of Mr Fox, and to torment every eminent Dissenter in Great Britain; Lord Camden shall have large boxes of plums; Mr Rose receive permission to prefix to his name the appellative of virtuous; and to the Viscount Castlereagh* a round sum of ready money shall be well and truly paid into his hand. Lastly, what remains to Mr George Canning, but that he ride up and down Pall Mall glorious upon a white horse, and that they cry out before him, Thus shall it be done to the statesman who hath written *The Needy Knife-Grinder*, and the German play? Adieu only for the present; you shall soon hear from me again; it is a subject upon which I cannot long be silent.

VIII

NOTHING can be more erroneous than to suppose that Ireland is not bigger than the Isle of Wight or of more consequence than Guernsey or Jersey; and yet I am almost inclined to believe, from the general supineness which prevails here respecting the dangerous state of that country, that such is the rank which it holds in our statistical tables. I have been writing to you a great deal about Ireland, and perhaps it may be of some use to state to you concisely the nature and resources of the country which has been the subject of our long and strange correspondence. There were returned, as I have before observed, to the hearth tax, in 1791, 701,132 houses, which Mr Newenham shows from unquestionable documents to be nearly 80,000 below the real number of houses in that country. There are 27,457 square English miles in Ireland, and more than five millions of people.

By the last survey it appears that the inhabited houses in England and Wales amount to 1,574,902, and the population to 9,343,578, which gives an average of $5\frac{7}{8}$ to each house, in a country where the density of population is certainly less considerable than in Ireland. It is commonly supposed that two-fifths of the army and navy are Irishmen, at periods when political

* This is a very unjust imputation on Lord Castlereagh.

disaffection does not avert the Catholics from the service. The current value of Irish exports in 1807 was £9,314,854 17s. 7d.; a state of commerce about equal to the commerce of England in the middle of the reign of George II. The tonnage of ships entered inward and cleared outward in the trade of Ireland, in 1807, amounted to 1,567,430 tons. The quantity of home spirits exported amounted to 10,284 gallons in 1796, and to 930,800 gallons in 1804. Of the exports which I have stated, provisions amounted to four millions, and linen to about four millions and a half. There was exported from Ireland, upon an average of two years ending in January 1804, 591,274 barrels of barley, oats, and wheat; and by weight 910,848 cwts. of flour, oatmeal, barley, oats, and wheat. The amount of butter exported in 1804, from Ireland, was worth, in money, £1,704,680 sterling. The importation of ale and beer, from the immense manufactures now carrying on of these articles, was diminished to 3209 barrels, in the year 1804, from 111,920 barrels, which was the average importation per annum, taking from three years ending in 1792; and at present there is an export trade of porter. On an average of the three years ending March 1783 there were imported into Ireland, of cotton wool 3326 cwts., of cotton yarn 5405 lbs.; but on an average of three years ending January 1803 there were imported, of the first article, 13,159 cwts, and of the latter, 628,406 lbs. It is impossible to conceive any manufacture more flourishing. The export of linen has increased in Ireland from 17,776,862 yards, the average in 1770, to 43,534,971 yards, the amount in 1805. The tillage of Ireland has more than trebled within the last twenty-one years. The importation of coals has increased from 230,000 tons in 1783, to 417,030 in 1804; of tobacco, from 3,459,861 lbs. in 1783, to 6,611,543 in 1804; of tea, from 1,703,855 lbs. in 1783, to 3,358,256, in 1804; of sugar, from 143,117 cwts. in 1782, to 309,076, in 1804. Ireland now supports a funded debt of above 64 millions, and it is computed that more than three millions of money are annually remitted to Irish absentees resident in this country. In Mr Foster's report, of 100 folio pages, presented to the House of Commons in the year 1806, the total expenditure of Ireland is stated at £9,760,013. Ireland has increased about two-thirds in its population within twenty-five years, and yet, and in about the same space of time, its exports of beef, bullocks, cows, pork, swine, butter, wheat, barley, and oats, collectively taken, have doubled; and this in spite of two years' famine and the presence of an immense army that is always at hand to guard the most valuable appanage of our empire from joining our most inveterate enemies. Ireland has the greatest possible facilities for carrying on commerce with the whole of Europe. It contains, within a circuit of 750 miles, 66 secure harbours, and presents a western frontier against Great Britain reaching from the Firth of Clyde north to the Bristol Channel south and varying in distance from 20 to 100 miles; so that the subjugation of Ireland would compel us to guard with ships and soldiers a new line of coast certainly amounting, with all its sinuosities, to more than 700 miles—an addition of polemics, in our present state of hostility with all the world, which must highly gratify the vigorists and give them an ample opportunity of displaying that foolish energy upon which their claims to distinction are founded. Such is the country which the Right Reverend the Chancellor of the Exchequer would drive into the arms of France, and for the conciliation of which we are requested to wait, as if it were one of those sinecure places which were given to Mr Perceval snarling at the breast, and which cannot be abolished till his decease.

How sincerely and fervently have I often wished that the Emperor of the French had thought as Mr Spencer Perceval does upon the subject of government; that he had entertained doubts and scruples upon the propriety of admitting the Protestants to an equality of rights with the Catholics, and that he had left in the middle of his empire these vigorous seeds of hatred and disaffection: but the world was never yet conquered by a blockhead. One of the very first measures we saw him recurring to was the complete establishment of religious liberty; if his subjects fought and paid as he pleased, he allowed them to believe as they pleased: the moment I saw this, my best hopes were lost. I perceived in a moment the kind of man we had to do with. I was well aware of the miserable ignorance and folly of this country upon the subject of toleration; and every year has been adding to the success of that game which it was clear he had the will and the ability to play against us.

You say Bonaparte is not in earnest upon the subject of religion, and that this is the cause of his tolerant spirit; but is it possible you can intend to give us such dreadful and unamiable notions of religion? Are we to understand that the moment a man is sincere he is narrow-minded; that persecution is the child of belief; and that a desire to leave all men in the quiet and unpunished exercise of their own creed can only exist in the mind of an infidel? Thank God, I know many men whose principles are as firm as they are expanded, who cling tenaciously to their own modification of the Christian faith, without the slightest disposition to force that modification upon other people. If Bonaparte is liberal in subjects of religion because he has no religion, is this a reason why we should be illiberal because we are Christians? If he owes this excellent quality to a vice, is that any reason why we may not owe it to a virtue? Toleration is a great good, and a good to be imitated, let it come from whom it will. If a sceptic is tolerant, it only shows that he is not foolish in practice as well as erroneous in theory. If a religious man is tolerant, it evinces that he is religious from thought and inquiry, because he exhibits in his conduct one of the most beautiful and important consequences of a religious mind,— an inviolable charity to all the honest varieties of human opinion.

Lord Sidmouth, and all the anti-Catholic people, little foresee that they will hereafter be the sport of the antiquarian; that their prophecies of ruin and destruction from Catholic emancipation will be clapped into the notes of some quaint history and be matter of pleasantry even to the sedulous housewife and the rural dean. There is always a copious supply of Lord Sidmouths in the world; nor is there one single source of human happiness against which they have not uttered the most lugubrious predictions. Turnpike roads, navigable canals, inoculation, hops, tobacco, the Reformation, the Revolution—there are always a set of worthy and moderately-gifted men who bawl out death and ruin upon every valuable change which the varying aspect of human affairs absolutely and imperiously requires. I have often thought that it would be extremely useful to make a collection of the hatred and abuse that all those changes have experienced which are now admitted to be marked improvements in our condition. Such a history might make folly a little more modest, and suspicious of its own decisions.

Ireland, you say, since the Union, is to be considered as a part of the whole kingdom; and therefore, however Catholics may predominate in that particular spot, yet, taking the whole empire together, they are to be considered as a much more insignificant quota of the population. Consider them in what light you please, as part of the whole, or by themselves, or in what manner may be most consentaneous to the devices of your holy mind—I say in a very few words, if you do not relieve these people from the civil incapacities to which they are exposed, you will lose them; or you must employ great strength and much treasure in watching over them. In the present state of the world, you can afford to do neither the one nor the other. Having stated this, I shall leave you to be ruined, Puffendorf in hand (as Mr Secretary Canning says), and to lose Ireland, just as you have found out what proportion the aggrieved people should bear to the whole population before their calamities meet with redress. As for your parallel cases, I am no more afraid of deciding upon them than I am upon their prototype. If ever any one heresy should so far spread itself over the principality of Wales that the Established Church were left in a minority of one to four, if you had subjected these heretics to very severe civil privations, if the consequence of such privations were a universal state of disaffection among that caseous and wrathful people, and if at the same time you were at war with all the world, how can you doubt for a moment that I would instantly restore them to a state of the most complete civil liberty? What matters it under what name you put the same case? Common sense is not changed by appellations. I have said how I would act to Ireland, and I would act so to all the world.

I admit that, to a certain degree, the Government will lose the affections of the Orangemen by emancipating the Catholics; much less, however, at present, than three years past. The few men who have ill-treated the whole crew live in constant terror that the oppressed people will rise upon them and carry the ship into Brest:—they begin to find that it is a very tiresome thing to sleep every night with cocked pistols under their pillows, and to breakfast, dine, and sup with drawn hangers. They suspect that the privilege of beating and kicking the rest of the sailors is hardly worth all this anxiety, and that if the ship does ever fall into the hands of the disaffected, all the cruelties which they have experienced will be thoroughly remembered and amply repaid. To a short period of disaffection among the Orangemen, I confess I should not much object: my love of poetical justice

does carry me as far as that; one summer's whipping, only one:
the thumb-screw for a short season: a little light easy torturing
between Lady-day and Michaelmas; a short specimen of Mr
Perceval's rigour. I have malice enough to ask this slight atonement for the groans and shrieks of the poor Catholics, unheard
by any human tribunal, but registered by the Angel of God
against their Protestant and enlightened oppressors.

Besides, if you who count ten so often can count five, you
must perceive that it is better to have four friends and one enemy
than four enemies and one friend; and the more violent the
hatred of the Orangemen, the more certain the reconciliation
of the Catholics. The disaffection of the Orangemen will be the
Irish rainbow; when I see it, I shall be sure that the storm is over.

If those incapacities from which the Catholics ask to be relieved
were to the mass of them only a mere feeling of pride, and if the
question were respecting the attainment of privileges which could
be of importance only to the highest of the sect, I should still
say, that the pride of the mass was very naturally wounded by
the degradation of their superiors. Indignity to George Rose
would be felt by the smallest nummary gentleman in the king's
employ; and Mr John Bannister could not be indifferent to anything which happened to Mr Canning. But the truth is, it is a
most egregious mistake to suppose that the Catholics are contending merely for the fringes and feathers of their chiefs. I will
give you a list, in my next Letter, of those privations which are
represented to be of no consequence to anybody but Lord Fingal,
and some twenty or thirty of the principal persons of their sect.
In the meantime, adieu, and be wise.

IX

Dear Abraham,
No Catholic can be chief Governor or Governor of this Kingdom,
Chancellor or Keeper of the Great Seal, Lord High Treasurer,
Chief of any of the Courts of Justice, Chancellor of the Exchequer,
Puisne Judge, Judge in the Admiralty, Master of the Rolls,
Secretary of State, Keeper of the Privy Seal, Vice-Treasurer or
his Deputy, Teller or Cashier of Exchequer, Auditor or General
Governor or Custos Rotulorum of Counties, Chief Governor's

Secretary, Privy Councillor, King's Counsel, Serjeant, Attorney, Solicitor General, Master in Chancery, Provost or Fellow of Trinity College Dublin, Postmaster-General, Master and Lieutenant-General of Ordnance, Commander-in-Chief, General on the Staff, Sheriff, Sub-Sheriff, Mayor, Bailiff, Recorder, Burgess, or any other officer in a City or a Corporation. No Catholic can be guardian to a Protestant, and no priest guardian at all: no Catholic can be a gamekeeper, or have for sale, or otherwise, any arms or warlike stores: no Catholic can present to a living, unless he choose to turn Jew in order to obtain that privilege; the pecuniary qualification of Catholic jurors is made higher than that of Protestants, and no relaxation of the ancient rigorous code is permitted, unless to those who shall take an oath prescribed by 13 & 14 Geo. III. Now if this is not picking the plums out of the pudding and leaving the mere batter to the Catholics, I know not what is. If it were merely the Privy Council, it would be (I allow) nothing but a point of honour for which the mass of Catholics were contending, the honour of being chief-mourners or pall-bearers to the country; but surely no man will contend that every barrister may not speculate upon the possibility of being a puisne Judge; and that every shopkeeper must not feel himself injured by his exclusion from borough offices.

One of the greatest practical evils which the Catholics suffer in Ireland is their exclusion from the offices of Sheriff and Deputy Sheriff. Nobody who is unacquainted with Ireland can conceive the obstacles which this opposes to the fair administration of justice. The formation of juries is now entirely in the hands of the Protestants; the lives, liberties, and properties of the Catholics in the hands of the juries; and this is the arrangement for the administration of justice in a country where religious prejudices are inflamed to the greatest degree of animosity! In this country, if a man is a foreigner, if he sells slippers, and sealing wax, and artificial flowers, we are so tender of human life that we take care half the number of persons who are to decide upon his fate should be men of similar prejudices and feelings with himself: but a poor Catholic in Ireland may be tried by twelve Percevals, and destroyed according to the manner of that gentleman in the name of the Lord, and with all the insulting forms of justice. I do not go the length of saying that deliberate and wilful injustice is done. I have no doubt that the Orange Deputy Sheriff thinks it would be a most unpardonable breach of his duty if he did not summon a Protestant panel. I can easily believe that the Protestant panel may conduct themselves very conscientiously in hanging the gentlemen of the crucifix; but I blame the law which does not guard the Catholic against the probable tenor of those feelings which must unconsciously influence the judgments of mankind. I detest that state of society which extends unequal degrees of protection to different creeds and persuasions; and I cannot describe to you the contempt I feel for a man who, calling himself a statesman, defends a system which fills the heart of every Irishman with treason and makes his allegiance prudence, not choice.

I request to know if the vestry taxes in Ireland are a mere matter of romantic feeling, which can affect only the Earl of Fingal? In a parish where there are four thousand Catholics and fifty Protestants, the Protestants may meet together in a vestry meeting, at which no Catholic has the right to vote, and tax all the lands in the parish 1s 6d per acre, or in the pound, I forget which, for the repairs of the church—and how has the necessity of these repairs been ascertained? A Protestant plumber has discovered that it wants new leading; a Protestant carpenter is convinced the timbers are not sound, and the glazier who hates holy water (as an accoucheur hates celibacy because he gets nothing by it) is employed to put in new sashes.

The grand juries in Ireland are the great scene of jobbing. They have a power of making a county rate to a considerable extent for roads, bridges, and other objects of general accommodation. 'You suffer the road to be brought through my park, and I will have the bridge constructed in a situation where it will make a beautiful object to your house. You do my job, and I will do yours.' These are the sweet and interesting subjects which occasionally occupy Milesian gentlemen while they are attendant upon this grand inquest of justice. But there is a religion, it seems, even in jobs; and it will be highly gratifying to Mr Perceval to learn that no man in Ireland who believes in seven sacraments can carry a public road, or bridge, one yard out of the direction most beneficial to the public, and that nobody can cheat that public who does not expound the Scriptures in the purest and most orthodox manner. This will give pleasure to Mr Perceval: but, from his unfairness upon these topics, I appeal to the justice and the proper feelings of Mr Huskisson. I ask him if the human mind can experience a more dreadful sensation than to see its own jobs refused, and the jobs of another religion perpetually succeeding? I ask him his opinion of a job-less faith, of a creed which dooms a man through life to a lean and plunderless integrity. He knows that human nature cannot and will not bear it; and if we were to paint a political Tartarus, it would be an endless series of snug expectations and cruel disappointments. These are a few of many dreadful inconveniences which the Catholics of all ranks suffer from the laws by which they are at present oppressed. Besides, look at human nature:—what is the history of all professions? Joel is to be brought up to the bar: has Mrs Plymley the slightest doubt of his being Chancellor? Do not his two shrivelled aunts live in the certainty of seeing him in that situation, and of cutting out with their own hands his equity habiliments? And I could name a certain minister of the Gospel who does not, in the bottom of his heart, much differ from these opinions. Do you think that the fathers and mothers of the holy Catholic Church are not as absurd as Protestant papas and mammas? The probability I admit to be, in each particular case, that the sweet little block-head will in fact never get a brief;—but I will venture to say there is not a parent from the Giant's Causeway to Bantry Bay who does not conceive that his child is the unfortunate victim of the exclusion, and that nothing short of positive law could prevent his own dear pre-eminent Paddy from rising to the highest honours of the State. So with the army, and parliament; in fact, few are excluded; but, in imagination, all: you keep twenty or thirty Catholics out, and you lose the affections of four millions; and let me tell you that recent circumstances have by no means tended to diminish in the minds of men that hope of elevation beyond their own rank which is so congenial to our nature: from pleading for John Roe to taxing John Bull, from jesting Mr Pitt and writing in the Anti-Jacobin, to managing the affairs of Europe—these are leaps which seem to justify the fondest dreams of mothers and of aunts.

I do not say that the disabilities to which the Catholics are exposed amount to such intolerable grievances that the strength and industry of a nation are overwhelmed by them: the increasing prosperity of Ireland fully demonstrates to the contrary. But I repeat again, what I have often stated in the course of our correspondence, that your laws against the Catholics are exactly in that state in which you have neither the benefits of rigour nor of liberality: every law which prevented the Catholic from gaining strength and wealth is repealed; every law which can irritate remains: if you were determined to insult the Catholics you should have kept them weak; if you resolved to give them strength you should have ceased to insult them:—at present your conduct is pure unadulterated folly.

Lord Hawkesbury says, We heard nothing about the Catholics till we began to mitigate the laws against them; when we relieved them in part from this oppression they began to be disaffected. This is very true; but it proves just what I have said, that you have either done too much or too little; and as there lives not, I hope, upon earth, so depraved a courtier that he would load the Catholics with their ancient chains, what absurdity it is then not to render their dispositions friendly, when you leave their arms and legs free!

You know, and many Englishmen know, what passes in China; but nobody knows or cares what passes in Ireland. At the beginning of the present reign, no Catholic could realize property or carry on any business; they were absolutely annihilated, and had no more agency in the country than so many trees. They were like Lord Mulgrave's eloquence and Lord Camden's wit; the legislative bodies did not know of their existence. For these twenty-five years last past, the Catholics have been engaged in commerce; within that period the commerce of Ireland has doubled:—there are four Catholics at work for one Protestant and eight Catholics at work for one Episcopalian; of course, the proportion which Catholic wealth bears to Protestant wealth is every year altering rapidly in favour of the Catholics. I have already told you what their purchases of land were the last year: since that period, I have been at some pains to find out the actual state of the Catholic wealth: it is impossible, upon such a subject, to arrive at complete accuracy; but I have good reason to believe that there are at present 2000 Catholics in Ireland, possessing an income from £500 upwards, many of these with incomes of one, two, three, and four thousand, and some amounting to fifteen and twenty thousand per annum:—and this is the kingdom, and these the people, for whose conciliation we are to wait Heaven knows when, and Lord Hawkesbury why! As for me, I never think of the situation of Ireland without feeling the same necessity for immediate interference as I should do if I saw blood flowing from a great artery. I rush towards it with the instinctive rapidity of a man desirous of preventing death, and have no other feeling but that in a few seconds the patient may be no more.

I could not help smiling, in the times of No Popery, to witness the loyal indignation of many persons at the attempt made by the last ministry to do something for the relief of Ireland. The general cry in the country was, that they would not see their beloved Monarch used ill in his old age, and that they would stand by him to the last drop of their blood. I respect good feelings, however erroneous be the occasions on which they display themselves; and therefore I saw in all this as much to admire as to blame. It was a species of affection, however, which reminded me very forcibly of the attachment displayed by the servants of the Russian ambassador at the beginning of the last century. His Excellency happened to fall down in a kind of apoplectic fit when he was paying a morning visit in the house of an acquaintance. The confusion was of course very great, and messengers were despatched in every direction to find a surgeon; who, upon his arrival, declared that his Excellency must be immediately blooded, and prepared himself forthwith to perform the operation: the barbarous servants of the embassy, who were there in great numbers, no sooner saw the surgeon prepared to wound the arm of their master with a sharp shining instrument, than they drew their swords, put themselves in an attitude of defence, and swore in pure Slavonic, 'that they would murder any man who attempted to do him the slightest injury: he had been a very good master to them, and they would not desert him in his misfortunes, or suffer his blood to be shed while he was off his guard, and incapable of defending himself'. By good fortune, the secretary arrived about this period of the dispute, and his Excellency, relieved from superfluous blood and perilous affection, was, after much difficulty, restored to life.

There is an argument brought forward with some appearance of plausibility in the House of Commons, which certainly merits an answer: You know that the Catholics now vote for members of parliament, in Ireland, and that they outnumber the

Protestants in a very great proportion; if you allow Catholics to
sit in Parliament, religion will be found to influence votes more
than property, and the greater part of the 100 Irish members
who are returned to parliament will be Catholics. Add to these
the Catholic members who are returned in England, and you
will have a phalanx of heretical strength which every minister
will be compelled to respect, and occasionally to conciliate by
concessions incompatible with the interests of the Protestant
Church. The fact is, however, that you are at this moment
subjected to every danger of this kind which you can possibly
apprehend hereafter. If the spiritual interest of the voters are
more powerful than their temporal interests, they can bind down
their representatives to support any measures favourable to the
Catholic religion, and they can change the objects of their choice
till they have found Protestant members (as they easily may do)
perfectly obedient to their wishes. If the superior possessions of
the Protestants prevent the Catholics from uniting for a common
political object, then the danger you fear cannot exist: if zeal,
on the contrary, gets the better of acres, then the danger at
present exists, from the right of voting already given to the
Catholics, and it will not be increased by allowing them to sit
in parliament. There are, as nearly as I can recollect, thirty
seats in Ireland for cities and counties, where the Protestants
are the most numerous, and where the members returned must
of course be Protestants. In the other seventy representations, the
wealth of the Protestants is opposed to the number of the Catholics;
and if all the seventy members returned were of the Catholic persuasion, they must still plot the destruction of our religion in the
midst of 588 Protestants. Such terrors would disgrace a cook-maid,
or a toothless aunt—when they fall from the lips of bearded and
senatorial men, they are nauseous, anti-peristaltic, and emetical.

How can you for a moment doubt of the rapid effects which
would be produced by the emancipation?—In the first place,
to my certain knowledge, the Catholics have long since expressed
to his Majesty's Ministers their perfect readiness *to vest in his
Majesty, either with the consent of the Pope, or without it if it cannot
be obtained, the nomination of the Catholic prelacy.** The Catholic

* [One wonders what warrant Sydney Smith can have imagined he had
for this statement. Roman Catholics will be the first to agree that such a
concession on their part would have been out of the question.]

prelacy in Ireland consists of twenty-six bishops and the warden of Galway, a dignitary enjoying Catholic jurisdiction. The number of Roman Catholic priests in Ireland exceeds one thousand. The expenses of his peculiar worship are, to a substantial farmer or mechanic, five shillings per annum; to a labourer (where he is not entirely excused) one shilling per annum: this includes the contribution of the whole family, and for this the priest is bound to attend them when sick, and to confess them when they apply to him: he is also to keep his chapel in order, to celebrate divine service, and to preach on Sundays and holy days. In the northern district a priest gains from £30 to £50; in the other parts of Ireland from £60 to £90 per annum. The best paid Catholic bishops receive about £400 per ann.; the others from £300 to £350. My plan is very simple; I would have 300 Catholic parishes at £100 per annum, 300 at £200 and 400 at £300 per annum; this, for the whole thousand parishes, would amount to £190,000. To the prelacy I would allot £20,000 in unequal proportions, from £1000 to £500; and I would appropriate £40,000 more for the support of Catholic schools and the repairs of Catholic churches; the whole amount of which sums is £250,000, about the expense of three days of one of our genuine, good, English, *just and necessary wars*. The clergy should all receive their salaries at the Bank of Ireland, and I would place the whole patronage in the hands of the Crown. Now, I appeal to any human being, except Spencer Perceval, Esq., of the parish of Hampstead, what the disaffection of a clergy would amount to, gaping after this graduated bounty of the Crown, and whether Ignatius Loyala himself, if he were a living blockhead instead of a dead saint, could withstand the temptation of bouncing from £100 a year at Sligo, to £300 in Tipperary? This is the miserable sum of money for which the merchants and land-owners and nobility of England are exposing themselves to the tremendous peril of losing Ireland. The sinecure places of the Roses and the Percevals, and the 'dear and near relations', put up to auction at thirty years' purchase, would almost amount to the money.

I admit that nothing can be more reasonable than to expect that a Catholic priest should starve to death, genteelly and pleasantly, for the good of the Protestant religion; but is it equally reasonable to expect that he should do so for the Protestant pews and Protestant brick and mortar? On an Irish Sabbath the bell of a neat parish church often summons to church only the parson and an occasionally conforming clerk; while, two hundred yards off, a thousand Catholics are huddled together in a miserable hovel and pelted by all the storms of heaven. Can anything be more distressing than to see a venerable man pouring forth sublime truths in tattered breeches, and depending for his food upon the little offal he gets from his parishioners?

I venerate a human being who starves for his principles, let them be what they may; but starving for anything is not at all to the taste of the honourable flagellants: strict principles and good pay is the motto of Mr Perceval: the one he keeps in great measure for the faults of his enemies, the other for himself.

There are parishes in Connaught in which a Protestant was never settled, nor even seen: in that province, in Munster, and in parts of Leinster, the entire peasantry for sixty miles are Catholics; in these tracts the churches are frequently shut for want of a congregation, or opened to an assemblage of from six to twenty persons. Of what Protestants there are in Ireland, the greatest part are gathered together in Ulster, or they live in towns. In the country of the other three provinces the Catholics see no other religion but their own, and are at the least as fifteen to one Protestant. In the diocese of Tuam they are sixty to one; in the parish of St Mullins, diocese of Leghlin, there are four thousand Catholics and *one Protestant*; in the town of Grasgenamana, in the county of Kilkenny, there are between four and five hundred Catholic houses, and three Protestant houses. In the parish of Allen, county Kildare, there is no Protestant, though it is very populous. In the parish of Arlesin, Queen's County, the proportion is one hundred to one. In the whole county of Kilkenny, by actual enumeration, it is seventeen to one: in the diocese of Kilmacduagh, province of Connaught, fifty-two to one, by ditto. These I give you as a few specimens of the present state of Ireland;—and yet there are men impudent and ignorant enough to contend that such evils require no remedy, and that mild family man who dwelleth in Hampstead can find none but the cautery and the knife,

omne per ignem
Excoquitur vitium.

I cannot describe the horror and disgust which I felt at hearing Mr Perceval call upon the then ministry for measures of vigour in Ireland. If I lived at Hampstead upon stewed meats and claret; if I walked to church every Sunday before eleven young gentlemen of my own begetting, with their faces washed, and their hair pleasingly combed; if the Almighty had blessed me with every earthly comfort,—how awfully would I pause before I sent forth the flame and the sword over the cabins of the poor, brave, generous, open-hearted peasants of Ireland! How easy it is to shed human blood—how easy it is to persuade ourselves that it is our duty to do so—and that the decision has cost us a severe struggle—how much in all ages have wounds and shrieks and tears been the cheap and vulgar resources of the rulers of mankind—how difficult and how noble it is to govern in kindness, and to found an empire upon the everlasting basis of justice and affection!—But what do men call vigour? To let loose hussars and to bring up artillery, to govern with lighted matches, and to cut, and push, and prime—I call this, not vigour, but the *sloth of cruelty and ignorance*. The vigour I love consists in finding out wherein subjects are aggrieved, in relieving them, in studying the temper and genius of a people, in consulting their prejudices, in selecting proper persons to lead and manage them, in the laborious, watchful, and difficult task of increasing public happiness by allaying each particular discontent. In this way Hoche pacified La Vendée—and in this way only will Ireland ever be subdued. But this, in the eyes of Mr Perceval, is imbecility and meanness: houses are not broken open—women are not insulted— the people seem all to be happy; they are not rode over by horses and cut by whips. Do you call this vigour?—Is this government?

X

You must observe that all I have said of the effects which will be produced by giving salaries to the Catholic Clergy only proceeds upon the supposition that the emancipation of the laity is effected:—without that, I am sure, there is not a clergyman in Ireland who would receive a shilling from Government; he could not do so, without an entire loss of credit among the members of his own persuasion.

What you say of the moderation of the Irish Protestant Clergy in collecting tithes, is, I believe, strictly true. Instead of collecting what the law enables them to collect, I believe they seldom or ever collect more than two-thirds; and I entirely agree with you, that the abolition of agistment tithe in Ireland by a vote of the Irish House of Commons, and without any remuneration to the Church, was a most scandalous and jacobinical measure. I do not blame the Irish Clergy; but I submit to your common sense, if it is possible to explain to an Irish peasant upon what principle of justice or common sense he is to pay every tenth potato in his little garden to a clergyman in whose religion nobody believes for twenty miles around him and who has nothing to preach to but bare walls. It is true, if the tithes are bought up the cottager must pay more rent to his landlord; but the same thing, done in the shape of rent, is less odious than when it is done in the shape of tithe: I do not want to take a shilling out of the pockets of the clergy, but to leave the substance of things, and to change their names. I cannot see the slightest reason why the Irish labourer is to be relieved from the real onus, or from anything else but the name of tithe. At present he rents only nine-tenths of the produce of the land, which is all that belongs to the owner; this he has at the market price; if the landowner purchase the other tenth of the Church, of course he has a right to make a correspondent advance upon his tenant.

I very much doubt, if you were to lay open all civil offices to the Catholics and to grant salaries to their clergy in the manner I have stated, if the Catholic laity would give themselves much trouble about the advance of their Church; for they would pay the same tithes under one system that they do under another. If you were to bring the Catholics into the daylight of the world, to the high situations of the army, the navy, and the bar, numbers of them would come over to the Established Church and do as other people do; instead of that, you set a mark of infamy upon them, rouse every passion of our nature in favour of their creed, and then wonder that men are blind to the follies of the Catholic religion. There are hardly any instances of old and rich families among the Protestant Dissenters: when a man keeps a coach, and lives in good company, he comes to church, and gets ashamed of the meeting-house; if this is not the case with the father it is almost always the case with the son. These things would never

be so if the dissenters were in *practice* as much excluded from all
the concerns of civil life as the Catholics are. If a rich young
Catholic were in parliament, he would belong to White's and
to Brookes's, would keep race-horses, would walk up and down
Pall Mall, be exonerated of his ready money and his constitution,
become as totally devoid of morality, honesty, knowledge, and
civility, as Protestant loungers in Pall Mall, and return home
with a supreme contempt for Father O'Leary and Father
O'Callaghan. I am astonished at the madness of the Catholic
clergy in not perceiving that Catholic emancipation is Catholic
infidelity; that to entangle their people in the intrigues of a
Protestant parliament and a Protestant court is to insure the loss
of every man of fashion and consequence in their community.
The true receipt for preserving their religion is Mr Perceval's
receipt for destroying it: it is to deprive every rich Catholic of
all the objects of secular ambition, to separate him from the
Protestant, and to shut him up in his castle, with priests and relics.

We are told, in answer to all our arguments, that this is not
a fit period,—that a period of universal war is not the proper
time for dangerous innovations in the constitution: this is as
much as to say, that the worst time for making friends is the
period when you have made many enemies; that it is the greatest
of all errors to stop when you are breathless, and to lie down
when you are fatigued. Of one thing I am quite certain: if the
safety of Europe is once completely restored, the Catholics may
for ever bid adieu to the slightest probability of effecting their
object. Such men as hang about a court not only are deaf to
the suggestions of mere justice, but they despise justice; they
detest the word *right*; the only word which rouses them is *peril*;
where they can oppress with impunity they oppress for ever, and
call it loyalty and wisdom.

I am so far from conceiving the legitimate strength of the
Crown would be diminished by those abolitions of civil incapacities in consequence of religious opinions, that my only objection
to the increase of religious freedom is, that it would operate as
a diminution of political freedom: the power of the Crown is so
overbearing at this period, that almost the only steady opposers
of its fatal influence are men disgusted by religious intolerance.
Our establishments are so enormous, and so utterly dispropor-
tioned to our population, that every second or third man you

meet in society gains something from the public : my brother the commissioner,—my nephew the police justice,—purveyor of small beer to the army in Ireland,—clerk of the mouth,—yeoman to the left hand,—these are the obstacles which common sense and justice have now to overcome. Add to this that the King, old and infirm, excites a principle of very amiable generosity in his favour; that he has led a good, moral, and religious life, equally removed from profligacy and methodistical hypocrisy; that he has been a good husband, a good father, and a good master; that he dresses plain, loves hunting and farming, hates the French, and is, in all his opinions and habits, quite English :— these feelings are heightened by the present situation of the world and the yet unexploded clamour of Jacobinism. In short, from the various sources of interest, personal regard, and national taste, such a tempest of loyalty has set in upon the people that the 47th proposition in Euclid might now be voted down with as much ease as any proposition in politics; and therefore if Lord Hawkesbury hates the abstract truths of science as much as he hates concrete truth in human affairs, now is his time for getting rid of the multiplication table, and passing a vote of censure upon the pretensions of the *hypotheneuse*. Such is the history of English parties at this moment: you cannot seriously suppose that the people care for such men as Lord Hawkesbury, Mr Canning, and Mr Perceval, on their own account; you cannot really believe them to be so degraded as to look to their safety from a man who proposes to subdue Europe by keeping it without Jesuit's Bark. The people, at present, have one passion, and but one—

A Jove principium. Jovis omnia plena.

They care no more for the ministers I have mentioned, than they do for those sturdy royalists who for £60 per annum stand behind his Majesty's carriage, arrayed in scarlet and in gold. If the present ministers opposed the Court instead of flattering it, they would not command twenty votes.

Do not imagine by these observations that I am not loyal: without joining in the common cant of the best of kings, I respect the King most sincerely as a good man. His religion is better than the religion of Mr Perceval, his old morality very superior to the old morality of Mr Canning, and I am quite certain he has a safer understanding than both of them put together. Loyalty within the bounds of reason and moderation is one of the great instruments of English happiness; but the love of the King may easily become more strong than the love of the kingdom, and we may lose sight of the public welfare in our exaggerated admiration of him who is appointed to reign only for its promotion and support. I detest Jacobinism; and if I am doomed to be a slave at all, I would rather be the slave of a king than a cobbler. God save the King, you say, warms your heart like the sound of a trumpet. I cannot make use of so violent a metaphor; but I am delighted to hear it when it is the cry of genuine affection; I am delighted to hear it when they hail not only the individual man but the outward and living sign of all English blessings. These are noble feelings, and the heart of every good man must go with them; but God save the King, in these times, too often means God save my pension and my place, God give my sisters an allowance out of the privy purse,—make me clerk of the irons, let me survey the meltings, let me live upon the fruits of other men's industry, and fatten upon the plunder of the public.

What is it possible to say to such a man as the Gentleman of Hampstead, who really believes it feasible to convert the four million Irish Catholics to the Protestant religion, and considers this as the best remedy for the disturbed state of Ireland? It is not possible to answer such a man with arguments; we must come out against him with beads, and a cowl, and push him into an hermitage. It is really such trash, that it is an abuse of the privilege of reasoning to reply to it. Such a project is well worthy the statesman who would bring the French to reason by keeping them without rhubarb, and exhibit to mankind the awful spectacle of a nation deprived of neutral salts. This is not the dream of a wild apothecary indulging in his own opium; this is not the distempered fancy of a pounder of drugs, delirious from smallness of profits: but it is the sober, deliberate, and systematic scheme of a man to whom the public safety is entrusted and whose appointment is considered by many as a masterpiece of political sagacity. What a sublime thought, that no purge can now be taken between the Weser and the Garonne; that the bustling pestle is still, the canorous mortar mute, and the bowels of mankind locked up for fourteen degrees of latitude! When, I should be curious to know, were all the powers of crudity and flatulence fully explained to his Majesty's Ministers? At what period was this great plan of conquest and constipation fully developed? In whose mind was the idea of destroying the pride and the plasters of France first engendered? Without castor oil they might for some months, to be sure, have carried on a lingering war; but can they do without bark? Will the people live under a government where antimonial powders cannot be procured? Will they bear the loss of mercury? 'There's the rub.' Depend upon it, the absence of the materia medica will soon bring them to their senses, and the cry of *Bourbon and bolus* burst forth from the Baltic to the Mediterranean.

You ask me for any precedent in our history where the oath of supremacy has been dispensed with. It was dispensed with to the Catholics of Canada in 1774. They are only required to take a simple oath of allegiance. The same, I believe, was the case in Corsica. The reason of such exemption was obvious; you could not possibly have retained either of these countries without it. And what did it signify whether you retained them or not? In cases where you might have been foolish without peril you were wise; when nonsense and bigotry threaten you with destruction it is impossible to bring you back to the alphabet of justice and common sense. If men are to be fools I would rather they were fools in little matters than in great; dulness turned up with temerity is a livery all the worse for the facings; and the most tremendous of all things is the magnanimity of a dunce.

It is not by any means necessary, as you contend, to repeal the Test Act if you give relief to the Catholic: what the Catholics ask for is to be put on a footing with the Protestant Dissenters, which would be done by repealing that part of the law which compels them to take the oath of supremacy and to make the declaration against transubstantiation: they would then come into parliament as all other Dissenters are allowed to do, and the penal laws to which they were exposed for taking office would be suspended every year, as they have been for this half century past towards Protestant Dissenters. Perhaps, after all, this is the best method,—to continue the persecuting law, and to suspend it every year,—a method which, while it effectually destroys the persecution itself, leaves to the great mass of mankind the exquisite gratification of supposing that they are enjoying some advantage from which a particular class of their fellow creatures are excluded. We manage the Corporation and Test Acts at present much in the same manner as if we were to persuade parish boys who had been in the habit of beating an ass to spare the animal, and beat the skin of an ass stuffed with straw; this would preserve the semblance of tormenting without the reality, and keep boy and beast in good humour.

How can you imagine that a provision for the Catholic clergy affects the 5th article of the Union? Surely I am preserving the Protestant Church in Ireland if I put it in a better conditon than that in which it now is. A tithe proctor in Ireland collects his tithes with a blunderbuss, and carries his tenth hay-cock by storm, sword in hand: to give him equal value in a more pacific shape cannot, I should imagine, be considered as injurious to the Church of Ireland; and what right has that Church to complain, if parliament chooses to fix upon the empire the burthen of supporting a double ecclesiastical establishment? Are the revenues of the Irish Protestant clergy in the slightest degree injured by such provision? On the contrary, is it possible to confer a more serious benefit upon that Church, than by quieting and contenting those who are at work for its destruction?

It is impossible to think of the affairs of Ireland without being forcibly struck with the parallel of Hungary. Of her seven millions of inhabitants, one half were Protestants, Calvinists, and Lutherans, many of the Greek Church, and many Jews: such was the state of their religious dissensions that Mahomet had often been called in to the aid of Calvin, and the crescent often glittered on the walls of Buda and of Presburg. At last, in 1791, during the most violent crisis of disturbance, a diet was called, and by a great majority of voices a decree was passed which secured to all the contending sects the fullest and freest exercise of religious worship and education; ordained (let it be heard in Hampstead) that churches and chapels should be erected for all on the most perfectly equal terms; that the Protestants of both confessions should depend upon their spiritual superiors alone; liberated them from swearing by the usual oath, 'the holy Virgin Mary, the saints, and chosen of God'; and then, the decree adds, '*that public offices and honours, high or low, great or small, shall be given to natural born Hungarians who deserve well of their country, and possess the other qualifications, let their religion be what it may.*' Such was the line of policy pursued in a diet consisting of four hundred members, in a state whose form of government approaches nearer to our own than any other, having a Roman Catholic establishment of great wealth and power, and under the influence of one of the most bigoted Catholic Courts in Europe. This measure has now the experience of eighteen years in its favour; it has undergone a trial of fourteen years of revolution such as the world never witnessed, and more than equal to a century less convulsed: What have been its effects? When the French advanced like a torrent within a few days' march of Vienna, the Hungarians rose in a mass; they formed what they called the sacred insurrection, to defend their sovereign, their rights and liberties, now common to all; and the apprehension of their approach dictated to the reluctant Bonaparte the immediate signature of the treaty of *Leoben*. The Romish hierarchy of Hungary exists in all its former splendour and opulence; never has the slightest attempt been made to diminish it; and those revolutionary principles to which so large a portion of civilized Europe has been sacrificed have here failed in making the smallest successful inroad.

The whole history of this proceeding of the Hungarian Diet is so extraordinary, and such an admirable comment upon the Protestantism of Mr Spencer Perceval, that I must compel you to read a few short extracts from the law itself:—'The Protestants of both confessions shall in religious matters depend upon their own spiritual superiors alone. The Protestants may likewise retain their trivial and grammar schools. The Church dues which the Protestants have hitherto paid to the Catholic parish priests, schoolmasters, or other such officers, either in money, productions, or labour, shall in future entirely cease, and after three months from the publishing of this law be no more anywhere demanded. In the building or repairing of churches, parsonage-houses, and schools, the Protestants are not obliged to assist the Catholics with labour, nor the Catholics the Protestants. The pious foundations and donations of the Protestants which already exist, or which in future may be made for their churches, ministers, schools and students, hospitals, orphan-houses and poor, cannot be taken from them under any pretext, nor yet the care of them; but rather the unimpeded administration shall be entrusted to those from among them to whom it legally belongs, and those foundations which may have been taken from them

under the last government shall be returned to them without
delay. All affairs of marriage of the Protestants are left to their
own consistories; all landlords and masters of families, under the
penalty of public prosecution, are ordered not to prevent their
subjects and servants, whether they be Catholic or Protestant,
from the observance of the festivals and ceremonies of their
religion,' &c. &c. &c.—By what strange chances are mankind
influenced! A little Catholic barrister of Vienna might have
raised the cry of *No Protestantism*, and Hungary would have
panted for the arrival of a French army as much as Ireland
does at this moment; arms would have been searched for;
Lutheran and Calvinist houses entered in the dead of the night;
and the strength of Austria exhausted in guarding a country
from which, under the present liberal system, she may expect,
in a moment of danger, the most powerful aid: and let it be
remembered that this memorable example of political wisdom
took place at a period when many great monarchies were yet
unconquered in Europe; in a country where the two religious
parties were equal in number, and where it is impossible to
suppose indifference in the party which relinquished its exclusive
privileges. Under all these circumstances, the measure was
carried in the Hungarian Diet by a majority of 280 to 120. In
a few weeks we shall see every concession denied to the Catholics
by a much larger majority of Protestants, at a moment when
every other power is subjugated but ourselves, and in a country
where the oppressed are four times as numerous as their oppressors. So much for the wisdom of our ancestors—so much for the
nineteenth century—so much for the superiority of the English
over all the nations of the Continent!

Are you not sensible, let me ask you, of the absurdity of
trusting the lowest Catholics with offices correspondent to their
situation in life, and of denying such privilege to the higher? A
Catholic may serve in the militia, but a Catholic cannot come
into Parliament; in the latter case you suspect combination, and
in the former case you suspect no combination; you deliberately
arm ten or twenty thousand of the lowest of the Catholic people;
—and the moment you come to a class of men whose education,
honour, and talents, seem to render all mischief less probable,
then you see the danger of employing a Catholic, and cling to
your investigating tests and disabling laws. If you tell me you

have enough of members of parliament, and not enough of militia, without the Catholics, I beg leave to remind you that by employing the physical force of any sect at the same time when you leave them in a state of utter disaffection you are not adding strength to your armies, but weakness and ruin. If you want the vigour of their common people, you must not disgrace their nobility and insult their priesthood.

I thought that the terror of the Pope had been confined to the limits of the nursery, and merely employed as a means to induce young master to enter into his small-clothes with greater speed and to eat his breakfast with greater attention to decorum. For these purposes, the name of the Pope is admirable; but why push it beyond? Why not leave to Lord Hawkesbury all farther enumeration of the Pope's powers? For a whole century you have been exposed to the enmity of France, and your succession was disputed in two rebellions; what could the Pope do at the period when there was a serious struggle whether England should be Protestant or Catholic, and when the issue was completely doubtful? Could the Pope induce the Irish to rise in 1715? Could he induce them to rise in 1745? You had no Catholic enemy when half this island was in arms; and what did the Pope attempt in the last rebellion in Ireland? But if he had as much power over the minds of the Irish as Mr Wilberforce has over the mind of a young Methodist converted the preceding quarter, is this a reason why we are to disgust men who may be acted upon in such a manner by a foreign power? or is it not an additional reason why we should raise up every barrier of affection and kindness against the mischief of foreign influence? But the true answer is, the mischief does not exist. Gog and Magog have produced as much influence upon human affairs as the Pope has done for this half century past; and by spoiling him of his possessions, and degrading him in the eyes of all Europe, Bonaparte has not taken quite the proper method of increasing his influence.

But why not a Catholic king, as well as a Catholic member of parliament, or of the cabinet?—Because it is probable that the one would be mischievous, and the other not. A Catholic king might struggle against the Protestantism of the country, and if the struggle was not successful, it would at least be dangerous; but the efforts of any other Catholic would be quite insignificant, and his hope of success so small, that it is quite improbable the effort would ever be made: my argument is that in so Protestant a country as Great Britain the character of her parliaments and her cabinet could not be changed by the few Catholics who would ever find their way to the one or the other. But the power of the Crown is immeasurably greater than the power which the Catholics could obtain from any other species of authority in the state; and it does not follow, because the lesser degree of power is innocent, that the greater should be so too. As for the stress you lay upon the danger of a Catholic chancellor, I have not the least hesitation in saying that his appointment would not do a ten thousandth part of the mischief to the English Church that might be done by a Methodistical chancellor of the true Clapham breed; and I request to know, if it is really so very necessary that a chancellor should be of the religion of the Church of England, how many chancellors you have had within the last century who have been bred up in the Presbyterian religion?—And again, how many you have had who notoriously have been without any religion at all?

Why are you to suppose that eligibility and election are the same thing, and that all the cabinet *will* be Catholics whenever all the cabinet *may* be Catholics? You have a right, you say, to suppose an extreme case and to argue upon it—so have I: and I will suppose that the hundred Irish members will one day come down in a body and pass a law compelling the King to reside in Dublin. I will suppose that the Scotch members, by a similar stratagem, will lay England under a large contribution of meal and sulphur: no measure is without objection, if you sweep the whole horizon for danger; it is not sufficient to tell me of what may happen, but you must show me a rational probability that it will happen: after all, I might, contrary to my real opinion, admit all your dangers to exist; it is enough for me to contend that all other dangers taken together are not equal to the danger of losing Ireland from disaffection and invasion.

I am astonished to see you, and many good and well-meaning clergymen beside you, painting the Catholics in such detestable colours; two-thirds, at least, of Europe are Catholics,—they are Christians, though mistaken Christians; how can I possibly admit that any sect of Christians, and above all that the oldest and the

R

most numerous sect of Christians, are incapable of fulfilling the common duties and relations of life: though I do differ from them in many particulars, God forbid I should give such a handle to infidelity and subscribe to such blasphemy against our common religion!

Do you think mankind never change their opinions without formally expressing and confessing that change? When you quote the decisions of ancient Catholic councils, are you prepared to defend all the decrees of English convocations and universities since the reign of Queen Elizabeth? I could soon make you sick of your uncandid industry against the Catholics, and bring you to allow that it is better to forget times past and to judge and be judged by present opinions and present practice.

I must beg to be excused from explaining and refuting all the mistakes about the Catholics made by my Lord Redesdale; and I must do that nobleman the justice to say, that he has been treated with great disrespect. Could anything be more indecent than to make it a morning lounge in Dublin to call upon his Lordship and to cram him with Arabian-night stories about the Catholics? Is this proper behaviour to the representative of Majesty, the child of Themis, and the keeper of the conscience in West Britain? Whoever reads the Letters of the Catholic Bishops, in the Appendix to Sir John Hippesly's very sensible book, will see to what an excess this practice must have been carried with the pleasing and Protestant nobleman whose name I have mentioned, and from thence I wish you to receive your answer about excommunication, and all the trash which is talked against the Catholics.

A sort of notion has by some means or another crept into the world, that difference of religion would render men unfit to perform together the offices of common and civil life: that Brother Wood and Brother Grose could not travel together the same circuit if they differed in creed, nor Cockell and Mingay be engaged in the same cause if Cockell was a Catholic and Mingay a Muggletonian. It is supposed that Huskisson and Sir Harry Englefield would squabble behind the Speaker's chair about the Council of Lateran, and many a turnpike bill miscarry by the sarcastical controversies of Mr Hawkins Brown and Sir John Throckmorton upon the real presence. I wish I could see some of these symptoms of earnestness upon the subject of

religion; but it really seems to me that, in the present state of
society, men no more think about inquiring concerning each
other's faith than they do concerning the colour of each other's
skins. There may have been times in England when the quarter
sessions would have been disturbed by theological polemics: but
now, after a Catholic justice had once been seen on the bench,
and it had been clearly ascertained that he spoke English, had
no tail, only a single row of teeth, and that he loved port wine,
—after all the scandalous and infamous reports of his physical
conformation had been clearly proved to be false,—he would be
reckoned a jolly fellow, and very superior in flavour to a sly
Presbyterian. Nothing, in fact, can be more uncandid and
unphilosophical than to say that a man has a tail because you
cannot agree with him upon religious subjects: it appears to be
ludicrous, but I am convinced it has done infinite mischief to
the Catholics, and made a very serious impression upon the
minds of many gentlemen of large landed property.

In talking of the impossibility of Catholic and Protestant living
together with equal privilege under the same government, do
you forget the Cantons of Switzerland? You might have seen
there a Protestant congregation going into a church which had
just been quitted by a Catholic congregation: and I will venture
to say that the Swiss Catholics were more bigoted to their religion
than any people in the whole world. Did the kings of Prussia
ever refuse to employ a Catholic? Would Frederick the Great
have rejected an able man on this account? We have seen Prince
Czartorinski, a Catholic secretary of state in Russia: in former
times, a Greek patriarch and an apostolic vicar acted together
in the most perfect harmony in Venice; and we have seen the
Emperor of Germany in modern times entrusting the care of his
person and the command of his guard to a Protestant Prince,
Ferdinand of Wirtemberg. But what are all these things to Mr
Perceval? He has looked at human nature from the top of
Hampstead Hill, and has not a thought beyond the little sphere
of his own vision. 'The snail,' say the Hindoos, 'sees nothing
but his own shell, and thinks it the grandest palace in the
universe.'

I now take a final leave of this subject of Ireland; the only
difficulty in discussing it is a want of resistance, a want of something difficult to unravel, and something dark to illumine. To

agitate such a question is to beat the air with a club and cut down gnats with a scimitar; it is a prostitution of industry and a waste of strength. If a man says, I have a good place and I do not choose to lose it, this mode of arguing upon the Catholic question I can well understand; but that any human being with an understanding two degrees elevated above that of an Anabaptist preacher should conscientiously contend for the expediency and propriety of leaving the Irish Catholics in their present state, and of subjecting us to such tremendous peril in the present condition of the world, it is utterly out of my power to conceive. Such a measure as the Catholic question is entirely beyond the common game of politics; it is a measure in which all parties ought to acquiesce, in order to preserve the place where and the stake for which they play. If Ireland is gone, where are jobs? where are reversions? where is my brother Lord Arden? where are my dear and near relations? The game is up, and the Speaker of the House of Commons will be sent as a present to the menagerie at Paris. We talk of waiting from particular considerations, as if centuries of joy and prosperity were before us: in the next ten years our fate must be decided; we shall know, long before that period, whether we can bear up against the miseries by which we are threatened, or not: and yet, in the very midst of our crisis, we are enjoined to abstain from the most certain means of increasing our strength, and advised to wait for the remedy till the disease is removed by death or health. And now, instead of the plain and manly policy of increasing unanimity at home by equalizing rights and privileges, what is the ignorant, arrogant, and wicked system which has been pursued? Such a career of madness and of folly was, I believe, never run in so short a period. The vigour of the ministry is like the vigour of a grave-digger,—the tomb becomes more ready and more wide for every effort which they make. There is nothing which it is worth while either to take or to retain, and a constant train of ruinous expeditions have been kept up. Every Englishman felt proud of the integrity of his country; the character of the country is lost for ever. It is of the utmost consequence to a commercial people at war with the greatest part of Europe that there should be a free entry of neutrals into the enemy's ports; the neutrals who carried our manufactures we have not only excluded, but we have compelled them to declare war

against us. It was our interest to make a good peace, or convince
our own people that it could not be obtained; we have not made
a peace, and we have convinced the people of nothing but of
the arrogance of the Foreign Secretary: and all this has taken
place in the short space of a year, because a King's Bench
barrister and a writer of epigrams, turned into Ministers of
State, were determined to show country gentlemen that the late
administration had no vigour. In the mean time commerce stands
still, manufacturers perish, Ireland is more and more irritated,
India is threatened, fresh taxes are accumulated upon the
wretched people, the war is carried on without it being possible
to conceive any one single object which a rational being can
propose to himself by its continuation; and in the midst of this
unparalleled insanity we are told that the Continent is to be
reconquered by the want of rhubarb and plums. A better spirit
than exists in the English people never existed in any people
in the world; it has been misdirected, and squandered upon
party purposes, in the most degrading and scandalous manner;
they have been led to believe that they were benefiting the
commerce of England by destroying the commerce of America,
that they were defending their Sovereign by perpetuating the
bigoted oppression of their fellow-subject; their rulers and their
guides have told them that they would equal the vigour of
France by equalling her atrocity; and they had gone on wasting
that opulence, patience, and courage, which, if husbanded by
prudent and moderate counsels, might have proved the salvation
of mankind. The same policy of turning the good qualities of
Englishmen to their own destruction, which made Mr Pitt
omnipotent, continues his power to those who resemble him only
in his vices; advantage is taken of the loyalty of Englishmen to
make them meanly submissive; their piety is turned into persecution, their courage into useless and obstinate contention;
they are plundered because they are ready to pay, and soothed
into asinine stupidity because they are full of virtuous patience.
If England must perish at last, so let it be; that event is in the
hands of God; we must dry up our tears and submit. But that
England should perish swindling and stealing; that it should
perish waging war against lazar houses and hospitals; that it
should perish persecuting with monastic bigotry; that it should
calmly give itself up to be ruined by the flashy arrogance of one

man and the narrow fanaticism of another; these events are within the power of human beings, and I did not think that the magnanimity of Englishmen would ever stoop to such degradations.

Longum vale!

PETER PLYMLEY

MISCELLANEOUS EXTRACTS

[There are two notebooks in existence. They measure 6¼ inches by 4, and were probably carried in the pocket. Variations in calligraphy, and other considerations, suggest that they were both in use over many years. The other sources drawn upon for these miscellaneous extracts are: the EDINBURGH REVIEW essays, the Singleton pamphlets, talk reported by Saba Holland, and published letters.]

FROM NOTEBOOKS (HOLOGRAPH)

I AM bound by the laws of religion to forgive my enemies, but am not bound to forgive my friends.

When pearls are cast to swine, the jewels are nasty and the pork not good.

In his conversation there are the furrows of long thought.

Mrs M is a woman full of petty malignities. She would not have driven a nail into the head of Sisera, but she would have wounded him with tin tacks.

Though Truth lies at the bottom of a well, it comes up very dry when F works at the windlass.

What do you mean by Faith? Believing all that is told us. What do you mean by Grace? Bowing to the Duke of R.

The tomb speaks more than a thousand homilies.

Sensuality destroys health, talents, fame, fortune—and often makes others unhappy.

The Devil is the father of lies, and a very large family he has. This lie, I should imagine, has recently left the paternal mansion and must have been a great favourite there.

Every political eminence is a Tarpeian Rock.

He would trample on the Cross like a Dutchman in Japan, or lift it up like a Carmelite Friar, as best suited his interest.

The sands are numbered that made up my life.

The clergy are getting back from the cultivated ground that bread which their Master gave away in the wilderness.

He has not knowledge to ask a question which is not impertinent, nor sense to frame a wish which is not absurd. He multiplies the pillars of Hercules, and is always finding points beyond which human science ought not to penetrate.

He is for the mob and the moment. He shewed a great contempt of dirt in kissing his hand to me.

The liberality of churchmen is like the quantity of matter in a cone. Both get less and less as they mount higher and higher.

G is like a public house with the sign of an angel: spirituality without and debauchery within.

His talk is mere pothooks and hangers.

Those eminent dissenters—Shadrach, Meshec, and Abednego.

Shakes by the hand. Ordinary—digital—mortmain or sepulchral—rustic and vigorous—high official—horizontal—eternal and retentive—ecstatic and convulsive.

If he had been Adam we should have remained safe in Paradise, for nothing could ever have persuaded him to taste [of] the Tree of Knowledge.

Ajax was mad when he took a flock of sheep for his greatest enemies, but I shall never be sound till I have the same way of thinking.

John pleaded to L that he had broken nothing since he came into the house. But says L, not so: you have broke the Sabbath, the Ten Commandments, and a new set of French china.

B is always hovering about ladies and scratching up barley for them.

The clergy make the common people kneel like elephants, that they may more conveniently load their backs with burthens.

He would have missed the road, only it was in a position where he could not get at it.

Fumbling for his brains.

G takes time by the pigtail instead of by the forelock.

I lectured my friend G J on his conduct. Unjustifiable—if he succeeds immoral, if not he is made a fool of, a ridiculous figure, must be laughed at behind his back. He is in love with a handsome face—but a young handsome face has no love for him—old enough for a grandfather. He is living upon emotion and making of life good for nothing.

Mathematics—the pupils: If you Mr Professor will give us your word of honour that the problem is true, you may spare yourself the pain of proof.

Her looks are the natural food of my soul,

He has an understanding as pinched and small as the foot of a Chinese woman.

Among fallacies are objections to half-measures.

FROM PUBLISHED SOURCES

Letter to a Brother

DEAR Bobus, Pray take care of yourself. We shall both be a brown infragrant powder in thirty or forty years. Let us contrive to last out for the same or nearly the same time. Weary will the latter half of my pilgrimage be, if you leave me in the lurch. Ever your affectionate brother, Sydney Smith.

Free Men's Privilege

TO notice every singular train of reasoning into which Mr Bowles falls is not possible; and, in the copious choice of evils, we shall, from feelings of mercy, take the least. It must not be forgotten, he observes, that 'those rights of government, which, because they are ancient, are recognized by the moral sense as lawful, are the only ones which are compatible with civil liberty'. So that all questions of right and wrong, between the governors and the governed, are determinable by chronology alone. Every political institution is favourable to liberty, not according to its spirit, but in proportion to the antiquity of its date; and the slaves of Great Britain are groaning under the trial by jury, while the free men of Asia exult in the bold privilege transmitted to them by their fathers, of being trampled to death by elephants.

The Perils of Reviewing

AN accident which happened to the gentleman engaged in reviewing this Sermon [the Anniversary Sermon of the Royal Humane Society] proves in the most striking manner the importance of this charity for restoring to life persons in whom the vital power is suspended. He was discovered, with Dr Langford's discourse lying open before him, in a state of the most profound sleep; from which he could not by any means be awaked for a great length of time. By attending, however, to the rules prescribed by the Humane Society, flinging in the smoke of tobacco, applying hot flannels, and carefully removing the discourse itself to a great distance, the critic was restored to his disconsolate brothers.

Protest against Scepticism

I CERTAINLY, my dear Jeffrey, in conjunction with the Knight of the Shaggy Eyebrows [Francis Horner], do protest against your increasing and unprofitable scepticism. I exhort you to restrain the violent tendency of your nature for analysis, and to cultivate synthetical propensities. What is virtue? What's the use of truth? What's the use of honour? What's a guinea but a d———d yellow circle? The whole effect of your mind is to destroy. Because others build slightly and eagerly, you employ yourself in kicking down their houses, and contract a sort of aversion for the more honourable, useful, and difficult task of building well yourself.

Friendship

LIFE is to be fortified by many friendships. To love, and to be loved, is the greatest happiness of existence. If I lived under the burning sun of the equator it would be a pleasure to me to think that there were many human beings on the other side of the world who regarded and respected me; I could not and would not live if I were alone upon the earth and cut off from the remembrance of my fellow-creatures. It is not that a man has occasion often to fall back upon the kindness of his friends; perhaps he may never experience the necessity of doing so; but we are governed by our imaginations, and they stand there as a solid and impregnable bulwark against all the evils of life.

Very few friends will bear to be told of their faults, and if done at all it must be done with infinite management and delicacy; for if you indulge often in the practice, men think you hate, and avoid you. If the evil is not very alarming it is better to let it alone and not to turn friendship into a system of lawful and unpunishable impertinence. I am for frank explanations with friends in cases of affronts. They sometimes save a perishing friendship, and even place it on a firmer basis than at first; but secret discontent must always end badly.

Botany Bay

THIS land of convicts and kangaroos is beginning to rise into a
very fine and flourishing settlement; and great indeed must be
the natural resources and splendid the endowments of that land
that has been able to survive the system of neglect and oppression
experienced from the mother country, and the series of ignorant
and absurd governors that have been selected for the administration of its affairs. But mankind live and flourish not only in spite
of storms and tempests, but (which could not have been anticipated previous to experience) in spite of colonial secretaries expressly
paid to watch over their interests. The supineness and profligacy
of public officers cannot always overcome the amazing energy
with which human beings pursue their happiness, nor the
sagacity with which they determine on the means by which that
end is to be promoted.

Catering for Cannibals

THE advice I sent to the Bishop of New Zealand, when he had
to receive the cannibal chiefs there, was to say to them: 'I deeply
regret, sirs, to have nothing on my own table suited to your
tastes, but you will find plenty of cold curate and roasted clergyman on the sideboard.' And if, in spite of this prudent provision,
his visitors should end their repast by eating him likewise—why,
I could only add I sincerely hoped he would disagree with them.

Sermons

THE great object of modern sermons is to hazard nothing: their
characteristic is decent debility, which alike guards their authors
from ludicrous errors and precludes them from striking beauties.
Every man of sense, in taking up an English sermon, expects to
find it a tedious essay full of commonplace morality; and if the
fulfilment of such expectations be meritorious, the clergy have
certainly the merit of not disappointing their readers. Yet it is
curious to consider how a body of men so well educated and so
magnificently endowed as the English clergy should distinguish
themselves so little in a species of composition to which it is their
peculiar duty, as well as their ordinary habit, to attend. To
solve this difficulty it should be remembered that the eloquence

of the Bar and of the Senate force themselves into notice, power, and wealth; that the penalty which an individual client pays for choosing a bad advocate is the loss of his cause; that a prime minister must infallibly suffer in the estimation of the public who neglects to conciliate eloquent men and trusts the defence of his measures to those who have not adequate talents for that purpose: whereas, the only evil which accrues from the promotion of a clergyman to the pulpit, which he has no ability to fill as he ought, is the fatigue of the audience and the discredit of that species of public instruction; an evil so general that no individual patron would dream of sacrificing to it his particular interest.

A Leave-taking

JUST before his third journey Mr Waterton takes leave of Sir Joseph Banks and speaks of him with affectionate regret. 'I saw,' (says Mr W.) 'with sorrow, that death was going to rob us of him. We talked of stuffing quadrupeds; I agreed that the lips and nose ought to be cut off, and stuffed with wax.' This is the way great naturalists take an eternal farewell of each other! Upon stuffing animals, however, we have a word to say. Mr Waterton has placed at the head of his book the picture of what he is pleased to consider a nondescript species of monkey. In this exhibition our author is surely abusing his stuffing talents, and laughing at the public. It is clearly the head of a Master in Chancery—whom we have often seen backing in the House of Commons after he has delivered his message. It is foolish thus to trifle with science and natural history.

America

AMERICA seems, on the whole, to be a country possessing vast advantages and little inconveniences; they have a cheap government, and bad roads; they pay no tithes, and have stage coaches without springs. They have no poor laws and no monopolies— but their inns are inconvenient and travellers are teased with questions. They have no collections in the fine arts; but they have no Lord Chancellor, and they can go to law without absolute ruin. They cannot make Latin verses, but they expend immense sums in the education of the poor. In all this the balance is prodigiously in their favour: but then comes the great disgrace and danger of America—the existence of slavery. . . . A high-spirited nation, who cannot endure the slightest act of foreign aggression and who revolt at the very shadow of domestic tyranny, beat with cart-whips, and bind with chains, and murder for the merest trifles, wretched human beings who are of a more dusky colour than themselves; and have recently admitted into their Union a new State, with the express permission of ingrafting this atrocious wickedness into their constitution! No one can admire the simple wisdom and manly firmness of the Americans more than we do, or more despise the pitiful propensity which exists among Government runners to vent their small spite at their character; but on the subject of slavery the conduct of America is, and has been, most reprehensible. It is impossible to speak of it with too much indignation and contempt; but for it, we should look forward with unqualified pleasure to such a land of freedom and such a magnificent spectacle of human happiness.

A Plague of Dogs

WHEN I first went down into Yorkshire [Smith's daughter reports him as saying] there had not been a resident clergyman in my parish for a hundred and fifty years. Each farmer kept a huge mastiff dog, ranging at large, and ready to make his morning meal on clergy or laity, as best suited his particular taste. I could never approach a cottage in pursuit of my calling but I rushed into the jaws of one of those shaggy monsters. I scolded, preached, and prayed, without avail; so I determined to try what fear for their pockets would do. Forthwith appeared in the county papers a minute account of a trial of a farmer, at the Northampton sessions, for keeping dogs unconfined, where said farmer was not only fined five pounds and reprimanded by the magistrates but sentenced to three months' imprisonment. The effect was wonderful, and the reign of Cerberus ceased in the land.

An Aversion to Piccadilly

MR WATERTON is a Roman Catholic gentleman of Yorkshire, of good fortune, who, instead of passing his life at balls and assemblies, has preferred living with Indians and monkeys in the forests of Guiana. He appears in early life to have been seized with an unconquerable aversion to Piccadilly, and to that train of meteorological questions and answers which forms the great staple of polite English conversation. . . . The first thing which strikes us in this extraordinary chronicle [the book under review] is the genuine zeal and inexhaustible delight with which all the barbarous countries he visits are described. He seems to love the forests, the tigers, and the apes; to be rejoiced that he is the only man there, that he has left his species far away, and is at last in the midst of his blessed baboons! He writes with a considerable degree of force and vigour; and contrives to infuse into his reader that admiration of the great works and undisturbed scenes of Nature which animates his style and has influenced his life and practice. There is something, too, to be highly respected and praised in the conduct of a country gentleman, who, instead of exhausting life in the chase, has dedicated a considerable portion of it to the pursuit of knowledge. There are so many temptations to complete idleness in the life of a country gentleman, so many examples of it, and so much loss to the community from it, that every exception from the practice is deserving of great praise.

Candid Criticism

I MUST be candid with you, my dear Jeffrey, and tell you that I do not like your article on the Scotch Courts; and with me think many persons whose opinions I am sure you would respect. I subscribe to none of your reasonings, hardly, about juries; and the manner in which you have done it is far from happy. You have made, too, some egregious mistakes about English law, pointed out to me by one of the first lawyers in the King's Bench. I like to tell you these things because you never do so well as when you are humbled and frightened, and if you could be alarmed into the semblance of modesty you would charm everybody; but remember my joke against you about the moon: —'Damn the solar system! bad light—planets too distant—pestered with comets—feeble contrivance—could make a better with great ease.'

I sincerely hope you will be up here in the spring. It is long since we met, and I want to talk over old and new times with you. God bless you.

Invitation to Breakfast

I HAVE a breakfast of philosophers tomorrow at ten punctually; muffins and metaphysics, crumpets and contradiction. Will you come?

Law and Public Opinion

THE Judges and the Parliament would have gone on, to this day, hanging by wholesale for the forgeries of bank notes, if juries had not become weary of the continual butchery and resolved to acquit. The proper execution of laws must always depend in great measure upon public opinion; and it is undoubtedly most discreditable to any man entrusted with power, when the governed turn round upon their governors and say: 'Your laws are so cruel, or so foolish, we cannot and *will not* act upon them.'

Who is Peter Plymley?

JULY 14, 1807. My dear Lady Holland, Mr Allen has mentioned to me the letters of a Mr Plymley, which I have obtained from the adjacent market-town and read with some entertainment. My conjecture lies between three persons—Sir Samuel Romilly, Sir Arthur Pigott, or Mr Horner, for the name is evidently fictitious. I shall be very happy to hear your conjectures on this subject on Saturday, when I hope you will let me dine with you at Holland House.

Portrait of Mr Bull

THERE is nothing which an Englishman enjoys more than the pleasure of sulkiness, of not being forced to hear a word from anybody which may occasion to him the necessity of replying. It is not so much that Mr Bull disdains to talk, as that Mr Bull has nothing to say. His forefathers have been out of spirits for six or seven hundred years, and, seeing nothing but fog and vapour, he is out of spirits too; and when there is no selling or buying, or no business to settle, he prefers being alone and looking at the fire. If any gentleman was in distress, he would willingly lend a helping hand; but he thinks it no part of neighbourhood to talk to a person because he happens to be near him. In short, with many excellent qualities, it must be acknowledged that the English are the most disagreeable of all the nations of Europe—more surly and morose, with less disposition to please, to exert themselves for the good of society, to make small sacrifices, and to put themselves out of their way. They are content with Magna Charta and Trial by Jury, and think they are not bound to excel the rest of the world in small behaviour if they are superior to them in great institutions.

Giving Them Beans

A MAN gets well pummelled at a public school; is subject to every misery and every indignity which seventeen years of age can inflict upon nine and ten; has his eye nearly knocked out, and his clothes stolen and cut to bits; and twenty years afterwards, when he is a chrysalis, and has forgotten the miseries of his grub state, is determined to act a manly part in life, and says, 'I passed through all that myself, and I am determined my son shall pass through it as I have done'; and away goes his bleating progeny to the tyranny and servitude of the long chamber or the large dormitory. It would surely be much more rational to say, 'Because I have passed through it, I am determined my son shall not pass through it; because I was kicked for nothing, and cuffed for nothing, and fagged for everything, I will spare all these miseries to my child.' It is not for any good which may be derived from this rough usage; that has not been weighed and considered; few persons are capable of weighing its effects upon character; but there is a sort of compensatory and consolatory notion, that the present generation (whether useful or not, no matter) are not to come off scot-free, but are to have their share of ill-usage; as if the black eye and bloody nose which Master John Jackson received in 1800, are less black and bloody by the application of similar violence to similar parts of Master Thomas Jackson, the son, in 1830. This is not only sad nonsense, but cruel nonsense. The only use to be derived from the recollection of what we have suffered in youth, is a fixed determination to screen those we educate from every evil and inconvenience, from subjection to which there are not cogent reasons for submitting. Can anything be more stupid and preposterous than this concealed revenge upon the rising generation, and latent envy lest they should avail themselves of the improvements time has made, and pass a happier youth than their fathers have done?

Toucan and Sloth

THE Toucan has an enormous bill, makes a noise like a puppy dog, and lays his eggs in hollow trees. How astonishing are the freaks and fancies of nature! To what purpose, we say, is a bird placed in the woods of Cayenne with a bill a yard long, making a noise like a puppy dog, and laying eggs in hollow trees? The Toucans, to be sure, might retort, to what purpose were gentlemen in Bond Street created? To what purpose were certain foolish prating Members of Parliament created?—pestering the House of Commons with their ignorance and folly, and impeding the business of the country? There is no end of such questions. So we will not enter into the metaphysics of the Toucan.

The Sloth, in its wild state, spends its life in trees, and never leaves them but from force or accident. The eagle to the sky, the mole to the ground, the sloth to the tree; but what is most extraordinary, he lives not *upon* the branches, but *under* them. He moves suspended, rests suspended, sleeps suspended, and passes his life in suspense—like a young clergyman distantly related to a bishop.

The Forests of Cayenne

THE description of the birds is very animated and interesting; but how far does the gentle reader imagine the campanero may be heard, whose size is that of a jay? Perhaps 300 yards. Poor innocent, ignorant reader, unconscious of what Nature has done in the forests of Cayenne, and measuring the force of tropical intonation by the sounds of a Scotch duck! The campanero may be heard three miles!—this single little bird being more powerful than a belfry of a cathedral ringing for a new dean—just appointed on account of shabby politics, small understanding, and good family.

The Road to a Bishopric

I AM surprised it does not strike the mountaineers how very much the great emoluments of the Church are flung open to the lowest ranks of the community. Butchers, bakers, publicans, schoolmasters, are perpetually seeing their children elevated to the mitre. Let a respectable baker drive through the city from the west end of the town, and let him cast an eye on the battlements of Northumberland House, has his little muffin-faced son the smallest chance of getting in among the Percies, enjoying a share of their luxury and splendour, and of chasing the deer with hound and horn upon the Cheviot Hills? But let him drive his alum-steeped loaves a little farther, till he reaches St Paul's Churchyard, and all his thoughts are changed when he sees that beautiful fabric; it is not impossible that his little penny roll may be introduced into that splendid oven. Young Crumpet is sent to school; takes to his books; spends the best years of his life, as all eminent Englishmen do, in making Latin verses; knows that the *crum* in crumpet is long, and the *pet* short; goes to the University; gets a prize for an Essay on the Dispersion of the Jews; takes orders; becomes a Bishop's chaplain; has a young nobleman for his pupil; publishes a useless classic and a serious call to the unconverted; and then goes through the Elysian transitions of Prebendary, Dean, Prelate, and the long train of purple, profit, and power.

Latin Verse

THE prodigious honour in which Latin verses are held at public schools is surely the most absurd of all absurd distinctions. You rest all reputation upon doing that which is a natural gift and which no labour can attain. If a lad won't learn the words of a language, his degradation in the school is a very natural punishment for his disobedience or his indolence; but it would be as reasonable to expect that all boys should be witty, or beautiful, as that they should be poets. In either case, it would be to make an accidental, unattainable, and not a very important gift of nature, the only or the principal test of merit. This is the reason why boys who make a very considerable figure at school so very often make no figure in the world, and why other lads, who are passed over without notice, turn out to be valuable, important men. The test established in the world is widely different from that established in a place which is presumed to be a preparation for the world; and the head of a public school, who is a perfect miracle to his contemporaries, finds himself shrink into absolute insignificance because he has nothing else to command respect or regard but a talent for fugitive poetry in a dead language.

Relieving Distress

EVERYBODY is full of humanity and good-nature when he can relieve misfortune by putting his hand in his neighbour's pocket. Who can bear to see a fellow-creature suffering pain and poverty when he can order other fellow-creatures to relieve them? Is it in human nature that A should see B in tears and misery and not order C to assist him?

Advice to Parishioners

I MUST positively forbid all poaching; it is absolute ruin to yourself and your family. In the end you are sure to be detected, a hare in one pocket and a pheasant in the other. How are you to pay ten pounds? You have not ten pence beforehand in the world. Daniel's breeches are unpaid for; you have a hole in your hat, and want a new one; your wife, an excellent woman, is about to lie in; and you are, all of a sudden, called upon by the Justice to pay ten pounds. I shall never forget the sight of poor Cranford, hurried to Taunton Jail; a wife and three daughters on their knees to the Justice, who was compelled to do his duty and commit him. The next day, beds, chairs, and clothes sold, to get the father out of jail. Out of jail he came; but the poor fellow could not bear the sight of his naked cottage and to see his family pinched with hunger. You know how he ended his days. Was there a dry eye in the churchyard when he was buried? It was a lesson to poachers. It is indeed a desperate and foolish trade. Observe, I am not defending the game-laws, but I am advising you, as long as the game-laws exist, to fear them, and to take care that you and your family are not crushed by them.

Taking Care of the Bishops

THERE are very few men in either House of Parliament who ever think of the happiness and comfort of the working Clergy, or bestow one thought upon guarding them from the increased and increasing power of their encroaching masters. What is called taking care of the Church is taking care of the Bishops; and all Bills for the management of the Clergy are left to the concoction of men who very naturally believe they are improving the Church when they are increasing their own power. . . .

I give sincere credit to the Commissioners for good intentions —how can such men have intended anything but good? And I firmly believe that they are hardly conscious of the extraordinary predilection they have shown for Bishops in all their proceedings; it is like those errors in tradesmen's bills of which the retail arithmetician is really unconscious, but which somehow or another always happen to be in his own favour.

Acknowledging a Letter

MY dear Jeffrey, I thought you had entirely forgotten me, and was pleasing myself with the notion that you were rising in the world, that your income was tripling and quadrupling in value, and that you were going through the customary and concomitant process of shedding your old friends and the companions of your obscurity—when, behold, your letter arrived, diminished your income, blunted your fame, and restored your character.

Cheerfulness

PERSONS subject to low spirits should make the rooms in which they live as cheerful as possible; taking care that the paper with which the wall is covered should be of a brilliant lively colour, hanging up pictures or prints, and covering the chimney-piece with beautiful china. A bay-window looking upon pleasant objects, and above all a large fire whenever the weather will permit, are favourable to good spirits, and the tables near should be strewed with books and pamphlets. To this must be added as much eating and drinking as is consistent with health, and some manual employment for men, as gardening, a carpenter's shop, the turning-lathe, etc. Women have always manual employments enough, and it is a great source of cheerfulness. Fresh air, exercise, occupation, society, and travelling, are powerful remedies. The habit of taking very short views of human life may be acquired by degrees, and a great sum of happiness is gained by it.

The Miseries of Falling in Love

MANY thanks, dear Lady Dacre, for your beautiful translations in your beautiful book. I read forthwith several beautiful sonnets upon Love, which paint with great fidelity some of the worst symptoms of that terrible disorder, than which none destroys more completely the happiness of common existence, and substitutes, for the activity which Life demands, a long and sickly dream with moments of pleasure and days of intolerable pain. The Poets are full of false views: they make mankind believe that happiness consists in falling in love and living in the country. I say, live in London; like many people; fall in love with nobody. To these rules of life I add: read Lady Dacre's translations, and attend her Monday evening parties. Ever yours, Sydney Smith [*aetatis* 66].

Saying Goodbye

WE have been unpleasantly engaged for these two or three days past in bidding adieu to some very pleasant families who are quitting this place. All adieus are melancholy; and principally, I believe, because they put us in mind of the last of all adieus, when the apothecary, and the heir apparent, and the nurse who weeps for pay, surround the bed; when the curate, engaged to dine three miles off, mumbles hasty prayers; when the dim eye closes for ever in the midst of empty pill-boxes, gallipots, phials, and jugs of barley-water. At that time—a very distant one, I hope, my dear Madam—may the memory of good deeds support you.

SERMONS AND OTHER OCCASIONS

[This section contains two sermons, two letters to the MORNING CHRONICLE, and a speech on the Reform Bill. An account of the Dame Partington speech will be found on page 77.]

TOLERATION

That ye may be the children of your Father which is in heaven: for he maketh his sun to rise on the evil and the good, and sendeth rain on the just and the unjust. St Matthew, v. 45.

IT is not uncommon for the apostles to restrain with considerations of this nature the angry and vindictive passions of mankind. You would exterminate, they say, and root out those who offend you, but look to the ways of the Almighty, and observe the patient forbearance by which they are marked—the bow of his wrath is not always bent, nor is he constantly scattering his judgments among the sons of men;—he maketh the sun to rise among the evil and the good, and sendeth rain upon the just and the unjust.

Now if this argument of divine forbearance be calculated to teach men forbearance in cases where they themselves have been injured, it must necessarily, and with much greater force, inculcate the same turn of mind towards that class of injuries by which we conceive the interests of religion only to be affected. If the consideration of God's merciful forbearance make us forgive errors in practice, it should make us forgive errors in religion, and if it make us placable, it should make us tolerant; for I may say as the Apostle says, 'If God thought of the heretic as you think of him, would the earth be to him as it is to us; would he drink our air, would he be enlivened with our sun, would nature bud, and swell, and grow for him, as it does for us? But now while we are taking God's cause into our own hands, the Almighty, the most merciful Father of us all, 'God sendeth his rain upon the just and the unjust, and maketh the sun to shine upon the evil and the good'. I do not say that such a passage as this settles the question of religious benevolence, but it suggests a beautiful analogy—it provokes an useful train of thought and leads us to reflect seriously upon this great Christian duty. The subject is, I fear, too much connected with present passions to allow that I should be heard with all the impartiality I could wish. I have no intention whatever to avail myself of that connexion in the most remote degree. I mean only to treat the subject generally, to descant upon that spirit of religious forbearance which appears to me so perfectly congenial to the Christian religion, which is applicable to all times, which will allay the passions and promote the interest of mankind, when the present generation of living beings, with all their factions and intrigues, are swept away into the gulf of eternity.

In pursuance of this intention I propose to lay down some rules and points of consideration which may govern and fashion our opinions of those who differ from us in our religious persuasion. It is by no means derogatory to religion to say that, unless it be watched over with great care, it has a tendency to produce the feelings of intolerance: this inconvenience, and risk, springs out of the very nature of religion—the allurements it holds out are so irresistible, the punishments with which it menaces are so infinite, it excites so many passions and appeals to so many first principles, that it is scarcely possible to reason and to act here as we would reason and act in any case of human concern. I have studied the Scriptures diligently; I have endeavoured to gather from them just rules of action in this world—I have endeavoured to make them my guide to salvation—I think I have succeeded—I think I understand the Scriptures—I love the interpretations I have made—I am accustomed to them—I have gained them by laborious diligence, and they appear good in my eyes; but I come to you, and I find that your interpretation of the same subject is completely opposite to mine—I find you attacking my religious opinions and establishing your own. Is it any wonder that I should be heated when the question between us is a question of eternity? Is it any charge against religion that men cannot reason upon it as calmly, and as coolly, as they do upon the divisions of their lands, and the portions of their children, and the structure of their buildings? What does all this prove but that the most impassioned feeling which can occupy the heart of man is eternity? That the thought of God moves him more than all other thoughts—and that pain, labour, watchfulness, sorrow, wretchedness, are endured—fortune, fame, health, friends, country abjured—in the pursuit of an immortal existence?

But though no argument against religion in general can be

drawn from intolerance, it is still necessary to show that intolerance is a very great evil; that it leads to consequences the most pernicious, and requires on our part every effort for its prevention or its cure.

If the chances of life were to lead any of us into intimacy with the members of any other religious sect, and if they were to speak undisguisedly before us, we should soon come to hear from some a great deal of foolish anger against our religious opinions, from others a great deal of ignorant misrepresentation: we should wonder that some of them hated us so much, and be astonished that others knew us so little. What a pity (we should think) that so many men, not otherwise deficient in understanding or goodness, should suffer themselves to be thus blinded by religious prejudices! And yet, do you think, my brethren, if a sectary were to come and study us, and listen to our prejudices, that there is nothing of which he could complain? Would he not say, 'I perceive you have taken your notions of my creed from mere hearsay. You ascribe to me some doctrines which I have long since abjured, and others which I never professed. I find myself universally hated, because I am universally misrepresented. It is quite impossible among these people to find candour or justice.' It is the truth I fear of the great mass, in all religious sects; it is the tribe of Reuben against the tribe of Benjamin, and the threats of Issachar against the tribe of Manasses. Now the feeling which a good man derives from all this misrepresentation and exaggeration is a distaste for religious violence; a respect for calmness, charity, and moderation, a conviction that these feelings of hatred cannot be from God, and a determination to be rigidly just to every description of Christians. It is for this reason that the railings and hatred of different sects of Christians against each other ought to be noticed, and brought before Christian congregations, to make good men afraid of doing anything so pernicious, proud men ashamed of falling into any error so common, and to convince able men that their faculties are degraded by the reception of opinions so easy, so vulgar, and so false.

It will be of use, I think, to remember that this fault of intolerance or unjust abuse of other sects is very common; it will be of use also to reflect from what it proceeds. It proceeds, if I mistake not, from our supposing that there is only one road to heaven; whereas, God Almighty be thanked, there are many roads to heaven. The Church of England is the wisest and the most enlightened sect of Christians. I think so, or I would not belong to it another hour. But is it possible for me to believe that every Christian out of the pale of that Church will be consigned after this life to the never-ending wrath of God? If I were to preach such doctrines, who would hear me? Can I paint God as the protector of one Christian creed—deaf to all prayers, blind to all woes, but ours? God whom the Indian Christian, whom the Armenian Christian, whom the Greek Christian, whom the Catholic, whom the Protestant, adore in a varied manner, in another climate, with a fresh priest and a changed creed. Are you and I to live again, and are these Christians as well as us not to live again? Foolish arrogant man has said this, but God has never said this. He calls for the just in Christ; he tells us that through that name he will reward every good man and accept every just action; that if you take up the Cross of Christ he will reward you for every kind deed, repay you sevenfold for every example of charity, carefully note, and everlastingly recompense, the justice, the honour, the integrity, the benevolence of your present life; and yet, though God is the God of all Christians, each says to the other, 'He is not *your* God, but *my* God; for me and my brethren are the heavens spread out and the everlasting blessings of the just prepared; God accepts only my prayers, listens only to my hymns, sanctions only my glosses; he is not the God of the just in Christ, but the God of Calvin, the God of Luther, or the God of the Papal Crown.'

It seems, then, that every sincere Christian who leads a good life, and interprets the Scriptures in the best manner he is able, has an equal chance of salvation, let his creed be what it may. Is there any man will be hardy enough to deny this, or say that salvation is to be found only among one set of Christians? Why, then, see the immediate consequences which follows. God is tolerant, man is *not* tolerant; Omniscience pardons, frailty is inexorable; God opens wide the portals of heaven, but man says, 'Before you can enter in you must have the mark of my brotherhood, and the passport of my creed.' In the ages of ignorance he comes with his faggot, and his whip, and his sword, to teach that creed; and, after that, he comes with that creed to the Judge who sits in the judgment-seat, to the Captain of his hosts, to the Maker of his laws: this, he says, is the test of your righteousness, your valour, and your wisdom, and he tumbles from every power of civil life the man who will not reason as he reasons and pray as he prays; and when the increasing wisdom of ages has deprived him of these means of persecution, there are left to him only the bitter arms of calumny and misrepresentation. But if the Almighty did allow but one method of expounding the Scriptures, if it were a mortal sin in the eye of Heaven to deviate from the dogmas of one particular creed, is it therefore necessary that man should fight the battles of his Creator? If a man says that murder is lawful, or theft is lawful, he must be stopt and put down. Society could not exist if such sort of doctrines were tolerated; but why is man to interfere with questions which are purely speculative and theological? to punish opinions which are only between his Creator and the man who professes them, which have no sort of reference to the common order and decency of the world? But such doctrines are wrong.— Very likely.—Then refute them.—I have.—Your antagonist is so far from thinking so, that he believes himself to have refuted you.—But they are contrary to the glory of God.—Then let God avenge them.—They will be followed by his eternal punishments on the day of judgment.—If God then can wait till the day of judgment, why not you?—why think you not that you should be the children of your Father which is in heaven, who sendeth rain on the just and the unjust, and causeth the sun to rise on the evil and the good?

It would seem as if the Word of God armed us against sectaries, as the Jews were armed against the Hivites, the Jebusites, and the Perizzites, and sent out for their extermination—and yet the Gospel nowhere says, 'Do me this service, fight me this battle, rise up in judgment against these rebellious children, who will not fashion their prayers after your prayers, and interpret my word as you interpret it.' In the Gospel all is peace, all is forbearance; in the natural world there are no signs of God's immediate anger against any description of Christians: the blessings of nature are extended to us all, yet we are all eager to rush forward for the glory of God and religion, to protect Omnipotence, and stimulate the tardy vengeance of Heaven.

The fact is, and the plain truth must be told, that an intolerant spirit, though it often proceeds from a mistaken zeal for religion, often proceeds also from mere personal insolence; offended pride, that any man should presume to think differently from you on these subjects; that he should deny the force of arguments which have always appeared to you, from your very childhood, to be irresistible; that he should dare to differ from you in some religious ceremonies which you have been always taught to consider as of the last importance, and to refuse conversion too; to persevere in these errors, to maintain them after repeated discussions, to deny the force of such plain arguments and the inference from such unquestionable fact. So feels the Calvinist against the Lutheran, and so feels the Lutheran against the Calvinist. The affairs of religion become a mere question of pique and passion; each man feels his understanding insulted, and then would call in the civil power, if he could, to disgrace and disqualify his antagonist, declaring to others, and firmly believing himself, that he is actuated only by an earnest zeal for the glory of God and the dearest interests of religion.

This very feeling of insolence in the mask of religious zeal has thrust millions of human beings into the flames or mangled them upon scaffolds. The state of the world is changed, and its sphere of action is limited. I know not a better, or a more useful, or a more Christian, or a more thankless, or a more perilous office than to strive every nerve, and to exert every faculty, to make those little limits less, and to bring out Christianity in its true and genuine nature—a mild religion, a tolerating religion, a generous and a magnanimous religion; a religion which allows to every man that unlimited freedom of inquiry which every man ought to possess whose eternal salvation depends on whether he inquires well or ill. Infidels tell us Christianity is intolerant. Christianity is not intolerant: most men would force their opinions upon others if they could; but they do it in spite of the Gospel, which never in one page or one line from the stable where our Redeemer was born to the cross on which he died, never mentions pain for any creed, punishment for any mode of worship—never breathes the slightest thought of anger, blame, penalty, shame, or degradation, against any one honest diversity of human opinion. I would suggest as a check upon the spirit of intolerance this reflection: That the obstinacy of mankind on these points cannot be overcome; they are not to be forced by violence, intimidated by threats, or turned from their purpose by any effort of hatred or persecution. If experience teaches us any one thing in the world, it teaches us the impossibility of doing any good by interfering with religious opinions, the absolute necessity of leaving human beings to think and act for themselves on subjects of this nature; therefore there is this reason for excluding from the mind that class of hatreds and disgusts, that they are absolutely useless and powerless. You may be as angry as you please that men will entertain this or that religious opinion: your anger does no good, it will go on in spite of you. It is better to let it alone, to pass it by with calmness, to leave it to the unerring decision of time, which strengthens reasonable piety without the aid of law, and dissipates that fervour, and exposes that folly, against which the sceptre, and the sword, and the mitre, conspire in vain.

I must stipulate for another principle which circumscribes and calms the tumultuous passions of intolerance—a rooted conviction that all men have a perfect right to think and act as they please on religious subjects, where they do nothing, and say nothing, incompatible with the public peace; whereas the notion by which we are too often actuated is, that dissent from established opinions is a crime; that the law has settled a certain mode of salvation; not, which every man is wisely and properly invited to adopt (that would be true enough), but which every man is bound to adopt;—that he becomes accountable to the civil magistrate if he does not:—perhaps the proposition is not drawn out so clearly, but there is certainly a confused sort of notion that a dissenter is a criminal; that he has done something which stamps him a bad subject of the commonwealth and marks him out as an object of persecution. It is this feeling which has ever been the great parent of religious slavery all over the world, and for the suppression of which every honest minister of the Gospel ought to raise his voice. No human being has a right to dictate to another in what way he shall make his peace with God or ask for an humble and contrite heart the blessings of eternity. Here ends, and here ought to end, all human authority; here begins that commerce between the Creator and the created being—the secret sigh, the dawning thought of piety, the ascending prayer, the descending grace, the great workings of the human heart, struggling to get up to another order of beings—the sacred feelings which all the unbridled licence of human tyrants has

T

never been able to repress:—the only point where every base man is noble, and every abject spirit free.

It is our duty to probe to the bottom this feeling of religious hatred: it is not pleasant but is useful; for if a man does not hear truth here, where can he ever reach it? We do not come to the temple of God to be confirmed in pleasing opinions, but to get at religious truth, to get at righteousness, to get at heaven, to get at God; to burst through all the delusions of the world; to proclaim a sabbath in the soul, and to be more pure in mind, at the same time that we put on the postures of adoration and of prayer. I fear then very much that there is a selfish pleasure in seeing other sects beneath us; the Pharisee loves to have the Sadducee beneath his feet; the Jew keeps down the Samaritan, and he says, 'That man's disgrace is my glory. If I let him rise he will become equal to me; he will range his altar beside my altar; and the cloud of his burnt offering will go up to heaven like mine'. But the warm and expanded heart says, 'Let God hear us all! Why punish you for your honest prayer? why mark and degrade you because you will not come under the roof of my temple, and join in my hymn? I love freedom, and I know you love it. I enjoy every right of worship, and I wish you to enjoy them like me; I seek not to build my distinction on your shame, nor is that happiness only grateful to me which is purchased by the disgrace and persecution of my fellow-creatures.' This is the best and most beautiful picture of the Christian faith, and in this way does the true disciple of Christ govern the thoughts of his heart; he loves religious truth ardently and he seeks it diligently; but he remembers always that the pursuit is difficult and the conclusion not certain: he detests levity in religion, but he does not punish error, because he feels the comfort of enjoying a free and unmolested creed; he cordially wishes to extend that comfort to the utmost boundaries of the Christian world; he feels religious persecution and religious hatred to be unjust, and he knows it to be useless; he thinks it folly to protect mankind in their flocks, and their fields, and to carry tyranny into their vows and prayers: such a man leaves penalty and vengeance to God, in God's concerns; he uses religion not for the advancement of his sect but for the subjugation of his soul: through all the diversities of Christian opinion he searches for the holy in desire, for the good in council, for the just in works, and he loves the good under whatever temple, at whatever altar, he may find them. He defends his creed by his labour, by his talent, by his zeal, by his knowledge; and he scorns to ask that aid from the sword of the magistrate which he ought to derive from the honest exertions of his own mind. If I have read well my gospel, such is the character of a good and a sincere servant of Christ; and in such wise should he imitate the patient forbearance of our common Father, who pities that frailty we do not pity, who forgives that error we do not forgive, who maketh his sun to rise on the evil and on the good, and sendeth rain on the just and the unjust.

THE FORGIVENESS OF INJURIES

Forgive, and ye shall be forgiven. Luke, vi. 37.

AS I always wish to make my sermons practical and useful, I mean to preach today upon the forgiveness of injuries; for I know no better way of making men Christians than by taking those vices in detail which are opposed to the Christian character, examining the causes from which they proceed, and suggesting the means by which they may be opposed. A real Christian is he who has established in his mind many good qualities and got rid of many bad ones; and this can only be done, sin by sin, and fault by fault, and excellence by excellence; slowly, cautiously, and carefully. And therefore you must not think it singular that I often take up very narrow points of conduct and descant upon single virtues, for I think it the best and surest way of building up the Christian character.

It is not bad counsel to give to a Christian congregation, to request, before they indulge in any scheme of resentment, and put on that horrid character of implacability which is so foreign to our religion—it is not, I say, bad advice to exhort them seriously to consider, and most anxiously to weigh, whether they have really suffered the injury upon which their anger and resentment are founded, or whether self-love and furious passions may not have rendered them mistaken in the fact and mistaken in the author of the fact. Perhaps they may have suffered no injury, perhaps the person whom they considered to be the author of an injury which is real may not be the author of it; and in treating the subject of forgiveness of injuries which I purpose to do this day, it may be as well to begin here, to make it sure that there is even that frail and faulty basis for revenge which even human tribunals and the opinions of the world would require—to be sure that you are not left even without the shadow of an excuse for a fault so abhorrent to every principle of our faith.

You have suffered an injury. Are you sure it *is* an injury? Have you laid it before good, and just, and wise men, and are they satisfied as well as you are, that you have been really injured? Are you not the cause of what you are pleased to term an injury? Have you not brought it upon yourself by your own violence and injustice? and inflicted much greater injury than you have received? Look abroad and see how often others are deceived, how often the sufferer appears to have suffered justly, how often the complainant has given birth to the complaint; and if these errors exist in others, why may they not exist in any one of us? Why may not we justify our revenge upon a base as instable, deceive ourselves with conclusions as hasty, rush into dangerous passions upon principles as foolish and as false? And then think what the error is!—not an error in calculations which make us more or less rich, or more or less powerful, but an error in the work of salvation; a blindness which darkens the view of heaven, a false step in the road to God; for remember what says our great Christian prayer—'Forgive us as we forgive those who have trespassed against us'. What then is our chance of forgiveness if we forgive not them who have never trespassed against us? If we rage with implacable revenge against the innocent, and offer up a miserable error as an atonement for an unpardonable sin, which sin it could not expiate if it were no error at all, but as true as we (deceived by our miserable passions) believe it to be.

But what matters whether it be a real injury or not? If it *is*, you must forgive it, at least you must forgive it if you wish to be forgiven.

The precept may appear hard, but obedience to it brings many immediate rewards; and it is the best plan of life for your immediate happiness, as the precepts of the Gospel are ever found to be. You will find the pain of forgiving to be of short duration, the pleasure of forgiving to be for ever recurring; causing a man to love and respect himself; breathing a satisfaction over the whole of life; remembered the hour before dissolution; offered to God as an atonement for sin; rising up to you in sickness and pain, and in all the miseries of the flesh, when power is forgotten and glory is despised.

And don't be tempted to the unchristian sin of not forgiving, by the pleasure of revenge: there is a pleasure in revenge, but it is a short-lived pleasure, and always followed by bitter remorse. When you have humbled all you wish to humble, and destroyed all you wished to destroy, when you cease to be supported by strong passions, when you cannot retract, and cannot repair, you will then begin to repent! You will then be conscious that you have lived in opposition to one of the most sacred rules of the Gospel; that in a religion of peace your life has been a life of hatred; that under a law of forgiveness you have indulged in malicious rancour; that, expecting to be forgiven only as you forgive, you have lost all right to implore the mercy of God, because you have spurned the condition on which that right is founded. And will it never come? Are you rash and foolish enough to suppose that the violation of this condition will never flash across your mind; that when you lose your children by sudden disease, when you are in the agonies of pain or the depression of sickness or the bitterness of death, that you will not be driven to ask help from God, and mercy for a bad life, and forbearance for the many sins of your soul? Believe me, the stoutest, and the bravest, and the youngest amongst you, will all come to this! And then the dreadful answer! the man within the breast! the dreadful dialogue with your own soul! Were *you* merciful? Did tears soften you? Did entreaties bend you? Was your heart an heart of flesh? Remember the man in the prison!—the debtor seized, the goods confiscated, the bitterness of speech, the destruction of fame, and the long work of wrath and strife! Think of this in your losses, think of it in your pain, think of it at your death; but above all, think of it *now*, that you may turn aside those losses, when you may lessen that pain by pleasing remembrances, that you may feel in that death the piercing hope of everlasting life.

Again, common observation on human character shows us that great schemes of resentment commonly give way. No man can hate for a whole life: the passion which *seemed* to be immortal is at length swept off by the current of impressions, and at the close of life, when little time remains for affection, the dictates of reason resume their empire and the feelings of reason return. Year after year has past away in silent indignation. Every emotion of affection stifled, every office of kindness lost; all the sweet consolations of existence lavished away; and then when the grave admonishes enemies to forgive, they mourn over the kindness they have lost, to renew it for a moment and to lose it again for ever! Therefore, as the Apostle says, 'Repent, for the kingdom of heaven is at hand.' I say, Forgive, for the kingdom of heaven is at hand!—forgive, while forgiveness is worth having; forgive, while there remains enough of life for the reward of kindness; forgive, while you have something else to bestow on repentance than lingering looks and faltering words. And what does this solemn Christian injunction of forgiving do, but eradicate from the mind the most painful and unquiet of all human passions. What wretchedness to sacrifice all the quietness of life, to sicken on the bosom of joy, still after the lapse of years to feel and to suffer with the freshness of yesterday, and in the midst of blessings to explain, 'All this availeth me nothing, while Mordecai the Jew sitteth at the king's gate'.

Some men are so far from being ashamed of not forgiving injuries that they often glory in revenge; they believe it to be united with courage and dignified pride; belonging to a nature jealous of insult, firm above others in what it purposes, vivid above others in what it feels; yet after all, what virtue or what great quality can an unforgiving disposition possibly imply? Who is most likely longest to retain the sense of injured dignity? The man who has given no pledge to his fellow-creatures of excellence, the man who feels himself vulnerable, who is least fortified by a long tenour of just intentions and wise actions. If there be virtue and merit in these feelings of revenge, let *us* at least draw our virtues from a source where the weakest and worst of mankind cannot draw in common with us. Let *them* darken the sunshine of life with the inquietude of resentment, and hover year after year over expiring injuries! If such be the creed of the world, this is the creed of the Gospel. If there be any who have sinned against me, and I have not forgiven him, if the shadows be long and the sun going down and I am stirred up against any one of my brethren—if there be any man on the earth, the latchet of whose shoe, the hair of whose head, I would injure—if that man come to me and hold out his hand and say, 'It repenteth me sore that I have sinned against thee',—if I turn that man away in the bitterness of his heart, if I run not forward to meet him, may God turn away from me in the bitterness of *my* heart; and while mine enemy rests in the bosom of Abraham, may there be no drop of water to cool my thirst!

I beg you to remember, as sincere Christians, that there are many occasions in life where it is possible to effect by forgiveness every object which you propose to effect by resentment. It is possible, by forgiveness, to open the mind of an enemy to a sense of his injustice, it is possible to excite his admiration, to conciliate his affection, and to turn his heart. This is true Christianity, and it is high and difficult Christianity, and it is human nature in its most beautiful aspect. Who did me this kindness? Not my kinsman, not my brother, not my child, not mine own familiar friend, but mine enemy—the man whom I have been pursuing with inveterate malice, and for whose soul I have been preparing every variety of affliction. While I have been doing the work of the devil, he has been praying to God for me; and been labouring for my happiness, while I have been labouring to blacken his reputation and to embitter his life. I will arise and go to that man, and say, 'I have sinned against Heaven and against thee, and I am not worthy to be called thy friend.'

It is well worthy of attention to a serious and devout Christian, who is always looking to the inward man and always pressing forward to the prize of the high calling, that while other duties are only made the object of separate precepts this duty of forgiveness of injuries is the very condition upon which we are permitted to prefer any petition to the throne of grace. It is not said simply, 'Thou shalt forgive him that trespasseth against thee', but we are made to say, 'Forgive us our trespasses as we forgive them that trespass against us'. Here, then, is the history of a Christian who indulges in the violent emotions of hatred and revenge. You live on with a load of passion and folly on your own heart, knowing your sins, trembling at your sins, daily asking pardon of God for them, and yet without one atom of mercy for the passions, the follies, and vices of others. You implore the Being above, and you threaten the being beneath; the very prayer you use condemns you: you place the Redeemer, Jesus, between you and Omnipotence—you, who have never forgiven, nor redeemed, nor wept, nor listened, nor lifted up, the bruised, contrite, repentant spirit! What! when the great book of your life is laid open before you, when all your pretences are weak, when all your artifices are disclosed, when all your excuses fail, and before the congregation of nations you fall down before the judging angel, and with groans and tears, and with the place of torments before you, say to the judging angel that you were but a weak, frail, and powerless mortal, and try to awaken in the beings of heaven their own native feelings of pity! 'But,' says the heavenly Judge to you at that moment, 'Did you pity? had you mercy on weakness? Did *you* forget while you lived? Did you forgive? Did you earn this pardon for your own trespasses by pardoning the trespasses of others?' This will come as sure as you live and have your being—all this *must* come. Forgive then in time, and lay up treasures in the book of God. A right expression this, and one of frequent occurrence in the Bible, 'laying up treasures in heaven'; and perhaps there may be some persons here present who may deride this expression, and perhaps they may despise me for using it; but if there is a day of judgment there *are* treasures in heaven; there are records which ensure the mercy of God; there are remembrances which plead for the intercession of Christ. Every charitable act is a treasure; gentleness and kindness are treasures; every act of forgiveness is a treasure; and I counsel the lowest and the poorest man here present not to hear this language as a matter of course, and of daily repetition, but I counsel him to believe that these are real treasures, and I counsel the richest men here present to consider themselves as bare and destitute if they have not laid up these treasures. Your day will come, let the good believe; your day will come; be patient, trust firmly in the promise of the Gospel; give up the bad passions of hatred and revenge. You are hastening to your reward as the seed is hastening to its fruit. You must see that all this is a preparation for another world. Your day is coming. Forgive, and ye shall be forgiven!

There is this collateral advantage to be derived from the Christian lesson I have thought it my duty to give you this day, and that is, that he who keeps a clear mind, and is disposed to forgive injuries, is less likely to commit them; for being in the habit of accounting with himself he is more likely to reflect upon the consequences of actions, having experienced all the pain and indignation which the injuries of others have inflicted upon him; remembering the odious light in which the guilty person has appeared to him, the punishment he might have inflicted, the effort it has cost him to forbear, and the deep satisfaction he has felt when that effort has been crowned with success, he is not likely to change his high seat of religion for the path of sin; he is not likely to offend his Saviour by committing against others those trespasses which, in obedience to that law, he has forgiven when committed against himself. Physicians tell you that there are certain signs and appearances which indicate the presence of disease before the patient is disabled by it. So there are signs which show to the moral and religious teacher that the soul is dark, and that the lamp of the Gospel is not burning and shining within. You are not Christian if you hate, you are not Christian if you revenge: they are feelings which do not belong to the Christian climate, which has none of these fierce blasts but is always temperate and gentle. If you feel these bad passions, if you cannot master them, if they hurry you away, be exceedingly alarmed for your soul. God is not with you, you are wandering from your Redeemer, you are not of the family of Christ, and therefore don't wonder at the vehement anxiety with which preachers guard you from irascible passions. And be assured that prayers, and professions, and all outward demonstrations of faith, are vain, if you do not steadily rule all those violent passions whose inroads upon human happiness it is the constant object of the Gospel to restrain. I have much more to say on this subject than it will be possible to say in my present discourse, and it will be necessary to resume it on some future occasion. To say too much upon it will not be easy for a minister of the Gospel. In every occasion of this life our blessed Saviour preached forgiveness of injuries to Sadducee, to Pharisee, to Gentile, and to Jew; to rich and to poor. Mercy to others, if you wish for mercy, was his doctrine. God forgiveth the forgiver: he that smiteth shall be smitten. So, our blessed Saviour taught, and, dying as he lived, prayed for his destroyers—'God forgive them, they know not what they do!'

'LOCKING IN' ON RAILWAYS

[In the summer of 1842 Sydney Smith addressed three letters on this subject to the MORNING CHRONICLE. In the first he expatiates on two evil effects of having the carriage doors locked: (i) the possibility of the passengers being burnt alive, without chance of escape, as had recently happened on the Paris railway, and (ii) the effect of this possibility on the imagination: railway travel 'is inseparably connected with abominable tyranny and perilous imprisonment'. The railways are in the hands of a monopoly, which nothing can make tolerable 'but the most severe and watchful jealousy of the manner in which its powers are exercised'. The second and third letters here follow.]

7 June, 1842

SINCE the letter upon railroads, which you were good enough to insert in your paper, I have had some conversation with two gentlemen officially connected with the Great Western. Though nothing could be more courteous than their manner, nor more intelligible than their arguments, I remain unshaken as to the necessity of keeping the doors open.

There is, in the first place, the effect of imagination, the idea that all escape is impossible, that (let what will happen) you must sit quiet in first class No. 2, whether they are pounding you into a jam, or burning you into a cinder, or crumbling you into a human powder. These excellent directors, versant in wood and metal, seem to require that the imagination should be sent by some other conveyance, and that only loads of unimpassioned, unintellectual flesh and blood should be darted along on the Western rail; whereas, the female *homo* is a screaming, parturient, interjectional, hysterical animal, whose delicacy and timidity, monopolists even (much as it may surprise them) must be taught to consult. The female, in all probability, never would jump out; but she thinks she may jump out when she pleases; and this is intensely comfortable.

There are two sorts of dangers which hang over railroads. The one retail dangers, where individuals only are concerned; the other, wholesale dangers, where the whole train, or a considerable part of it, is put in jeopardy. For the first danger there is a remedy in the prudence of individuals; for the second, there is none. No man need be drunk, nor need he jump out when the carriage is in motion; but in the present state of science it is impossible to guard effectually against the fracture of the axle-tree, or the explosion of the engine; and if the safety of the one party cannot be consulted but by the danger of the other, if the foolish cannot be restrained but by the unjust incarceration of the wise, the prior consideration is due to those who have not the remedy for the evil in their own hands.

But the truth is—and so (after a hundred monopolizing experiments on public patience) the railroad directors will find it—there can be no other dependence for the safety of the public than the care which every human being is inclined to take of his own life and limbs. Every thing beyond this is the mere lazy tyranny of monopoly, which makes no distinction between human beings and brown paper parcels. If riding were a monopoly, as travelling in carriages is now become, there are many gentlemen whom I see riding in the Park upon such false principles, that I am sure the cantering and galloping directors would strap them, in the ardour of their affection, to the saddle, padlock them to the stirrups, or compel them to ride behind a policeman of the stable; and nothing but a motion from O'Brian, or an order from Gladstone, could release them.

Let the company stick up all sorts of cautions and notices within their carriages and without; but, after that, no doors locked. If one door is allowed to be locked, the other will soon be so too; there is no other security to the public than absolute prohibition of the practice. The directors and agents of the Great Western are individually excellent men; but the moment men meet in public boards, they cease to be collectively excellent. The fund of morality becomes less, as the individual contributors increase in number. I do not accuse such respectable men of any wilful violation of truth, but the memoirs which they are about to present will be, without the scrupulous cross-examination of a committee of the House of Commons, mere waste paper.

But the most absurd of all legislative enactments is this hemiplegian law—an act of Parliament to protect one side of the body and not the other. If the wheel comes off on the right, the open door is uppermost, and every one is saved. If, from any sudden avalanche on the road, the carriage is prostrated to the left, the locked door is uppermost, all escape is impossible, and the rail-road martyrdom begins.

Leave me to escape in the best way I can, as the fire-offices very kindly permit me to do. I know very well the danger of getting out on the off-side; but escape is the affair of a moment; suppose a train to have passed at that moment, I know I am safe from any other trains for twenty minutes or half an hour; and if I do get out on the off-side, I do not remain in the valley of death between the two trains, but am over to the opposite bank in an instant—only half-roasted, or merely browned, certainly not done enough for the Great Western directors.

On Saturday morning last, the wheel of the public carriage, in which a friend of mine was travelling, began to smoke, but was pacified by several buckets of water, and proceeded. After five more miles, the whole carriage was full of smoke, the train was with difficulty stopped, and the flagrant vehicle removed. The axle was nearly in two, and in another mile would have been severed.

Railroad travelling is a delightful improvement of human life. Man is become a bird; he can fly longer and quicker than a Solan goose. The mamma rushes sixty miles in two hours to the aching finger of her conjugating and declining grammar boy. The early Scotchman scratches himself in the morning mists of the North, and has his porridge in Piccadilly before the setting sun. The Puseyite priest, after a rush of 100 miles, appears with his little volume of nonsense at the breakfast of his bookseller. Everything is near, everything is immediate—time, distance, and delay are abolished. But, though charming and fascinating as all this is, we must not shut our eyes to the price we shall pay for it. There will be every three or four years some dreadful massacre—whole trains will be hurled down a precipice, and 200 or 300 persons will be killed on the spot. There will be every now and then a great combustion of human bodies, as there has been at Paris; then all the newspapers up in arms—a thousand regulations, forgotten as soon as the directors dare—loud screams of the velocity whistle—monopoly locks and bolts, as before.

The locking plea of directors is philanthropy; and I admit that to guard men from the commission of moral evil is as philanthropical as to prevent physical suffering. There is, I allow, a strong propensity in mankind to travel on railroads without paying; and to lock mankind in till they have completed their share of the contract is benevolent, because it guards the species from degrading and immoral conduct; but to burn or crush a whole train merely to prevent a few immoral insides from not paying is, I hope, a little more than Ripon or Gladstone will bear.

We have been, up to this point, very careless of our railway regulations. The first person of rank who is killed will put every-thing in order, and produce a code of the most careful rules. I hope it will not be one of the bench of bishops; but should it be so destined, let the burnt bishop—the unwilling Latimer—remember that, however painful gradual concoction by fire may be, his death will produce unspeakable benefit to the public. Even Sodor and Man will be better than nothing. From that moment the bad effects of the monopoly are destroyed; no more fatal deference to the directors; no despotic incarceration, no barbarous inattention to the anatomy and physiology of the human body; no commitment to locomotive prisons with warrant. We shall then find it possible '*Voyager libre sans mourir.*'

18 *June*, 1842

HAVING gradually got into this little controversy respecting the burning human beings alive on the railroads, I must beg leave, preparatory to the introduction of the bill, to say a few more words on the subject. If I could have my will in these matters, I would introduce into the bill a clause absolutely prohibitory of all locking doors on railroads; but as that fasci-nating board, the Board of Trade, does not love this, and as the public may, after some repetitions of roasted humanity, be better prepared for such peremptory legislation, the better method perhaps will be to give to the Board of Trade the power of opening doors (one or both), with the customary penalties against the companies for disobedience of orders, and then the board may use this power as the occasion may require.

To pass a one-legged law, giving power over one door and not the other, would, perhaps, be too absurd for human en-

durance. If railroad companies were aware of their real and
extended interests, they would not harass the public by vexatious
regulations, nor, under the plea of humanity (though really for
purposes of economy), expose them to serious peril. The country
are very angry with themselves for having granted the monopoly,
and very angry for the instances of carelessness and oppression
which have appeared in the working of the system: the heaviest
fines are inflicted by coroner's juries, the heaviest damages are
given by common juries. Railroads have daily proofs of their
unpopularity. If Parliament get out of temper with these metallic
ways, they will visit them with Laws of Iron, and burst upon
them with the high pressure of despotism.

The wayfaring men of the North will league with the wayfaring men of the West; South and East will join hand in hand
against them. All the points of the compass will combine against
these vendors of velocity and traders in transition. I hope a
clause will be introduced, compelling the Board of Trade to
report twice a year to Parliament upon the accidents of railroads,
their causes, and their prevention. The public know little or
nothing of what happens on the rail. All the men with letters
upon the collars of their coats are sworn to secrecy—nothing
can be extracted from them; when anything happens they
neither appear to see nor hear you.

In case of conflagration, you would be to them as so many
joints on the spit. It has occurred to 500 persons, that soft impedi-
ments behind and before (such as wool) would prevent the
dangers of meeting or overtaking. It is not yet understood why
a carriage on fire at the end of the train cannot be seen by the
driver of the engine. All this may be great nonsense; but the
public ought to know that these points have been properly
considered; they should know that there are a set of officers paid
to watch over their interests, and to guard against the perpetual
encroachments, the carelessness, the insolence, and the avarice
of monopoly.

Why do not our dear Ripon and our youthful Gladstone see
this, and come cheerfully to the rescue? and, instead of wrapping
themselves up in transcendental philosophy and the principles
of letting-aloneness, why do they not at once do what ought to
be done—what must be done—and what, after many needless
butcheries, they will at last be compelled to do?

SPEECH ON THE REFORM BILL

STICK to the Bill—it is your Magna Charta and your Runnymede. King John made a present to the Barons. King William has made a similar present to you. Never mind, common qualities good in common times. If a man does not vote for the Bill, he is unclean—the plague-spot is upon him—push him into the lazaretto of the last century, with Wetherell and Sadler—purify the air before you approach him —bathe your hands in chloride of lime, if you have been contaminated by his touch.

So far from its being a merely theoretical improvement, I put it to any man who is himself embarked in a profession, or has sons in the same situation, if the unfair influence of Borough-mongers has not perpetually thwarted him in his lawful career of ambition and professional emoluments? 'I have been in three general engagements at sea,' said an old sailor—'have been twice wounded. I commanded the boats when the French frigate, the Astrolabe, was cut out so gallantly.' 'Then you are made a Post Captain?' 'No. I was very near it; but—Lieutenant Thomson cut me out, as I cut out the French frigate; his father is Town Clerk of the Borough for which Lord F—— is Member, and there my chance was finished.' In the same manner, all over England you will find great scholars rotting on curacies, brave captains starving in garrets, profound lawyers decayed and mouldering in the Inns of Court, because the parsons, warriors, and advocates of Boroughmongers must be crammed to saturation before there is a morsel of bread for the man who does not sell his votes and put his country up to auction; and though this is of every-day occurrence, the Borough system, we are told, is no practical evil.

Who can bear to walk through a slaughter-house? blood, garbage, stomachs, entrails, legs, tails, kidneys, horrors—I often walk a mile about to avoid it. What a scene of disgust and horror is an election—the base and infamous traffic of principles

—a candidate of high character reduced to such means—the perjury and evasion of agents—the detestable rapacity of voters —the ten days' dominion of Mammon and Belial. The Bill lessens it—begins the destruction of such practices—affords some chance and some means of turning public opinion against bribery and of rendering it infamous.

But the thing I cannot and will not bear is this;—what right has *this* Lord, or *that* Marquis, to buy ten seats in Parliament, in the shape of Boroughs, and then to make laws to govern me? And how are these masses of power re-distributed? The eldest son of my Lord is just come from Eton; he knows a good deal about Æneas and Dido, Apollo and Daphne; and that is all. And to this boy his father gives a six-hundredth part of the power of making laws, as he would give him a horse, or a double-barrelled gun. Then Vellum the steward is put in—an admirable man;—he has raised the estates—watched the progress of the family Road and Canal Bills—and Vellum shall help to rule over the people of Israel. A neighbouring country gentleman, Mr Plumpkin, hunts with my Lord—opens him a gate or two while the hounds are running—dines with my Lord—agrees with my Lord—wishes he could rival the South Down sheep of my Lord—and upon Plumpkin is conferred a portion of the government. Then there is a distant relation of the same name, in the County Militia, with white teeth, who calls up the carriage at the Opera and is always wishing O'Connell was hanged, drawn, and quartered—then a barrister, who has written an article in the Quarterly, and is very likely to speak, and refute M'Culloch; and these five people, in whose nomination I have no more agency than I have in the nomination of the toll-keepers of the Bosphorus, are to make laws for me and my family—to put their hands in my purse and to sway the future destinies of this country; and when the neighbours step in and beg permission to say a few words before these persons are chosen, there is an universal cry of ruin, confusion, and destruction;—we have become a great people under Vellum and Plumpkin—under Vellum and Plumpkin our ships have covered the ocean—under Vellum and Plumpkin our armies have secured the strength of the Hills—to turn out Vellum and Plumpkin is not Reform, but Revolution.

Was there ever such a Ministry? Was there ever before a real

U

Ministry of the people? Look at the condition of the country
when it was placed in their hands: the state of the house when
the incoming tenant took possession: windows broken, chimneys
on fire, mobs round the house threatening to pull it down, roof
tumbling, rain pouring in. It was courage to occupy it; it was a
miracle to save it; it will be the glory of glories to enlarge and
expand it, and to make it the eternal palace of wise and temperate
freedom.

Proper examples have been made among the unhappy and
misguided disciples of Swing: a rope has been carried round
O'Connell's legs, and a ring inserted in Cobbett's nose. Then
the Game Laws!!! Was ever conduct so shabby as that of the
two or three governments which preceded that of Lord Grey?
The cruelties and enormities of this code had been thoroughly
exposed; and a general conviction existed of the necessity of a
change. Bills were brought in by various gentlemen, containing
some trifling alteration in this abominable code, and even these
were sacrificed to the tricks and manœuvres of some noble
Nimrod, who availed himself of the emptiness of the town in
July, and flung out the Bill. Government never stirred a step.
The fulness of the prisons, the wretchedness and demoralization
of the poor, never came across them. The humane and considerate
Peel never once offered to extend his aegis over them. It had
nothing to do with the state of party; and some of their double-
barrelled voters might be offended. In the mean time, for every
ten pheasants which fluttered in the wood, one English peasant
was rotting in gaol. No sooner is Lord Althorp Chancellor of
the Exchequer than he turns out of the House a trumpery and
(perhaps) an insidious Bill for the improvement of the Game
Laws; and in an instant offers the assistance of Government for
the abolition of the whole code.

Then look at the gigantic Brougham, sworn in at 12 o'clock,
and before 6 has a Bill on the table abolishing the abuses of a
Court which has been the curse of the people of England for
centuries. For twenty-five long years did Lord Eldon sit in that
Court, surrounded with misery and sorrow, which he never
held up a finger to alleviate. The widow and the orphan cried
to him as vainly as the town crier cries when he offers a small
reward for a full purse; the bankrupt of the Court became the
lunatic of the Court; estates mouldered away and mansions fell

down; but the fees came in, and all was well. But in an instant the iron mace of Brougham shivered to atoms this house of fraud and of delay; and this is the man who will help to govern you; who bottoms his reputation on doing good to you; who knows that to reform abuses is the safest basis of fame and the surest instrument of power; who uses the highest gifts of reason, and the most splendid efforts of genius, to rectify those abuses which all the genius and talent of the profession* have hitherto been employed to justify and to protect. Look to Brougham, and turn you to that side where he waves his long and lean finger; and mark well that face which nature has marked so forcibly—which dissolves pensions—turns jobbers into honest men—scares away the plunderer of the public—and is a terror to him who doeth evil to the people. But, above all, look to the Northern Earl [Grey], victim, before this honest and manly reign, of the spitefulness of the Court. You may now, for the first time, learn to trust in the professions of a Minister; you are directed by a man who prefers character to place, and who has given such unequivocal proofs of honesty and patriotism that his image ought to be amongst your household gods, and his name to be lisped by your children: two thousand years hence it will be a legend like the fable of Perseus and Andromeda: Britannia chained to a mountain—two hundred rotten animals menacing her destruction, till a tall Earl, armed with Schedule A and followed by his page Russell, drives them into the deep and delivers over Britannia in safety to crowds of ten-pound renters, who deafen the air with their acclamations. Forthwith, Latin verses upon this—school exercises—boys whipt, and all the usual absurdities of education. Don't part with the Administration composed of Lord Grey and Lord Brougham; and not only these, but look at them all—the mild wisdom of Lansdowne—the genius and extensive knowledge of Holland, in whose bold and honest life there is no varying nor shadow of change—the unexpected and exemplary activity of Lord Melbourne—and the rising parliamentary talents of Stanley. You are ignorant of your best interests if every vote you can bestow is not given to such a Ministry as this.

You will soon find an alteration of behaviour in the upper

---

* Lord Lyndhurst is an exception; I firmly believe he had no wish to perpetuate the abuses of the Court of Chancery.

orders when elections become real. You will find that you are raised to the importance to which you ought to be raised. The merciless ejector, the rural tyrant, will be restrained within the limits of decency and humanity, and will improve their own characters at the same time that they better your condition.

It is not the power of aristocracy that will be destroyed by these measures, but the unfair power. If the Duke of Newcastle is kind and obliging to his neighbours, he will probably lead his neighbours; if he is a man of sense, he will lead them more certainly and to a better purpose. All this is as it should be; but the Duke of Newcastle at present, by buying certain old houses, could govern his neighbours and legislate for them even if he had not five grains of understanding and if he were the most churlish and brutal man under heaven. The present state of things renders unnecessary all those important virtues which rich and well-born men, under a better system, would exercise for the public good. The Duke of Newcastle, I mention him only as an instance, Lord Exeter will do as well, but either of those noblemen, depending not upon walls, arches, and abutments, for their power—but upon mercy, charity, forbearance, indulgence, and example—would pay this price, and lead the people by their affections; one would be the God of Stamford, and the other of Newark. This union of the great with the many is the real healthy state of a country; such a country is strong to invincibility—and this strength the Borough System entirely destroys.

Cant words creep in, and affect quarrels; the changes are rung between Revolution and Reform; but, first settle whether a wise Government ought to attempt the measure—whether anything is wanted—whether less would do—and, having settled this, mere nomenclature becomes of very little consequence. But, after all, if it is Revolution, and not Reform, it will only induce me to receive an old political toast in a twofold meaning and with twofold pleasure. When King William and the great and glorious Revolution are given, I shall think not only of escape from bigotry, but exemption from corruption; and I shall thank Providence, which has given us a second King William for the destruction of vice, as the other of that name was given us for the conservation of freedom.

All former political changes, proposed by these very men, it is said, were mild and gentle compared to this; true, but are you on Saturday night to seize your apothecary by the throat and say to him: 'Subtle compounder, fraudulent posologist, did not you order me a dram of this medicine on Monday morning, and now you declare that nothing short of an ounce can do me any good?' 'True enough,' would he of the phials reply, '*but you did not take the dram on Monday morning*—that makes all the difference, my dear Sir; if you had done as I advised you at first, the small quantity of medicine would have sufficed; and instead of being in a night-gown and slippers upstairs, you would have been walking vigorously in Piccadilly. Do as you please—and die if you please; but don't blame me because you despised my advice and by your own ignorance and obstinacy have entailed upon yourself tenfold rhubarb and unlimited infusion of senna.'

Now see the consequences of having a manly Leader, and a manly Cabinet. Suppose they had come out with a little old-fashioned seven months' reform; what would have been the consequence? The same opposition from the Tories—that would have been quite certain—and not a single Reformer in England satisfied with the measure. You have now a real Reform, and a fair share of power delegated to the people.

The Anti-Reformers cite the increased power of the press—this is the very reason why I want an increased power in the House of Commons. *The Times, Herald, Advertiser, Globe, Sun, Courier,* and *Chronicle,* are a heptarchy, which govern this country, and govern it because the people are so badly represented. I am perfectly satisfied that with a fair and honest House of Commons the power of the press would diminish—and that the greatest authority would centre in the highest place.

§

The great majority of persons returned by the new Boroughs would either be men of high reputation for talents, or persons of fortune known in the neighbourhood; they have property and character to lose. Why are they to plunge into mad and revoluntary projects of pillaging the public creditor? It is not the interest of any such man to do it; he would lose more by the destruction of public credit than he would gain by a remission of what he paid for the interest of the public debt. And if it is not the interest of any one to act in this manner, it is not the interest of the mass. How many also of these new Legislators would there be, who were not themselves creditors of the State? Is it the interest of such men to create a revolution, by destroying the constitutional power of the House of Lords or of the King? Does there exist in persons of that class any disposition for such changes? Are not all their feelings, and opinions, and prejudices, on the opposite side? The majority of the new Members will be landed gentlemen: their genus is utterly distinct from the revolutionary tribe; they have molar teeth; they are destitute of the carnivorous and incisive jaws of political adventurers.

There will be mistakes at first, as there are in all changes. All young Ladies will imagine (as soon as this Bill is carried) that they will be instantly married. Schoolboys believe that gerunds and supines will be abolished, and that currant tarts must ultimately come down in price; the corporal and sergeant are sure of double pay; bad poets will expect a demand for their epics; fools will be disappointed, as they always are; reasonable men, who know what to expect, will find that a very serious good has been obtained.

What good to the hewer of wood and the drawer of water? How is he benefited if Old Sarum is abolished and Birmingham members created? But if you ask this question of Reform, you must ask it of a great number of other great measures? How is he benefited by Catholic Emancipation, by the repeal of the Corporation and Test Act, by the Revolution of 1688, by any great political change? by a good government? In the first place, if many are benefited, and the lower orders are not injured, this alone is reason enough for the change. But the hewer of wood and the drawer of water *are* benefited by Reform. Reform will produce economy and investigation; there will be fewer jobs and a less lavish expenditure; wars will not be persevered in for years after the people are tired of them; taxes will be taken off the poor, and laid upon the rich; demotic habits will be more common in a country where the rich are forced to court the poor for political power; cruel and oppressive punishments (such as those for night poaching) will be abolished. If you steal a pheasant you will be punished as you ought to be, but not sent away from your wife and children for seven years. Tobacco will be 2d per lb cheaper. Candles will fall in price. These last results of an improved government will be felt. We do not pretend to abolish poverty, or to prevent wretchedness; but if peace, economy, and justice, are the results of Reform, a number of small benefits, or rather of benefits which appear small to us but not to them, will accrue to millions of the people; and the connection between the existence of John Russell and the reduced price of bread and cheese will be as clear as it has been the object of his honest, wise, and useful life to make it.

Don't be led away by such nonsense; all things are dearer under a bad government and cheaper under a good one. The real question they ask you is: What difference can any change of government make to you? They want to keep the bees from buzzing and stinging, in order that they may rob the hive in peace.

Work well! How does it work well, when every human being in doors and out (with the exception of the Duke of Wellington) says it must be made to work better or it will soon cease to work at all? It is little short of absolute nonsense to call a government good which the great mass of Englishmen would, before twenty years were elapsed, if Reform were denied, rise up and destroy. Of what use have all the cruel laws been of Perceval, Eldon, and Castlereagh, to extinguish Reform? Lord John Russell and his abettors would have been committed to gaol twenty years ago for half only of his present Reform; and now relays of the people would drag them from London to Edinburgh; at which latter city we are told, by Mr Dundas, there is no eagerness for Reform. Five minutes before Moses struck the rock, this gentleman would have said that there was no eagerness for water.

There are two methods of making alterations: the one is to despise the applicants, to begin with refusing every concession, then to relax by making concessions which are always too late; by offering in 1831 what is then too late but would have been cheerfully accepted in 1830—gradually to O'Connellize the country, till at last, after this process has gone on for some time, the alarm becomes too great, and everything is conceded in hurry and confusion. In the meantime fresh conspiracies have been hatched by the long delay, and no gratitude is expresesd for what has been extorted by fear. In this way peace was concluded with America, and Emancipation granted to the Catholics; and in this way the war of complexion will be finished in the

West Indies. The other method is to see at a distance that the thing must be done, and to do it effectually, *and at once;* to take it out of the hands of the common people, and to carry the measure in a manly liberal manner, so as to satisfy the great majority. The merit of this belongs to the Administration of Lord Grey. He is the only Minister I know of who has begun a great measure in good time, conceded at the beginning of twenty years what would have been extorted at the end of it, and prevented that folly, violence, and ignorance, which emanate from a long denial and extorted concession of justice to great masses of human beings. I believe the question of Reform, or any dangerous agitation of it, is set at rest for thirty or forty years; and this is an eternity in politics.

§

If any man doubts of the power of Reform, let him take these two memorable proofs of its omnipotence. First, but for the declaration against it, I believe the Duke of Wellington might this day have been in office; and, secondly, in the whole course of the debates at County Meetings, and in Parliament, there are not twenty men who have declared against Reform. Some advance an inch, some a foot, some a yard—but nobody stands still—nobody says we ought to remain just where we were— everybody discovers that he is a Reformer and has long been so— and appears infinitely delighted with this new view of himself. Nobody appears without the cockade—bigger or less—but always the cockade.

An exact and elaborate census is called for—vast information should have been laid upon the table of the House—great time should have been given for deliberation. All these objections, being turned into English, simply mean that the chances of another year should have been given for defeating the Bill. In that time the Poles may be crushed, the Belgians Orangized, Louis Philip dethroned; war may rage all over Europe—the popular spirit may be diverted to other objects. It is certainly provoking that the Ministry foresaw all these possibilities, and determined to model the iron while it was red and glowing.

It is not enough that a political institution works well practically: it must be defensible; it must be such as will bear discussion, and not excite ridicule and contempt. It might work well for aught I know, if, like the savages of Onelashka, we sent out to catch a King: but who could defend a coronation by chase? who can defend the payment of £40,000 for the three hundredth part of the power of Parliament, and the resale of this power to Government for places to the Lord Williams and Lord Charleses, and others of the Anglophagi? Teach a million of the common people to read—and such a government (work it ever so well) must perish in twenty years. It is impossible to persuade the mass of mankind that there are not other and better methods of governing a country. It is so complicated, so wicked, such envy and hatred accumulate against the gentlemen who have fixed themselves on the joints, that it cannot fail to perish, and to be driven as it *is* driven from the country, by a general burst of hatred and detestation. I meant, Gentlemen, to have spoken for another half-hour, but I am old and tired. Thank me for ending— but, Gentlemen, bear with me for another moment; one word before I end. I am old, but I thank God I have lived to see more than my observations on human nature taught me I had any right to expect. I have lived to see an honest King, in whose word his Ministers can trust; who disdains to deceive those men whom he has called to the public service, but makes common cause with them for the common good; and exercises the highest powers of a ruler for the dearest interests of the State. I have lived to see a King with a good heart, who, surrounded by nobles, thinks of common men; who loves the great mass of English people and wishes to be loved by them; who knows that his real power, as he feels that his happiness, is founded on their affection. I have lived to see a King who, without pretending to the pomp of superior intellect, has the wisdom to see that the decayed institutions of human policy require amendment; and who, in spite of clamour, interest, prejudice, and fear, has the manliness to carry these wise changes into immediate execution. Gentlemen, farewell: shout for the King.

INDEX